THE POPE SPEAKS

THE
POPE
SPEAKS

Dialogues of Paul VI with

JEAN GUITTON

English Translation by Anne and Christopher Fremantle

MEREDITH PRESS: NEW YORK

First U.S. edition

Library of Congress Catalog Card Number: 68–15204

Manufactured in The United States of America for Meredith Press by American Book–Stratford Press, Inc.

Designed by Stefan Salter Associates

What the reader will find in this work is something unusual. He will not find an interview, a recording of the words of Paul VI, such as a mechanical device—impressionable wax hard or soft, a silent secretary—could have registered. No single one of these meetings was taken down on tape, or recorded; nor were notes made. The words of Socrates were not transcribed by his disciple but rediscovered with desperate, inimitable art; Plato created of old the literary form that has since been called the dialogue.

The reader will be disappointed if he looks in this book for surprises, indiscretions, anecdotes. Certainly everything is true, even as to detail, but no secret is revealed here, no gossip, no off-the-record contemporary history.

And the reader would make an even greater mistake were he to compare this attempt with the indirect confidences which certain exceptional human beings made in order to extend or to prolong their influence, as, for example, the *Mémorial* of Las Cases at St. Helena, or the *Conversations* of Eckermann with Goethe at Weimar. Paul VI never knew of my undertaking until it was completed on December 25, 1966.

A Pope's situation cannot be compared with that of anyone else in the world. A statesman, the founder of an empire, a great mind or a great artist can permit himself confidences. He can explain his personal viewpoint, reveal himself. And even some saints have told their own story. A Pope's duty is the exact opposite. As Pope he is no longer his own master. He is no longer himself, since he has received a new name which separates him from himself. Since Simon Bar-Jona received the name of Cephas-Peter, he no longer exists as an individual. Through his being Christ must appear. And his whole desire, his whole torment is that within him ceaselessly Jesus may grow and Peter shrink, to the apparently impossible point when, the person of Peter being effaced, there may appear as on Mount Tabor Jesus only.

Several times, over five years, I suspended this work; I felt that, in spite of my wish to make a wholly living portrait, it was humanly impossible to make the Pope speak, as Plato made Socrates. Yet an interior voice admonished me: "Bear witness to the unseen greatness. Do not obscure the light. Do not be the cloud which hides the sight of the city set upon a hill."

The Holy Father, in his magnanimous humility that seeks the common good, was aware of this aspect of his vocation when he permitted the publication of this study, where I attempt to set forth, by the device of a dialogue with the Pope, eternal Christian principles in their application to this deeply anguished and vital moment in human history. At this moment, every layman is duty-bound to be an apostle. That is to say, he must do everything possible, according to his capacity, in order that the voice of Jesus, overlaid with so much propaganda and indeed with so much silence, reaches by all means every type of mind. My idea was to make an enduring book that would survive and still find readers, friends, after the people and the circumstances have vanished. For the theme of these discussions is a constant here on earth: It is the dialogue within us of the man of eternity with the man of the moment.

But however great my desire to write an extratemporal book in the wake of the Council, I would have thrown this work into the fire had I thought I had displeased Paul VI. That is why it was a moment of joy when on the morning of December 27 (the day the Church celebrates the feast of an evangelist who is also my patron saint), I received a telegram from Paul VI containing these words of gentle absolution: NIMIS BENE DE NOBIS SCRIPSISTI. (You have written very well of Us.)

I return to the indiscreet question. Many of the Pope's remarks are historic, and in his very words, which I have respected insofar as my memory allows; this is the case, for example, in the first chapter. Much of the dialogue is the outcome of a slow osmosis, sixteen years long, between the speaking and the writing. I have made use of some almost unknown texts. Let the expert discover which is which. All I can say is that beyond the reproduction of literal words, which is often tiresome, unreliable, and useless, there exists a more faithful, deeper, more intimate, and truer reproduction, which proceeds from a saturation of the whole soul. I have just written down the most important word: truth. These sayings are not all historical. But, insofar as I am concerned, I have made every possible effort to be able to say: These sayings are all authentic. They are all *true*.

Having explained the problems of my sources, I would like to explain what I have tried to do, which seems to me to correspond to the aspirations of a large number of free men.

Today, the citizen and the believer are no longer children. They wish to know, they wish to understand. They do not care to be neglected or deceived. Similarly, the faithful wish to be treated as the daughters and sons are in modern families. The father is in full sight in the midst of his family; his face is visible, he is known for what he is. He does not appear from among the clouds, he does not rise up out of a cave. He speaks. He brings his children up to date. This does not impair his authority. On the contrary, when he indicates his wishes, his wishes will be understood. His difficulties, his anxieties are shared. And the unity without which there can be no common action is realized without need for recourse to that surgical method, the injunction.

More than any other Pope of our times, Paul VI, who is a young pontiff, appears as a brotherly father, wanting to talk with his fellow men, his brothers and his sons, wanting to be heard, to be understood. This he said in his first encyclical. And could there be, via some satellite, a worldwide universal television where the miracle of Pentecost would be renewed, then we could see him each Sunday talking with every member of the human family in a cordial, simple and familiar conversation, as the sun's light . . .

> *Pour bénir chaque front et mûrir chaque miel*
> *Entrant dans chaque coeur et dans chaque chaumière*
> *Se partage et demeure entière*
> *Ainsi que l'amour maternel.*[1]

Soon will come the time when the tiny screen will permit this intimacy of one man with millions of other men, perhaps with four or five billion, the little family of the inhabitants of this planet: the human race.

While waiting for this to happen, it is possible to imagine still

[1] To bless each head and honey hive with fire,
Enters each croft and every heart,
Wholly divided, always yet entire,
Like mother love in every part.

more intimate means of communication between the Holy Father and his own, such as these dialogues, imaginary in one sense, but more real, as I have said, than recorded dialogues. In ordinary interviews the risks of conversation, the carelessness of language, the absence of order cause the line of thought to be dissipated and lost; often the essential is suppressed. In order for a dialogue to be clear, the words of both speakers should have been meditated upon at length, they should have sojourned in the heart and the memory; they should be oracles coming from the depths, while retaining the casualness of those human conversations where one can dare to be wholly oneself, where one can speak freely on whatever subject occurs. The Gospel of St. John seems to have used this method toward the end of the first century.

When the Pope speaks, he does so in a necessarily simple way. Every one of us tends to be marked by some viewpoint, some talent, some system, some originality, some manner: Each one can only be himself by accentuating a single aspect, he is almost obliged to be partial. On the contrary, the man who is placed at the summit must be common, must be universal. He has the authority of truth, which is single; he reminds everyone of what he knows and hides. Let no one expect from this book any revelations except the revelation of what is just, honorable, pure, amiable, and of good report.

No one can pretend to know a Pope. His lonely and mysterious charge obliges him to a greater reserve than is incumbent on any other man in power. More than any other man he is dedicated to universal love, obliged to mortify in himself any too human expression, any too personal judgment. Finally, he is constrained to that vigilant courtesy which is an exquisite form of love.

Yet every pontiff remains himself. He keeps his moods, his human way of being. Without wishing to, perhaps without being aware of it, he stamps his office with his humanity as a seal. I would even say that in that high office where one is no longer judged except by God, the personality can sometimes blossom into ease and joviality, as was seen in the case of John XXIII, who resolved to be plainly and simply himself. Yet Pope Paul's way cannot be that of Pope John.

Nothing can prevent a Pope's eyes from being of a certain color, his voice having a certain resonance. Curiously enough, in the Gospel of St. Mark—written by the interpreter, the disciple of St. Peter—in this stony Gospel, concentrated on the Master alone, Cephas-Peter is seen more lucidly, with the contrasts in his character, than in the other Gospels.

This book, as will be seen, does not solely contain dialogues. With some history of his origins, of his background and his early education, it offers a portrait of Paul VI that I have tried to paint by juxtaposing colors, in a sequence of brushstrokes, after the fashion of Cézanne and of several painters of his era.

Once Monsignor Montini told me that in Milan, after an exhausting day, he would "find a little refreshment" by opening at random my book *Monsieur Pouget*. I think that this book reminded him of his beloved master, Father Bevillacqua, who is recalled in one chapter of this book. On January 1, 1967, the Holy Father had the goodness to write to me:

From the first day of your *Monsieur Pouget* with its dialogue of deepening self-awareness and its simultaneous deepening of communication with others, We have never ceased to follow with sympathy the development of the work you were writing, for the extension of that universe of thought, where faith and intelligence meet and enrich each other by their fruitful exchange.

I had written *Monsieur Pouget* while observing my model ceaselessly for fifteen years. In this case, for fifteen years it has been almost the reverse. I have been able to see and to hear only on rare occasions, separated by long intervals—circumstances conducive to thought. In both cases, the same method: saturation, as I have said, osmosis. To shut the eyes in order to see, listen, question: to leave aside the trivial, to go straight to the essential. To lift problems to their mystery. To hearken to silence.

"A high friendship," Pascal has said, "fulfills a man's heart far better than a common. And small things float away on its vastness. Only big things remain there forever." I have carried this book with me in all the moments of my thoughts, by night and by day, in all the interstices of my other work, and if I dare say it, in all the folds of my heart. It is the portrait of a mind at work, in certain of its memories, in the spiral of its reflections, in its anxieties, in its joys, in its absolute hope. It is a view from a rocket which has jettisoned its first stage of the conciliar period, and which proceeds, together with us all, with the whole of humanity, toward that time so near, so unimaginable, when God, as the Apostle Paul says, will be all in all.

My wish would be that this work of my declining years should reflect and sum up all the others, and that it should be, as St. Paul puts it, a letter inscribed in hearts and read by all men.

Rome, December 31, 1966   J. G.

CONTENTS

PART ONE

A Destiny in Perspective

1

THE EIGHTH OF SEPTEMBER, 1950

In my memory everything is contemporary. But the images are super-imposed; those present awaken those past, their forerunners.

In listening to Paul VI speak of his first experiences as Supreme Pontiff, I could not help thinking of the memories I had of him when he had been a man—a priest among others—whom one could address as an equal. Always when I shall speak of him in this book I shall place myself in front of that unfathomable mystery: How can there exist united in a single being a man like myself and a father of all men? And for those who knew him before he became Sovereign Pontiff, how was the transition made, the union between what he was and what he has become? The well-known axiom for every destiny, "Become that thou truly art"—how did it echo in his story, in his consciousness? That is each man's mystery: How to become what one is not yet. Knowing the Pope, one tries to project the image of what he is on the memory one has kept. And so is produced a wonderful mixture which helps in understanding human nature.

I have looked through my old notes, where I had tried to crystallize our first meeting. The occasion was a book I had published in 1950 on the Virgin Mary. A few words must be said about this work.

It was a book I had written on the advice of a priest friend who had been, for five long, interminable years, a prisoner of war in Germany with me. I did it to keep faith, in friendship, but without effort, without thinking too deeply about it—as I let the present book flow out of my declining years—in a sort of peace and plenty. It was an attempt, not, I would say, to *think about* the Virgin, but to *think* the Virgin, with "all my mind," that is, all my philosophy, replenished from the sources but also at the fountain of modern thought. I was helped by beliefs, but also by negations, by disbeliefs; for I had discerned in Goethe, in Renan, in Auguste Comte—more recently still in Marcel Proust—a portrait of the Virgin in *negative* and one which I wished to *develop*, as in those dark rooms with a red light used by the early photographers, in which my father used to slide the hyposulfite of the *developer* over the plate. Armed with these ancient and modern weapons, I had tried to write an ecumenical book on the Virgin, addressed first and foremost to those who deny—rationalists—and also those, so numerous since the Reformation, who see in the Marian cult evidence of superstition. The book was dedicated to our Protestant brethren. I recalled that at Cana, according to St. John's Gospel, the prayer of the Virgin had advanced the time of the Messiah's manifestation. An ecumenical prayer to the Virgin, known, unknown, could advance the hour of reconciliation. Such were the intentions of this book. It was not well received in certain Roman circles. I had wished to retrace the development of the consciousness of the Virgin, to show that she had not understood everything at once, that she had needed time to admit the divinity of Him whom she held in her arms: the *Osservatore Romano* had found fault with this "layman's theology." All this took place in the pre-Council era.

Monsignor Montini made no allusion to my difficulties with

certain representatives of the Holy Office. He said to me: "I liked your book on the Virgin very much. It is the Virgin who brings us together today. Since the pages of Newman in his famous letter to Dr. Pusey, I do not believe I have read any pages on the Virgin which gave me as much satisfaction. One has to be at the same time ancient and modern, to speak according to tradition and also to speak taking into account our sensibilities. What purpose would be served by saying what is true, if one does not make it comprehensible to men of today? I hope," he added, "with the Holy Father, that your book will be spiritually fruitful."

"Perhaps it will not please everyone," I said.

He smiled, and it was the first time I saw that expression in his look and on his lips, an expression of indulgence, of joy, of distance, not without humor. In the art of sounds, one of the notes is silence, and it is necessary to know how to play upon silence, to express oneself, too, by silences.

It was, as I was saying, the eighth of September, 1950. Two o'clock had just struck. Monsignor Montini had certainly not had lunch. He was not the least hurried. A heavy morning of audiences had neither tired nor depressed him. In a black cassock, with no decoration, his neck enclosed in a Roman collar, but at ease, he appeared young, slender, elegant, above all available, lively, calm, in possession of himself and also of that French which he evidently enjoyed speaking, unfolding it like a roll of cloth, rather slowly.

I observed him for the first time, being alone and very much at my ease with him, not embarrassed by any ideas about his importance, for he was only the secretary of a nonexistent Secretary of State. I watched that face, which I was to study so often later as it acquired little by little the patina of time, the furrows and uncertainties of care. At that moment he was free and not responsible. That day I was to hear him say: "Liberty and responsibility are in inverse ratio."

In fact care has changed him little, time has hardly scratched him. But at that period he had all his youthfulness and elegance.

I am at pains to go back to the very first contact, to the shock, the spark, the thrill, at the first, so fleeting, glimpse, to me much truer than the continuing impression. I am impulsive, I only see well in a state of waking, when fresh. My retina tires rapidly after the first moments, when the opinions of others and, at the same time, a shadow of doubt as to my own judgment, are interjected. And when it concerns one of the great of this world, I am troubled by the procession of legends, images, and conventions. But in the *first impression* which Monsignor Montini made on me that eighth of September, there was something sudden and decisive, with an assurance for the future. I seemed to grasp something indefinably open, direct, immediate, without prelate's unction, which had nothing of the ecclesiastical, of the cautious: *un uomo vivo e un uomo fresco,* a lively and open man, not evasive ("reticences," he has said, "are unworthy of a priest"), and wholly without talkativeness, as with those too anxious to please.

He had a silvery grace, serious, gentle, pleasant, and fresh. I thought of that proverb: "Gravity is the shield of fools." A superior man who is gay, Mondor said to me about Paul Valéry, is always fascinating. He was like the angel of Rheims, who does not speak in a pedantic manner, but only smiles, inclining his head, as if he were announcing a little more happiness.

Thus he will be seen in this first dialogue, written almost at his dictation. He avoided no objection, was friendly about difficulties; he entered into you better than you did, from the start. In short, I

found myself in front of a man in his prime. Immediately I felt
confident. At that moment, as I have said, such an equality in our
relation was helped by the apparently modest situation and title of
Monsignor Montini. He was an apparently ordinary priest without
responsibilities, although in fact he had many, without either "red or
purple," like a simple black bird on the branch of an old oak, which
had just alighted, which might perhaps fly away as it had come,
without disturbing the leaves or making the twig snap.

On the other hand, as I represented nobody and was nothing
other than myself, already something difficult enough, unknown, a
layman, expecting nothing from him, asking nothing; as he knew
that with me he had nothing to suspect, nothing to refuse, nothing
even to answer, there was at that moment in the Vatican, where the
police and Swiss Guards were taking their siesta, an interval of
suspense, of rest, of liberty, which I can still savor: it was, as in the
Apocalypse, a silence of half an hour.

Where have I read that in the eyes of the ancient Romans the
world and its history began in the month of September, when the
Goddess Lavinia distributed her first gifts to men? I find in that idea
a certain plausibility: The fall, by its softness, its languor, its calm
magnificence, is a true springtime of the spirit. The spring saddens
me by promises which are not kept; the summer crushes me; the
autumn lends me good counsel. And I wonder if, in his famous
"Dispute of the Holy Sacrament," Raphael did not wish to paint the
altar, the "Sun" of the Eucharist, the landscape and conversation of
the saints, in a September evening; for the evenings in September are
conducive to thoughts leading to adoration.

So I had just seen Monsignor Montini smile.

The conversation began about what is today called ecumenism. I
told Monsignor Montini that since my youth I had been active in

the union of the Churches, and how I had known Lord Halifax and Cardinal Mercier during the talks at Malines. He replied:

"It is the great wish of the Holy See that there should be relations of this kind, conversations between Catholics and non-Catholics. If sometimes we have appeared to be opposed to them, it is because these dialogues [I did not know then that he would later invest the word *dialogue* with such significance], or rather, these 'colloquies,' demand that Catholics be represented by people of competence. You understand that if incompetent spokesmen in such conversations pronounce, I would not say errors, but only inexactitudes, as to our faith—and here the smallest shades of meaning have their weight and value—it is a matter of no small inconvenience. That explains the present discipline of the Holy Office, and particularly the recent decree on relations between Catholics and non-Catholics, in which a control by the bishops is required. But the method is not condemned. It is good. I would even say that it is, in itself, excellent."

We then spoke of the Halifax family. He knew the third Lord Halifax, whom he called the Viceroy, as he was Viceroy of India. He asked me about the second Lord Halifax, who promoted the Union of the Churches, whom I had known well. I described him, so human and Christian, a man who had devoted himself to the cause of Christian unity. Then, speaking of my book on the Virgin, he asked me, "But how have the Protestants received it in France?"

I answered that I had heard that Pastor Boegner appreciated it.

He took advantage of this to tell me the good things he had heard of Pastor Boegner. Then he told me that he had received in that same room Pastor Thurian, that it had been for him a wonderful thing to meet these Protestant pastors, and to realize how by their studies they were in the process of rediscovering this idea of "tradition," which, in fact, they had never abandoned. Then he spoke to me of the sincerity, good faith, and piety of the separated Christians, of the respect he had for their research; of the necessity for the Holy See, in spite of so much sympathy, in spite of its admiration, not to give the smallest offense, not to make the smallest breach of faith in the doctrine always accepted in the Church.

"But," he said, "you have known the pioneers of this union— Cardinal Mercier, Lord Halifax. I recall that splendid symbolic gesture, the dying Cardinal sending to Lord Halifax, the Anglican nobleman, his pastoral ring. A sublime symbol."

"Yes," I said. And Lord Halifax was never separated from that Cardinal's ring. He said to me, on February 3, 1926: "I have a little golden chain. I have put the Cardinal's ring on it and I shall always wear it round my neck. It is a relic of the greatest value and will always be a source for me of what is most important in life."

And in fact one day I was bold enough to ask him to show me this ring. He opened his shirt. The Roman ring swung from a modest chain against his heart.

"You speak in your book *Monsieur Pouget* of the problems which raise difficulties, and in particular of Anglican ordinations. I remember a meeting between the old Lord Halifax and the French priest."

The conversation passed to the encyclical *Humani generis*. I told him what I thought about this papal document, which sets out the fundamentals of faith, the relationship between faith and natural reason, and the power of reason. By the perspectives it opens and the precautions it demands, the encyclical seems to me opportune for setting right the possible weaknesses of contemporary thought, tempted as it is by fideism and relativism. "But," I added, "the encyclical needs to be interpreted; several of its passages, taken literally and out of context, would suggest that Rome holds the progress of thought suspect; many intellectuals, on reading the encyclical, will have an impression of fear, and still more, of discouragement."

He immediately answered me, and I reproduce here the notes I made that very evening:

"I know what you are saying. I understand what you are confiding. But [a silence] listen, please.

"In the first moment certain Catholics in France and elsewhere will have the impression you convey. I am sure that impression will be dissipated. Moreover, we will take care that it shall be dissipated. The encyclical *Humani generis* gives certain warnings. It places certain limits to right and left—in order that one may go forward along the path of progress in safety, especially so that the sources may be pure, so that a new age of cultural progress may open before the Church. I would say that it opens a royal road, that is, an open and secure road.

"You have doubtless yourself noted the shades of meaning written into this papal text. For example, the encyclical never speaks of *errors* (*errores*). It only speaks of *opinions* (*opiniones*). This indicates that the Holy See aims to condemn not errors, properly speaking, but modes of thought which could lead to errors, but which in themselves remain respectable."

Then I decided to present some further comments on the subject of the encyclical. "It is harsh," I said. "In fact, it gives consistence to certain tendencies which are, with us, still very innocent ones, and I would say almost inconsistent."

Monsignor Montini interrupted me at once. "I know. That is why the encyclical, you will note, does not speak of an evil which has taken root; it only speaks of predisposition. You will notice that it is in quite a different tone from the encyclical *Pascendi* which was brought out by Pius X against modernist doctrines. One might say that the intention of the Holy Father is precisely to avoid the need for a new *Pascendi* encyclical. The Holy See would much prefer not to have to say anything, but it cannot put aside its duties."

"That," I answered, "we too are aware of, Monsignor; but in France, at least, we do not always recognize ourselves in the guise of these 'false opinions' which are written of in the encyclical. We think there is often a danger in going too far ahead, but that there are also dangers in staying too far behind."

Monsignor Montini replied, "That also we too do not forget. In short," he added after a further silence, "the duties of pastors and the duties of laymen are different. We, the pastors of the Church, responsible for the preservation of the Deposit of Faith, ought to avoid the faults of sloth, tardiness, and excessive conservatism. You, the faithful, are in constant relation with the world, you ought to avoid the fault of an excessive tolerance of new things which are erroneous or not yet established; you should avoid the peril of giving way too far, for then you will advance on a terrain which is undermined. You will win souls to the Church, but to a Church in ruins. I repeat: Our obligations are different; they are complementary. I would say that we, the pastors, are tempted by 'dogmatism,' and you, the faithful, by 'relativism.' "

At the end of the meeting, I took the liberty of saying that the laity in France and elsewhere often found themselves torn and in a difficult situation between the Church leaders and the unbelievers; that often the former mistrusted them as too advanced, while the latter mistrusted them as too backward, and that I myself, especially, suffered profoundly from that difficulty.

He replied as he rose to take leave, "Your ordeal as a layman must be felt; I would even say, it must be *suffered*. There is no easy solution for what is in its nature difficult. When it is necessary to be torn, one ought to endure it out of love of being torn.

"In the Church, many live in the present coming to it from the past, and that is very fortunate. A number are in the present as though they came from the present. A few come from the future, and that also is very fortunate. Do not worry at not feeling at ease in this world. Nobody is at ease in this passage. And I will quote you the lines of one of your poets:

> *"Va ton chemin sans plus t'inquiéter*
> *La route est droite et tu n'as qu'à monter*
> *Portant d'ailleurs le seul trésor qui vaille"*[2]

Then, looking at me with the same smile, angelic, as I have said, but a trifle sibylline:

> *"Simple comme un enfant, gravis la côte!"*[3]

And he vanished. Three o'clock was striking. The sun began to decline. The morning was finished.

Such was our first encounter, on September 8, 1950.

[2] Go thy way without more disquiet
  The road runs straight, you have but to ascend,
  Bearing, besides, the only valid treasure.
[3] Childlike and simple, ascend the steep!

2

THREE SIGNS UPON THE EARTH

He took me in a very narrow elevator into the Cloister Belvedere, which was built on top of the palace to allow him repose, to breathe in the air, to take a deep breath out of sight, to visit unobserved—as do the angels—the Roman hearths with his propitiatory, vigilant presence. Although Paris, inhabited as it is by so many memories, by the whole history of France from the beginning, is more friendly to me than Rome, I never feel protected there, so to speak. Paris lacks a presence. Ah! If I knew that from some hill a cordial, diligent, and perspicacious look was casually cast on each street, on every roof, every crossroads, where one argues, where one loves, even where one conspires, where one plays as a child, where wisdom wearies you, crushes you, ah, well . . . if I could count on such a look, Paris would be Rome for me. John XXIII had reserved the tower of St. John for himself, at the end of the Vatican gardens, in order to pray and grow old there alone. But from what I have learned from witnesses of his retreats to this round tower, with its medieval mien, Pope John escaped from his cell, where he opened the window, the better to see the mediocre dwellings which surround the Vatican on every side, like waves of humanity and poverty, those waves that of old laid siege to the palaces of kings and broke against them, hourly reminding them of the poverty of most people's condition. I have been told that John XXIII relaxed while watching the laundry drying, the household chores, and the variegated life of humble folk under the Roman sun; the children at the street corners running this way and that; he needed to feel the pulse of these good folk. It is impossible to understand the Pope without situating him and plunging him into the multifarious common family life of the city whose bishop he is, and from which, since the Renaissance, our customs generally remove him.

It is quite understandable that for modern popes in this Vatican City, conventions as in a church prison, stifle the desire to escape, to visit the people and mingle with them, sometimes to be seen, always to see. "How sweet it is," Cardinal Richelieu wrote, "to feel Paris resting in the shadow of my vigils." But the Cardinal was satisfied with that lofty presence.

So we went up by the narrow elevator to this overhanging terrace. I was surprised to find a cloister, indeed, a Benedictine cloister, where, as I imagine on the slopes of Mount Athos, was a place of recollection, but where the architecture itself invites you to view the landscape between the columns and arches which break up the horizon, which multiply and frame the perspectives. Thus, to walk is an incipient ecstasy, to saunter a prayer; in short, body and soul are simultaneously happy. (That is why I had dreams of having a cloister on my roof, and failing this, a mansard with a dormer giving onto the tiles and the television antennae.) This roof, then, of the most contemplative of palaces, was arranged as a cloister: Is this a regret, a hint? At Avignon the popes had conceived their dwelling as a fortress. At Avignon, where I have lived, was the Castello di Sant' Angelo, carried by the breath of the mistral onto the banks of the rushing Rhone. The most obvious thing, which should have been done centuries ago, was to have built a convent, or rather, a monastery, where the Pope, living with Cardinal-monks, and renouncing all other garb than the monastic habit or the symbolical vestments of the liturgy, would receive the thronging crowds of visitors in bare halls.

This cloister—could it perhaps be a beginning, a sign? The Holy Father has simplified the elegance in his own manner, which is more Attic than antique. He conceived of this retreat as a place of prayer. In order to "take the air," he said; I translate: the air of earth and the air of heaven, onto which the earth gives. We walked back and forth in this hanging garden, safe from all eyes, and upon which only a helicopter could trespass. The elevator cage has made necessary the introduction of a square form which is neither belfry nor tower, like a night watchman's lantern. "The walls of my cloister are high enough to prevent me from being seen and even from seeing."

"They are, Holy Father, your closed eyelids."

The Holy Father has mounted a block of stone, his profile is visible: He is seen, or could be seen, by Romans, by visitors. The wind, just arisen, fills his cape. I know he rather likes its lively Samothracian pleats, indicative of movement. It is the hour before twilight; gentle, fading, and phosphorescent in our temperate clime; but swifter in Rome than in Paris, more evocative of the secrets of ramparts and of lands, and for me, more inspiring. For the ocher of the walls, this concentration of the light by the earth or the stone, this raw sienna, dry, damp or burnt, which is the perfume of *Italiae tellus* (Italian earth), seems at the moment of sunset to be dissolved and irradiated, like a thought suddenly become poetry. Every evening in Rome has this same kind of faded beauty; every evening is an autumn. Moreover, at the moment when everything dies and becomes indigo, opalescent, without passing through any livid languor, as if night suddenly succeeded day, then the lights are lighted in the squares and at the crossings, and later along the arteries of the town in long patterns like constellations. And suddenly the whole town is illuminated. In Rome every day is Christmas.

The Pope, leaning on the parapet and, as I said, bronzed by the sun, whipped by the sea breeze, watches the city smile in beauty. Came a moment where the houses melted in ocher and rose, the domes alone emerging from the rusty shadows, while the Alban hills disappeared. Now Rome was no more than an inverted sky full of new stars, of figureless forms, of lassitudes, of voids. And the whole eye, the whole thought of Paul VI was filled with this great city's mixture of sleep, of pleasure, and of sin. He was contemplating this mirror of the universe, a city in its evening fever and repose. The Pope was watching Rome's disappearance into night. He was silent; the wind was still blowing. His white shape had become a gleam, a shadow of light, yet milky like the cloud of a nebula, which seemed to keep vigil over the earth.

"Nothing more can be seen," I said.

"*Everything can be seen,*" he replied.

And he joined his hands, slightly bent his head, became a silhouette in the shadow that prayed, "*Urbi et Orbi.*" These syllables which I was in the habit of joining, I seemed to understand, thanks to this prayer in the night—prayer so natural, not in the least theatrical, but done in the most unnoticeable and simple way in the world. The town, I thought, is a reflection of the world. And if the Holy Father flew elsewhere, he would not carry Rome with him, as Corneille suggested. But the tiniest fragment of this earth of men, at which he would look from the top of a twilit dwelling, would be the sacrament of the whole earth, the mirror of this immense cosmos, which is perhaps empty of thought or love in spite of its universality.

The other side of the terrace, which does not give onto the city, overlooks the basilica. But how strange this famous cupola becomes seen so close: oval, vast, and somber, a sort of elegant cranium, more beautiful than the flattened brain pan of the anthropoids! By night, the lines imagined by Michelangelo looked to me simpler than by day; they were justified by their shapes alone. The dome is like an architectural image of what takes place in a mind which thinks and which prays, when the spheres of reflection diminish as they rise toward the summit. In the dome this ascent is made more harmoniously than in the pointed ogive, which is a broken figure, a crucified vault.

I no longer know if the dome is big or small. It might be a planet visiting the earth and about to leave. It might equally well be a jewel. From the high point where I am, and where I can consider the takeoff of the curves, the dome seems to spring up and to become refined, drawn out like a sonnet in its last tercet, like the end of a wise life. I picture to myself, for no apparent reason, the last evening of the world, humanity's "few remains" contained in a rocket, finally about to leave the earth for another dwelling, another gravitation. The dome is so luminous under the floodlights that it seems transparent. Its color? I don't know. I see it now blue, now rose in the night.

"That is beautiful," said the Holy Father, and I think there is nothing more to be said.

Pope Paul VI has lived for thirty years in this landscape of perhaps all-too-human beauty, in this setting of the popes of the Renaissance from whom we are so far removed, more removed still than from the medieval popes. I know that he dreams of an art which would unite the Florentine aesthetics to Christian pity and piety. And the Milanese painters whom he favors, those who decorated his chapel, find their inspiration in the Early Renaissance, that of Giotto, of Fra Angelico, rather than that of Caravaggio. I will tell later how well this art expresses the Resurrection: one cannot represent Jesus without endowing Him with something of His own glory.

I thought about all these things while looking at the dome and letting my gaze fall toward Bernini's colonnade, toward his fountains, jets of light from which a murmur rose. But one was too high to see clearly what was taking place in St. Peter's Square, around the obelisk.

"From the window of my office, which is under the terrace where we are, at noon, according to a custom introduced by the good Pope John XXIII, I say the Angelus, then a few words, and I bless the assembled people. I see them indistinctly because the distance is too great."

"But," I said to him, "they see you well. They catch you as you are in your place of work, in your workshop, in your laboratory; but they do not disturb you. And this contributes to an intimacy between the people and the father of those people. Of all sovereigns the Pope, almost without guards and without police, is the one who can be seen and approached most easily in the world. One of the functions of his office consists in letting himself be seen as much as possible, not as sovereign but as father."

"And that is why," he replied, "I am happy about everything that can bring me closer. Often I give up the famous *sedia* to move among the crowd, to be nearer them. But I have noticed that this uncomfortable sedia, which gives an impression of the sea, of the tide, at the same time allows of being nearer to all. One is raised above all, to be the better seen by each equally without formalities. But at noon, when the Angelus rings, and I look out on this gathering of visitors from all parts of the earth, I feel linked to them. This rapid contact between solitude and multitude is a force."

J.G.

"Solitude would be isolated without the multitude. And the multitude would be helpless unless it leaned on a single person."

THE POPE

"I think that of all the functions of a Pope the most enviable is that of fatherhood. Formerly I used to accompany Pius XII during the great ceremonies. He used to plunge into the crowd as into the pool of Bethesda. He was crushed and pulled to pieces. But he was radiant. His strength returned. But to witness fatherhood and to be oneself a father, that's quite different. Fatherhood is a feeling which invades the heart and mind, which accompanies you at all hours of the day; which cannot grow less but which increases as the number of children grows; which takes on breadth, which cannot be delegated, which is as strong and delicate as life, which only stops at the final moment; if the Pope is not in the habit of retiring before the end, it is because it is not a question only of function but of paternity. And one cannot stop being a father. Fatherhood is a universal sentiment which extends to all men. I feel it flow from me in concentric circles far beyond the visible frontiers of the Church. I feel myself father of the whole human family. And there is no need for the children to know a father for him to be such. But it is also a feeling which particularizes—I do not know if the word exists in French—but what I mean is, a feeling which attaches you to that particular person, which makes a whole world of that person, even if you only see him once, even if that person is a child. And it is a feeling which in the consciousness of the Pope is always nascent, always fresh, dewy, always free and creative. Would you believe it? It is a feeling which does not weary, does not tire, which refreshes from all fatigue. I have never, for a single instant, felt tired of lifting my hand in blessing. No, I shall never grow weary of blessing or forgiving. When I reached the airfield at Bombay, there was a distance of about twelve miles to reach the place of the Congress. Vast, innumerable crowds, dense, silent, motionless, lined the route— crowds poor and spiritual, avid, packed, naked; attentive crowds, that one only sees in India. I had to bless without ceasing. A friendly priest at my side finally held up my arm, like the servant of Moses. And yet I do not feel superior, but as a brother, lower than all because responsible for all. Fatherhood, in a Pope, I think that is what it is. When he looks at himself he feels very small. If I look back on my past life it appears as a mystery. All that has happened to me in my life is explained by what was to be asked of me at the last. My weakness has remained whole, the feeling of my limitations has grown, but a strength which does not come from me upholds me from moment to moment. I understand what St. Paul says about the misery of his being, of which he did not wish to be relieved. It is an overwhelming and delicious burden, this universal charge, which varies from day to day like pain of light, which like them is daily renewed. The help too is renewed."

"It is," I said, "the mystery of every human life. Only the mystery is more striking at the center of life and in the case of the charge which recapitulates all charges. So it comes about that we too raise our eyes toward you, as to an example given on the mountain, telling us what we should do in daily affairs, great and small alike. A father is not only a father, but a model of what we are. Pascal says that we should do small things like great, because God lives our life, and the great like the small, because he is all-powerful—or rather, I would say, 'because he is omnipresent.' "

"The life of a Pope," he resumed, "has no moment of respite and repose. There is no suspending fatherhood or sonship. And as his business is always beyond his possibility, there is no other way than abandonment to the present moment, which is the Lord. A Pope lives from crisis to crisis, from moment to moment; he goes, like the Hebrews in the desert, from manna to manna. And he has not much time to look back on the road traversed, nor forward all the way to come. John XXIII, who was so simple and jovial, noted that on several occasions. And I remember, too; Newman's lines: 'Lead, kindly Light. . . . /I do not ask to see/the distant scene; one step enough for me.' "

"I remember," I said to him, "that one day at Castel Gandolfo, John XXIII pointed out a distant observatory: 'Look,' he said, 'down over there are Jesuit fathers who know the constellations; I do not know them. I take a step forward in the dark, like Abraham.' "

"Yes, that is how he proceeded, even in great circumstances like the Council, of which the idea came to him suddenly, he always told me. Not everyone has the sudden grace of John XXIII! The gifts of the spirit are so varied. But, for all, there are moments when one must tear oneself away from preparations and fly among the clouds confidently, boldly.

"God does us the honor of His help when we let ourselves fall into His arms. It is a great grace, an experiment which every Christian has made and perhaps even every man.

"I saw it in the course of my journey. Several cardinals had given me to understand that it was not without risks, and I expect they were right, but it is so good to risk when one is in Almighty hands. Then, truly one feels that between God and us there is no longer an interval."

And then the Holy Father spoke to me of his journeys. He said: "Since they took place and have melted into the past, I can reflect on what in them is alike and what is different. *I ponder them in my heart* as the Gospel tells us the Virgin did. It is a good method. And in thus pondering in my heart, I understand better each one's grace."

I said to him: "The first was to Jerusalem. It was to be the first of all, and would in itself have sufficed. I remember everyone's surprise when you announced it; nobody had thought of it. Nobody had thought it possible or conceivable! All the same, one hour after the *news*, it appeared natural, how can I express it, *evident*. This is a good example of what happens with inventions, of what happened with the calling of the Council. *Before*, nobody had thought of it. *After*, everyone seemed to have always thought of it. Once again, one had to have the idea and start; it is like making a forward movement. If one had never seen anyone move or speak, one would say, 'It's impossible'; and after one says, 'It's necessary.' Before it seems incredibly complicated; *after*, how easy it is!"

The Pope smiled and said: "It is quite true that it was most natural. I had wanted, as I have said, to make a pilgrimage to the place where the Church was born and where Peter was chosen, where Christ was born, suffered, and rose again. For centuries, it was not possible, because of politics or because of the insufficiency of technical means. But as soon as conditions allowed, the voyage became obvious. It was necessary if it was possible. As for my second journey, to India, that was more difficult to imagine. Some said that this journey to such a faraway country, and so little Christian . . ."

"But, Holy Father," I said to him, "one could have foreseen the second after the first. One could deduce it, as it is possible to deduce faith from hope. The act of faith suggested going to the Land of the Incarnation, to the junction of the Arab world and Israel, to the meeting place of Abraham's two families. Whoever is searching for the secret impulse which guides you in the choice of these visits might suppose that you would gladly go where the children of Abraham adjoin the Indian peoples, at the boundaries of the Orient, where such a grave menace threatens the world's peace. St. Paul, whose name you bear, took as his program to visit the extreme limits of the then known world. It is said he went as far as Spain, to the famous Pillars of Hercules. From the moment that a Pope is in possession of ubiquity, thanks to the progress of human techniques, he should go to these new 'pillars' which are the borders of Asia. And this is what St. Francis Xavier, who was a new St. Paul, understood in his day. To evangelize is not always to penetrate, to found, to remain; it is also to announce, to visit briefly, to be seen, to show one's profile, to cry out, to offer oneself in silence. Allow me to quote you something the Archbishop of Milan said: 'If the dialogue is not possible, there will at least be a cry, a call, a prophecy.' Ratisbonne, at the time of the famous apparition of San Andrea delle Fratte, said: 'She said nothing to me and I understood everything.' An apparition in the Indian sky, where you were the man clad in white, as Gandhi had been, the man of peace whose symbols are the dove and whiteness. Had I been an Indian man or woman, had I only seen you from afar as an indistinct white form, I would have thought that my yearning was fulfilled, that which I felt inside myself, more essential than my own self, had suddenly appeared."

THE POPE

"It is true that this voyage to India was a revelation of an unknown universe to me. I saw, as the Apocalypse puts it, a multitude which none can number, a multitude, and all in a state of welcome. I divined in those thousands of glances something more than curiosity. I do not know what inexplicable sympathy. India is a spiritual land. By nature it has a feeling for the Christian virtues. I told myself that if there is one country where the beatitudes of the Sermon on the Mount could one day be lived, and not by the elite, but by a whole people, by a unanimous, innumerable mass, it was there. What is nearer to the heart of India than poverty *of spirit?* What is more Hindu than *gentleness,* to such a point that there this gentleness can be read in their glances, their attitude, their speech? What is nearer the soul of India than *peace, mercy,* than *purity of heart?* What is nearer to this soul than submissiveness full of hope, under persecution for justice's sake? We cannot tell what would happen if all these possibilities, everything which exists in the heart, and I repeat, in the yearnings, in the capacities of this great people, were suddenly brought to light.

"I also noticed that the leaders of this people were sages. In the West, those who are at the head of affairs are trained in politics. There, they are mystics and sages. Life passes in contemplation. Voices are low, gestures are slow and liturgical. These are countries born for the Spirit. And one cannot know *the future of the Spirit.*"

"But," said I, "Indian spirituality does not admit of the Incarnation and the Redemption; the whole mystery of Christianity escapes it. It is even possible to wonder if western atheism, of which we are so afraid, which dominates all our dialogues, is not a lesser danger than the oriental atheism of tomorrow, which will be a mystical atheism. India could well, through its thinkers and its masses, be at the point of a mysticism where one would lose consciousness in the pure spirit, in the nonaction, and where no resistance would be made to anything, which would accept everything, which would have no objection to Christianity, because it would believe it would go beyond it and understand it. Nonresistance is worse than persecution."

HE

"We can never know what are the destinies of peoples. Every destiny is faced with the better and the worse. Its depths can lead it toward a great good or a great evil. I would even say that the higher is the vocation, the more it can stray. India will not escape this law. But a spark is sufficient, a breath, a call in the night, sometimes a finger silently lifted in a certain direction, as Leonardo da Vinci represented St. John's finger in the 'Madonna of the Rocks.' "

I

"This journey to fabulous India was a marvel, a legend, a colored splendor of distant lands, a discovery, at the same time an invention, a lightning flash, a passage, something divine, fairy, Shakespearian, or romantic—if it is true that the essence of art is sometimes to surprise, to produce a happening without links to the past. I remember Paul Claudel telliing me, 'I used to like the novels of Eugène Sue; you are in France, then suddenly, without knowing why or how, you find yourself transported to the North Pole.' There are such metamorphoses in *The Satin Slipper*. By the journeys of the Holy Father an element of curiosity, of suspense, has been introduced into the Christian consciousness. One asks oneself: What will he do next? One tries to deduce the future from the past. After Jerusalem, it was difficult to imagine a pilgrimage to India. And after India, it was not so easy to guess whether there would be a third voyage during the Council and which direction it would take."

The Pope smiled again. "Do not think," he said, "that I try to surprise. I ask myself, things being as they are—and by things, I mean circumstances, conditions, the constellation of events, and that continual alliance of necessity and chance, all these *signs of the times*—I question myself before God to determine exactly which is the act, of minimal extent, easy to do, but rich in symbolism, in scope, which I could do, to help Catholics, Christians, mankind. Help them to understand each other better, to unite. That is what is implied in my first duty to be an apostle, the successor of him whom Christ called *Peter*. And I foresee nothing. I do not make a five-year plan of future journeys, not even an ideal list of possible journeys. As I told you, I go from moment to moment, from urgency to urgency, and, through the Divine Mercy, from grace to grace. Thus I came to envisage going to the UN Headquarters, because at Bombay I had issued an appeal for peace and for help to the Third-World, because this call was not lost in the desert, because it had been heard by U Thant. One thing followed upon another, without my wishing it."

I

"You did not know what was impelling you. We never know everything. After the voyage of faith and hope, it was a voyage of love, of universal love. You went to the Far West, in order to meet the nations gathered together. Never, I think, had the Pope spoken to the nations, I mean to all nations, what the Bible calls *omnes gentes*. Yet the command 'to evangelize' is to go to all peoples. But until today they were only gathered together under the hard and always rather fictitious and provisional symbol of imperial unity. There was a symbiosis of *gentes*, every time that this imperial form appeared, this idea of unity under a single scepter, under a single head, sometimes consecrated by the Pope, who saw there his antitype, his double, or his homologue. But it was an imperfect image, for the nations were not free to act, did not have their autonomy, their liberty. And I recall this saying—of Victor Hugo, I think it is: Nations should not be destroyed—the same could be said of churches—but seated around the common hearth, each with its own genius and its familiar face. Moreover, this hearth should have its location on the street, should correspond to an institution, so that one can find the nations in some place."

HE

"You well express what was the purpose of this journey: to go to the nations whose organization had taken the initiative of inviting the Supreme Roman Pontiff. I weighed the extent, the astonishing yet simple meaning of this gesture of invitation; the Papacy is not a nation, it has no place among the nations. Its territory is so tiny; merely a pretext for existing, only as much body as is necessary for a soul to be. But as I think I said, it is something else, and in a certain sense it is more than the nations. It has no function among the nations, but it can be invited among them, like the Child Jesus among the doctors. For twenty centuries we were waiting for just this. And finally, at last, quite simply, it happened."

I

"And when you found yourself alone in front of these nations, one couldn't help thinking of Paul in the Areopagus, becoming Greek among Greeks, speaking their language, until the moment when he was no longer understood."

HE

"I quoted St. Paul in my talk, but I did not have to evangelize. The talk I gave was situated on another plane—if I dare to say so, the plane of Socrates. I was looking for what was reasonable and just, equitable and salutary, what every responsible man ought to think. If I evangelized, it was to preach that Gospel virtually contained within the Gospel, which is the Gospel of reason and justice."

I

"And it so happens that it is characteristic of our time that reason and justice can no longer stand alone. They need another support. And it even happens, and will happen increasingly, that it is those who believe in something other than the visible who will be necessary in order that the visible may be loved; that a higher light will be indispensable in order to know the light; that in order to taste the flavor of common sense it will be necessary to call upon men of faith. And they alone will discreetly speak the language of common sense and will enable it to be realized. Yes, I do not know if this was evident in New York, it was an extraordinary moment: the Gospel of justice and of common sense, the Pope speaking like a sage, listened to by sages, and finding the common bond among all. What you said, anyone could have said; but it was good that it was the Pope who said it."

HE

"I needed much thought and prayer to be so denuded and stripped."

I

"And in fact, when we in Europe saw you on television, alone, a white form, while Mr. Fanfani introduced you so simply in that lay, simplified, and dry decor, you seemed like a man who was about to appear before his judges. Sometimes you seemed like the Master about to teach, sometimes like the accused who had come to plead his defense, and under these two aspects of Jesus in his Passion, either before Pilate of Caiphas, or the night before Easter, *the doors being already closed.''*

HE

"Every man carried these two aspects always, like a medal with two faces."

I

"It was a unique moment in history; everyone understood it to be so. An original moment which will not be repeated, but which could have so many consequences for peace."

HE

"This word *peace* has a new and absolute sense. Never has the paradox been more felt. What each people desires is also that which they cannot accomplish. And the more one wishes peace, the farther one draws away from it. Humanity has never been nearer, nor farther. Never has it been in a situation where the extremes were before it: either to be lost, or saved! Never has it been so strong and so helpless. That is why I could use that language: *with* one another, *for* one another. I spoke the language of love, which is the imperative by which we are driven at bay. Earlier the Gospel could seem a luxury; from now on it is a practical necessity, an urgent direction, an experimental solution: something to which, after having tried everything, we are obliged, not by hope of life but under pain of death. Circumstances permitted the Pope to be heard in silence, not as Pope, but as a man having accumulated a long experience, authorized then to speak with simplicity as though he were an expert in humanity come from the depths of ages."

I

"And you did not speak only to New York. Thanks to the presence of this little screen, which multiplies you, which represents you in every group of men, I would say that you were also present in several millions of individual consciousnesses. Without breaking in, and even without being summoned, the Church entered with your white form, your very simple speech, into the homes of those unaware of it. This is what helps me to understand why among the twelve apostles Jesus nevertheless singled out one only, so that at some moments he was the twelve, he was all. The universe sometimes needs to see the unique. In certain circumstances it prefers only to hear a single voice to express everything.

"I remember my impressions as a television viewer on Monday, October 4, watching in a place quite close to the Vatican, which you had left at dawn, and to which you were returning the next day at noon. I saw you getting out of the cosmonaut's capsule of Alitalia's DC8. Having first appeared in the distance, it came closer, then made rather slow turns, then become motionless. The door did not open at once. There was a long wait. Unedited instant, that in which the Pope having the name of Paul, 'the Apostle of the Nations,' was about to appear to this New World—inexistent on medieval maps, unknown to Christianity then, and which was to double the surface of the earth. It must have been cold. In any event, the airport seemed icy; it seemed an uninhabited waste, windy, crude like a new land to conquer, 'still damp from the deluge,' as Victor Hugo would have said, a reservoir of men and of hormones for our aged West, capable of saving it."

HE

"When one has understood that an act is a duty, it becomes easier at once, the bird opens his wings and falls, but the impulse and the emptiness bear him up.

"I was never tired during this visit. And the voyage comforted me from the echo of my words in the hearts and the consciences of those who govern.

"It could be said that the Papacy became involved in politics. But, as I have already said, it is necessary to look at the context. The Council showed well this independence of the Papacy from the temporal. It was not even necessary to raise the question whether emperor or kings or ambassadors should be asked. The Papacy has become a voice, a sign above all voices and signs upon earth, without having to 'intervene,' as a surgeon puts it. The Papacy does not come nor does it intervene. It can assist, when the united efforts of all the nations, the community composed of all nations, needs a *little something* which is nothing, which is a lot, a confirmation, a blessing, an agreement, a breath, that little breath that says *yes*.

"I think this is a new situation, because for everyone, and all over the globe, even when there is no conflict, there is a sovereign, total, permanent danger, an underlying unexpressed anguish—what is the use of expressing it, as it is constant and clear, like the feeling of morality, like the fear of the judgment of God—an anguish which, being general, is a bond among all men, the like of which history has never known before. Certainly, there were anxieties, but limited anxieties, not yet universal ones. Anguish, I tell you, but also an aspiration toward peace, which is as universal as the anguish, which also unites all nations, even if only in the reciprocal mutual fear which is the sad consequence of sin. That is why, at this moment, an

incursion into politics is not a political gesture; it is the denial of
politics in the low sense, or, if you prefer, it is the fullness of politics
in the noble sense, in St. Augustine's sense, the fulfillment of the city
of man and of the city of God. It would be for the expert on St.
Augustine to correct me, if I am mistaken."

I

"The two cities for St. Augustine were rather two currents inter-
mingled. The city of evil or self-love divided men, opposed them in
rival factions, because it was founded on egoism, going as far as
hatred or negation of God. And there was the city of God, where the
love of God at last destroyed the separations of hatred so that finally
it persuaded the nations to love one another. That at least is what I
think I got from reading St. Augustine, and what he says that is
always pertinent."

HE

"It is still pertinent. But one can try to reconcile the two cities. St.
Augustine did not know what Father de Lubac calls atheistic
humanism. And this is truly specific to our times, its profound
problem, its scandal: that the love of man can appear to be opposed
to the very idea of God; that the love of God among those who love
Him and act in His name is not strong enough to counter schisms,
separations . . . the pooling of the energies, the resources, of all the
goods of faith, of the soul, of the body; that the love of mankind can
imagine that to be efficacious it must first deny, sweep out, silence, or
deny God; that those two laws of love that Jesus has so substantially
united are disassociated and opposed. *Thou shalt love thy God with
all thy strength. Thou shalt love the other as thou lovest thyself.*

"It is to try to bind what has been loosed that this unworthy and weak successor of the Apostle Peter, who has received the power to bind and to loose, that this sucessor, I repeat, went to the UN in the wake, in a continuation of the Council. For, in our time, everything is connected, marvelously, dramatically. This is another reason why the Pope should move, since his charitable function of universal audience symbolizes this link which henceforward everything has with everything else."

The conversation had risen to the point where it could only be completed by a certain silence, under the arcades of this little cloister filled with dusk, looking down toward the town which appeared only as a pink mist; modern cities are never completely dark.

The Holy Father had put politics in their place in the political context. And all the arguments that I had heard so often as to whether he did well or badly to go to UN, as to whether he had not compromised that unassignable prestige in going to support a disputed, divided, and powerless institution; or as to whether the Church was not going in the wrong direction by redreaming the temporal in a democratic form and for a new Christendom different from that of the Middle Ages or of the Holy Roman Empire but identical in principle; whether she should not rise above the abyss on the wings of the dove, isolate herself in the skies, restricting her action to her doves' coos and to the shadow of her wings—all these perfectly valid thoughts that I also had cogitated, all this was settled by a simple and superior viewpoint, which could be resumed as follows: "What is my duty as the leader of humanity, as the vicar of Christ, at the present moment, this only moment where the infinite puts on the finite as in the Host?" In our epoch, so different from the others, it is difficult to think in comparison with ancient times, to envisage precedents. And I also thought that, by gestures, by symbols, and by some few very general words—to which are limited those who execute arbitrary and supreme power and are obliged to inhabit the high places—the Holy Father had furthermore risen above contradictory theses. It is by *rising,* as I see it, that problems should often be solved, not by oppositions, but by going higher, or also by suddenly descending from a Mount Thabor.

All his preceding life had been a preparation for that hour, especially the evenings, the family vigils in the old house at Brescia, close to his father who had taught him to think of public matters, not to be content with a life without commitment, who taught him too not to despair of reason, to believe that Christianity can penetrate everything. St. Paul was *civis romanus* (a Roman citizen). He forgot it in ordinary circumstances, because he looked higher, because he was a Jew and full of the hopes of his race. But when it was necessary to remember that he was a Roman citizen, he did not fail to do so. In the same way young Montini, although a seminarian, although a priest, knew he was an Italian citizen and through Italy was associated with the world of nations. His brother Lodovico has continued the paternal tradition: He is a senator and vice-president of the Advisory Board of the European Council.

It so happened that I was placed very near this brother during the Council ceremonies and could observe the likenesses of their profiles, particularly the way their eyes are set in the sockets, the shape of the nose, the look of intense application which the Montini, these fiery mountaineers, bring to everything, with a deep-down tenderness and Vergilian gentleness. Brescia is in the plain not far from Mantua, Vergil's birthplace. In these districts, racially independent because they lived under foreign domination, the little visible city, made to human scale, is passionately loved; over the meadows, the mushrooms, and the teams of brown long-horned oxen, the town's profile of crenellated ramparts can be seen. *One goes up to Rome and its* ramparts, but as though to another city, stable and maternal, who will not destroy the municipalities, but will protect them, will found them anew by its patronage, just as the authority of the Pope protects and confirms the bishops, his equals, equally successors of the Apostles. I do not know if by situating the Montinis on their original lands, on their Vergilian or Lombard soil, I am grounding them too much. But no, no, indeed, on the contrary: I make it understandable how the Italian race which has given the world so many master politicians, how this free urban race is a citizen race—like St. Paul, who knew it when he asserted his claim to the title of *civis*, which claim caused his decapitation outside the walls. Young Giovanni Battista Montini breathed this "political" air in his city of Brescia, which is on a scale suited to human concerns: near enough to Milan and Venice to receive the western air, the eastern effluvia; far enough to enjoy that autonomy given by distance from dominations. And also because it had never been conquered for very long at any time, and even when it was (as when Napoleon Bonaparte in 1797 established himself and Josephine stayed there), it was never entirely submissive.

The visitor to Brescia still hears the heartbeat of a strong city, which no little reminds me of Grenoble and the Allobroges, of Clermont and the Arverni.

One can guess that in these much visited, but also solitary towns, there will always be a citadel to keep watch on the walls, but also that a school of artists can flourish at the same time as civil liberty can be organized. In spite of the insolence of the Fascist monuments disproportionate to the city's size, Brescia remained an unconquered center while Mussolini was in power, a city ready to foresee and to prepare the moment when liberty would reappear.

The Montini family worked there in the local press. The future

Pope lived in that atmosphere of continual creation, of uncertain but secure hope among the shocks and upheavals his father knew in his daily charge of infusing hope into newspaper articles. Giovanni Battista saw at its best the work of the Christian journalist which is to be reborn daily with a new spirit, to infuse into the flowing present something of the eternal. In one sense, the Pope too does this.

Every son of man transposes in an unedited way the call of his father and the voice of his mother. He too had to combine a resemblance to his father's activity with maternal contemplation, but he raised them to a higher state, in a more intimate union which is the renouncing of any family and civic work in order to be the servitor of the sole Spirit who wants us for Himself alone and by ways we know not. But transposition is not destruction. In the young priest the gifts and the tastes which would have made of him only an orator, a writer, a layer, a journalist, a senator were to be found in another guise.

I repeat that in a vocation a father's career and a mother's magic, her serious candor, her sacrificed tenderness live again. This is what happened yet once again in this Lombard province. Giovanni Battista consecrated himself to God. And his family habits, their occupations, their civic concern, these he raised much higher.

This anxiety to have a clear view of a situation, to seize what Cardinal de Retz called the precise point of possibility—the art of obtaining from men that they will do what secretly they wish when publicly they seem to do everything to prevent it—this is what animates the spirit of true politics. It is the art of preparing the common good by making use of individual goods. Politics is like the mariner who by tacking his ship arrives where he wishes in spite of contrary winds. And be it said in passing: Every art makes use of contrary and devilish means; writing uses dull and worn-out words. The churchman, who is an expert in the real and total good, is eminently political. And that is why a prelate often does no more than let himself slide down, need only put off ecclesiastical ways to become immediately a politician: Let us remember Retz, Mazarin, Talleyrand. Yet at home we are surprised when radical ministers who are politicians get on so easily with papal nuncios.

True politics are kin to charity, if love, as Leibniz taught, consists in taking another's viewpoint. The whole ecumenical discipline is, then, to see oneself not with one's own but with another's eye. What makes real politicians rather rare is that the art requires self-renunciation. But the demon wishes clever men to throw themselves into it, and that politics should become ambition's career.

Monsignor Montini first served under Pius XI, who was the first to notice his worth. The great esteem Pius XI had for him is not generally known; he consulted his views, to which he listened even when they did not agree with his own, in spite of the great difference in their ages and positions. Monsignor Montini was impressed by him whom he once in my hearing called *Rex tremendae majestatis* (King of awesome majesty). But it was under Pius XII that he completed his education in the handling of important matters. He was not his secretary of state, which indicates a function and division of labor, an obedience such as existed between Richelieu and Louis XIII, from minister to king. This was quite another thing. Monsignor Montini had a tactful title; he shared his office charge of "pro-secretary" with Monsignor Tardini. He was in the shadow of Monsignor Tardini, charged with the "first section" of the secretariat, but he was more in the presence. The Pope did not so much give him orders as make him party to his incipient thought: Pius XII thought and he tested his nascent thought on this first, mute echo. For a Montini, what an apprenticeship!

"On the whole," said the Pope, "these voyages were well received."

"Yes," I answered him, "the world was surprised. It was like an act of poesy, if it is true that poetry is, as John Keats said, to surprise 'by a fine excess.' And by excess must be understood that which takes a step forward, that which goes a little beyond what was expected."

"That is prophecy," Paul VI added, stressing the consonants, separating a little the first two syllables, as he does when speaking French, a language he has learned, which therefore is more filled with its primitive meaning.

By *prophecy* he does not here mean the divination of the future, but the language of heart speaking to heart, without the intermediary of concepts, which is what makes art. Prophecy is the language of that which it is impossible to say or is still unsayable. Prophecy is the language understood by the people, which sages can meditate, for it has *chiaroscuro*, it has several layered meanings. It does not wound. It is patient. It believes everything. It endures everything.

I have an idea that there exist three ways of expressing oneself. The first is language, but this gives up before the incommunicable part of us, or before the mystery one wishes to transmit. Silence then remains, a certain silence, I mean the silence which follows speech, silence in the face of others' suffering, the silence of compassion, or of respect, or of an unexpressed, inexpressible love. However, there exists an intermediary zone between these imperfect means of expression, that is, the symbolic gesture—mute like silence, but rich in meaning like speech. This is prophecy, which among the old-testament prophets included an act, a novel act, strange, but sometimes accompanied by its commentary. We see this even in the Bible; Jesus' great actions are also prophetic, like His baptism by John or His death. How they still speak to us, having traversed all the ages!

"It is thus that Your Holiness will—after having meditated upon them long, and prepared them secretly and circumspectly, without haste and foreseeing their every minute—that he will," said I, "have marked the earth with these three stigmata: Jerusalem, Bombay, New York. And stigmata are indelible. No one can make these places unvisited by the representative of Jesus Christ. This gives them a new dimension: depth. This is already noticeable in Jerusalem and Galilee, which cannot be visited anymore in the same way since the Pope has visited them. As for myself, not having returned there since 1935, I feel that they are no longer the same landscapes, simply because they have been seen by those eyes. This is some magic, perhaps some illusion; we have it for certain works of art. For example, one does not see the human face or nature in the same way since Rouault or Cézanne. Painters modify landscapes, they put their soul and substance into them. The commentaries are incorporated in the work."

I am quite sure that in future editions, Baedeker's guides, after having described the Holy Places, will add: "In 1964 *Pope Paul* VI *visited this site.*" The travelers will then no longer see it in the same way as when they read: "A battle was fought here."

I would say further: "A constellation is not stardust, it is a shape a face, a design—thus Leo, Virgo, or Gemini. I look at the constellation you have traced with your voyages. I look at the figure made by these three signs: It is this that instructs me. What I see in this constellation drawn during the Council which is its commentary is the link among these three cities, Jerusalem, Bombay, New York. It is the connection of these three intentions, of the past, the future, and the present, it is the agreement, the conspiracy of faith (by a return to the sources), of hope for the future, of love, by the desire of peace among men." I am sure that it would be possible to point out other bonds of affinity; when one looks for the connections among three related things, one finds more and more. It seems that a ray of light glides from one to another and reveals them, like a mutual gaze. For example:

At Jerusalem, at Capernaum, at Bethlehem, the mystery of the Incarnation was central. Not the Incarnation considered abstractly, as it sometimes happens in the Hellenized West, or reduced by certain Bible criticism to the status of being merely a revealed myth, but the Incarnation incarnated (if I may so put it) in the very land where Christ was born, emerged, grew, spoke, taught, died, and was born again in reality and glory. This *Holy Land* which reveals to us the historicity, the humanity, the benign presence of God among us. And more. It reveals Him who, shining from Galilee and Judea upon all the earth, made this whole planet a place of God's visitation, so that from henceforward the whole earth is holy.

Bombay was a homage to the Eucharistic mystery, so foreign to India, which rejects even the Incarnation, this mystery which the Holy Father was to extol before the last session of the Council as the highest point of the Faith. "It is only us whom God illuminates thus far," Pascal once said. And who is to say that one day there will not be in those lands so avid for the Spirit a deeper understanding than ours of this mystery of the divine humiliation?

And the New World that the Genoese Columbus dreamed of—in the city where Catherine of Genoa explored the hereafter—America, symbol of all that is virgin in the cosmos, ready to arise, rich in so

many ways of thinking and acting that we cannot as yet imagine.
It is the world of the conquistadores.

> *Penchés à l'avant des blanches caravelles*
> *Ils regardaient monter dans un ciel ignoré*
> *Du fond de l'Ocean, des étoiles nouvelles.*[1]

"But," I said to him then, "I now have to ask a question many have
asked me. May I formulate an objection? It is that this voyage will
introduce a new style of pontifical life, that the Papacy runs the risk
of seeing its prestige diminish to the extent in which it will get mixed
up with the world, that these voyages will fatally have a social and
political side, *whether you wish it or not*. And sometimes it seems as
though you wished it. Is not a Papacy, itinerant from now on,
faithless to its role of immovable arbiter, is it not obliged to take
sides, and consequently to engage itself in complications which it
will no longer be able to control? Will it not seem to prefer this
nation to that nation—thus, in Jerusalem to uphold the Jewish side
against Islam?"

THE POPE

"The Church is incarnated in time. She is spiritual and temporal.
She cannot not have a face; that face is of a time and a nation.

"I know that she is reproached for being Italian, as earlier she was
reproached for being French."

So the Pope would have to cease being a man, obliged to think
and to act successively. What is appropriate is that the Pope, when

---

[1] Leaning forth from their white caravels
They watched in the uncharted skies
New stars from Ocean's depths arise.

he chooses a site, a place, a people, a nation, a point in space, should rise above this point, and that he should visit it as Christ would have done. The Pope's words are different from those of a chief of state.

Whatever he does, or is, he speaks as the Universal Father. And that is what the people who receive him feel, and it is for this very reason that they receive him. You will notice that, on these three voyages, he never went to a really Catholic country. One might have thought that the first journeys of the Holy Father would be reserved for the old Catholic countries, for the great places of Catholic prayer. The Pope put out to sea. He advanced into the deep. He needed faith, a little confidence, some love of risk. He has been rewarded.

3

CONCESIO AND VEROLAVECCHIA

In thinking of his childhood I reflected that he had been fortunate in having lived close to the holy, and very close, too, to the world of men, in a small town, with a country house not faraway on the mountainside.

He had an active father, a contemplative mother, an old priest for a friend, a garden to dream in, and all this during the fragility, the susceptibility, the minor ills of childhood, which make one more perceptive, surrounded by affection.

I said to myself that this surely was also the story of the poet who, even before Christ was preached, formed our western sensitivity: Vergil.

I applied the following lines from the fourth Eclogue to the childhood of the young Giovanni Battista in that house in Concesio:

> And first, dear child, the unsubjected land
> Held lovely gifts for you; the scanty ivy
> With scented water lilies intertwined,
> And gay acanthus mingled with wild nard.[1]

This house at Concesio had as it were two faces, in the manner of oriental dwellings. On the street, or rather, on the road running

[1] *At tibi prima, puer nullo munuscula cultu*
Errantes hederas passim cum baccare tellus
Mixtaque ridenti colocasia fundet acantho.

through the village, little showed except the porch and a wrought-iron balcony, useful no doubt on feast days to deck with flags and to show oneself. All the beauty was within, and in the court, or rather in the yard, above all in the garden which was not, as with us, an enclosed garden—which creates a distinction between the garden proper and the orchards; here I could pass by imperceptible stages from the garden to the fields, from the fields to the countryside, and from the countryside to the lower slopes of the Alps.

Aggredere o magnos (aderit iam tempus), honores . . .

The days will come of your great magistracy . . .
Little one, learn to know your mother by her smile.
Ten months she has borne bitter weariness.[2]

These stanzas haunt our western memories; never, it would seem, have they been better applied than at Concesio.

The movement of a village, the peace of a dwelling, the shadows and openings of a mysterious garden, the sun and its realm, fields, adventures, little houses—in short, the different ways of being alone while remaining in contact with men, as from a cloister, which is, at the same time, an observatory. Apart from the world, mingling with the world, within the world . . .

The pines surrounded the old house, their shade was deep and cool with a slight scent of incense, with branches well arranged to tempt Lodovico, Giovanni Battista, and Francesco Montini, the three sons, to climb.

Nothing had changed. I meditated on this Italian family life familiar and patriarchal, where everything is more mixed and mingled than with us, even in Provence; where one sees so few walls,

2 Vergil: Eclogue 4, 20.

hedges, or fences; where the separation of thine and mine is by habit and custom more than by law or barriers, and is free from envy. This northern Italy has long remained a garden and what the orientals call a paradise. A critic said to me, "Italy lives in the present. The Italian does not have the French longing to grow up, he wants to prolong that beatific state of childhood, or at least to recapture it. And some get away with the ways of a spoiled child. After Modena you leave the world of scruples, of a torn conscience and regrets or even remorse, to enter the world of grace and of nature." He added mysteriously: "Every European man who reaches the age of thirty has had to abandon his early life. In Italy radiant childhood remains and carries a man along from age to age to his dying day. Only it is a divine game which replaces a childish one. St. Francis of Assisi, St. Philip Neri, and Don Bosco, perhaps John XXIII, too (Sotto il Monte is not so far from Concesio), will teach you this way of life, which we Gauls and Celts cannot imitate."

In the garden at Concesio I had these thoughts about childhood, its length, its extent, its possible transposition. It was at the end of March in the year 1965. I tried to recapture the image of this young boy who lived there a little as I had once lived, who found instruction in the garden, in the holidays, in prayer in that garden, in his mother's vigilance, who as an adolescent no doubt filled this harmonious, bounded, and secret landscape with his plans and laughter. Many a thoughtful boy has been in that sort of open cloister, that green close. And burgeoning thought must indeed be protected. The disadvantage—or advantage—would be a poetic, fantastic, reflective thought. But it is on a base of reflection that all deep thought is synthesized, and from thence it derives its oxygen and breath. And it is notable that the future Pope has nurtured in himself the imaginative, which was never desiccated by school. His journeys, his travels abroad have been few, secret, and swift. Devoted to getting to know the world, he has come to know it mostly through reading or through the visits he has so constantly received. The world has come to him, not he to the world. But an imaginative childhood creates an interworld; an ever-present poetry in which the whole world may come to dwell; it will be welcomed there and will have its place. And Marcel Proust, whose nature was reflective and who had also received education from a garden, from a journey to Venice which practically never took place, recreated and ruled a universe.

It was in the church of Concesio that Giovanni Battista was baptized on the thirtieth of September 1897. The same day at a quarter past seven in the evening, after a cruel agony, Thérèse of the Child Jesus expired at the Carmelite convent at Lisieux. The co-incidence would be less striking had there not been found in the journal of Sister Agnès of Jesus this passage full of interest and charm. On June 25, the day of the Feast of the Sacred Heart, Thérèse had shown her sister a passage in a pious work where was noted "the appearance of a beautiful Lady clothed in white near a baptized infant." And Thérèse had said to her sister: "Later I shall go like that to little children being baptized."

How similar that childhood was to my own I know from what the Holy Father said to me one day about my book on my mother: "I have found some of my own memories in your book. I think that I too owe much to my mother, to her way of thinking and feeling." He added, "There we enter the realm of the inexpressible."

The truly restful vacations, those which refresh and renew, were not passed at Concesio, too near Brescia to provide a peaceful country change. The true vacations for Don Battista, as for many children, were near his mother's birthplace, twenty miles from

Brescia at the del Dosso house in a village called Verolavecchia. It was flat country, full of sun and mist, and very fertile, the old marshlands having been dried out long ago and transformed into farm land by the labor of Benedictines. The Pope's father applied in the district the principles of *Rerum novarum* to raise the condition of the workers and free them from the vestiges of servitude.

It was, as I have said, the country of his mother, an Alghisi, who was born on July 17, 1874. She was an only daughter orphaned at the age of four. As Verolavecchia had no secondary school she was sent, when she was seven years old, to the college of the Marcelline Sisters at Milan. It was there that she found herself and forged her youthful freedom. Her guardian had chosen a fiancé for her. She did not accept him. At the age of eighteen, on a pilgrimage to Rome, she had noticed Giorgio Montini; she had admired his unembarrassed courage in affirming his faith. As her guardian did not accept this choice, she had to wait for her legal majority to marry as her heart bade. On July 17, 1895, she was twenty-one. On August 1 she married Giorgio Montini, who had studied law but dedicated his life to local government. The cast of her character was already evident: personal decision silently matured. The young couple went for their honeymoon to Switzerland to the Benedictine abbey of Einsiedeln.

She was pious and thoughtful; she had anticipated the decision of Pius X. Since 1892 she had been a daily communicant. How different she was from "worldly" people may be guessed. She has been described to me as incapable of having a frivolous conversation or of getting worked up about unimportant things.

"She gave short shrift to petty meanness," her sons Lodovico and Francesco told me. "And at the same time she had a lively wit. She was a delicious letter writer, and it was impossible to throw her letters away. She talked on paper; she set down family and local events, drawing from them suddenly a spiritual lesson; in the insignificant daily round she found the traces and reminders of God." All her actions 'had transcendent reference' the same witnesses told me. The children remember her conversations about the Gospel on Sunday evenings. They were simple and admirable explanations going straight to essentials. In 1909, she had read *The Story of a Soul* of St. Thérèse of the Child Jesus, then Gemma Galgani, then the Letters of Elisabeth Lesueur, Don Marmion, and Bossuet's *Elevations*. She was, like her husband, a Franciscan tertiary, and said the rosary every day.

"We still recall many friends whom my brother, so disposed to friendship, loved: the Abbé Francisco Galloni, an ardent and generous soul, who was a heroic military chaplain in the First World War before becoming, in Sofia, the friend of Monsignor Roncalli; the Abbé Enrico Soncini, a very fine man, very sensitive, who had translated from the French *A Sister's Story* by Pauline Craven de la Ferronays; Monsignor Defendente Salvetti; Longinotti; and Bazoli, whom he met on vacations in the Trentino.

"Sometimes the vacations were taken elsewhere. On the advice of an uncle, Joseph Montini, a physician and humanist, we went to Levico in the Trentino, then Austrian, where there were iron-rich waters. Or again to Recoaro Terme—or again to the mountains, to Borno and Bagolino. The holidays always ended on the eighth of September; then the whole family gathered together in Brescia, to be present at the feast of the birth of the Virgin, particularly solemn at the sanctuary, so near their family home, of Our Lady of All Grace.

"Our brother Battista was already full of apostolic zeal and charm. He won over his listeners. I remember what a good storyteller he was. At Concessio there are still shoemakers who remember his coming into their family shop while they worked and telling them the stories of Canon Christopho Schmidt, or the tales of Théophile: *The Orphan of the Valley*, and *The Good and the Wicked Fridolin*.

" 'Then,' they said, 'we stopped work and had to cry.'

"We remember how in 1912, to try out a bicycle, Giovanni Battista, who looked so fragile, had made the hard trip from Brescia to Bagolino without difficulty. Our mother was uneasy and reproached him with his rashness."

"Our mother," Dr. Francesco told me, "experienced very pure and deep joy when our brother was ordained priest. And we recall the peace, the consolation, and the joy which she brought to friends who regretted seeing their children choose the priesthood. Then she had a wonderful way of changing, in the Gospel words, their sorrow into joy.

"If," they added, "one were to include all the unknown and self-sacrificing souls who contributed, so to speak, to the destiny of our brother, several relatives should be mentioned, such as our aunt Elizabeth Montini, our grandmother Francesca, born Buffali, who was widowed at thirty, devoted herself to her six children, of whom our father was the eldest, and who cultivated in our minds devotion to the Church and affection for the Roman Pontiff.

"We have memories of this grandmother Giovanna Francesca, who was named for Jeanne Françoise de Chantal, and who, at a great age, read, or had read aloud, St. Francis of Sales' letters, which Don Battista had always loved and from which he has drawn, in part, his sense of Christian humanism. She gave them to him with tears of joy when our brother became a priest."

"Had the mother of the Holy Father a presentiment of what Don Battista was to become?" I asked Dr. Francesco one day. He replied, "Our mother was reserved and very modest. She was afraid to appear too much in public. Did she perhaps retard through this our father's entry into parliament? So far as our brother Giovanni Battista is concerned, she must have had both presentiment and fear. As for us, we had some sort of presentiment. But we told nobody, and kept it hidden in our hearts."

I took the liberty of questioning him about his brother's youth, the early influences on him, his early reading, those hidden sources in those first years so valuable for understanding an exceptional destiny.

"Our brother," he said, "was very orderly. He always studied with regularity, application, will, and determination. We think that it was at Pezzoro—a mountain village where we had gone for the holidays—that Battista learned to serve Mass in 1904.

"The priest who baptized him at Concesio and who was his very first teacher was called, if I remember well, Don Giovanni Fiorini. He had written an original and erudite book called *Fastidi teologici.* It is a difficult title to translate. 'The fastidious theologians' would give a wrong idea. It is about the insoluble and minor mysteries which worry theologians but which at the same time are exercises. For example, Don Giovanni indicated this question: 'Would our Lord have been made flesh if Adam and Eve had not sinned?' Translating it 'The nauseas of theologians' would be going too far. 'The *troubles* of theologians'? I do not know if that is strong enough."

"In short, Doctor," I said, "it is untranslatable."

"Perhaps. In any case the book was not read, with the exception, no doubt, of my attentive brother. In any case, I remember Don Giovanni Fiorini. He was a priest from a bygone age. He was a connection of my father and my father's mother. It was he who baptized us.

"I think that it was in 1913 that my brother decided to become a priest. His first director was Father Baroni, a most energetic Oratorian, of an austere spirituality, perhaps too austere for life in the world (he was to become a monk). At the Jesuit College of Arici and at the Oratory Fathers' Oratory of Peace my brother had for a friend a young man with a great clarity of soul, who died young, Lionello Nardini, and also Andrea Trebeschi, full of vivacity and genius, who, brought up in the State School, had a great reputation there for loyal courage. It was with these friends that he founded, in 1918, a student journal called *The Sling*, which was the organ of the Alessandro Manzoni Association. My brother collaborated in it with all his fervor and his talent.

"But, at the Oratory, his venerated master was the young Father Bevillacqua. With his colleagues the Father gave courses in religion to the students. My two brothers followed these courses with enthusiasm. They were passionately interested in the problem raised in so many ways by the speaker: the accord between culture and faith."

Later, under Fascism, Father Bevillacqua took refuge in Rome. There he found Don Battista, who was beginning his career at the Vatican, and who was the ecclesiastical assistant of the Italian Catholic University Federation. There it was that the almost supernatural friendship which has played so great a part in their two lives was confirmed.

This memorial would be incomplete if I did not inscribe in it with piety the names of unknown friends of the future Pope; they are always present in the memory of his heart and should in justice not be absent from that of the world: Mgr. Giovanni Marcoli, Mgr. Angelo Zammarchi, Mgr. Giorgio Bazani, Mgr. Domenico Menna, and the old Oratorian Father Paul Caresana, their only survivor at the present time. They were all collaborators and friends of the father of Paul VI. To each of them Paul VI owes some ray of his brightness.

"As the state of health of Don Battista always left much to be desired, and there was fear for him in the winters at Brescia, his bishop did not know how to employ him. He sent him to Rome to the Lombard Seminary, in the via del Mascherone, near to the Farnese Palace. I remember going to see him there; I noticed that his unwarmed cell was much colder than his room in Brescia, which was heated. The very day of his arrival in Rome, he went to enroll himself at the Gregorian University, for Theology, and at the State University, for Letters.

"In this solitary retreat one day there came to visit him M. Longinotti, who had been deputy for Brescia since 1907 and a friend of our father. He had been sub-secretary of state for Labor. He was a friend of Cardinal Gasparri. He was also well known to Pius XI. Through Longinotti, Cardinal Gasparri had my brother entered in the Academy of Nobles, where he assiduously pursued the courses of Monsignor Pizzardo, who later had him enter the Secretariat of State. And I remember Longinotti saying then to Cardinal Gasparri: 'Today it is I who should thank Your Eminence for facilitating the entry of Don Battista to the Academy in the Piazza Minerva, but perhaps one day it may be for Your Eminence to thank me for having been the occasion for making such a gift to the Church.' "

The father of Paul VI, who had such a great influence on his children, on his friends and his followers, was a pioneer of civic, social, and political action in Italy.

In the spirit of Leo XIII he had early understood that Italian Catholicism could not remain apart from the national life, that it must participate in that life, demand liberty, show itself in public,

take its place, and first place one day, in the press, in the municipalities, in the provincial councils, in parliament, and in government.
This pioneer was a prophet. Lawyer and jurist by training, writer
and man of letters, he directed a daily paper in Brescia, *Il Cittadino
di Brescia*. The daily effort of such an undertaking in a provincial
town may be appreciated. In fact, it is by a daily newspaper that a
beginning must always be made—each day showing the workings
and the wake of eternity in current affairs. Then to stand for election
everywhere, as soon as this was possible and permitted; an agreement between State and Church, at that time still hostile, was
necessary for this. Battles were fought for the liberty of teaching, for
"social Catholicism," for "Christian Democracy," without wishing
any honor for himself but only burdens, responsibilities, reverses,
suffering. Giorgio Montini was three times elected to the Italian
parliament. I have questioned those who saw him in civic action, full
of fire and yet serene. I have been able to observe the extraordinary
impression he left. In truth, Giorgio Montini was a kind of hero, a
modern knight whose modesty was as great as his spirit was enterprising, and who in my view proved Descartes' profound saying,
"The most generous are usually the humblest."

Courage he drew from his family, from the example of his sister
Elizabeth (Aunt Bettina) who died in 1941 after having dedicated
herself to child welfare; he drew it from his home as he watched his
three boys grow up faithful to his ideas. Courage equal to any test he
also drew from the sacrifices of his silent wife. His last words were
for her: *"Angelo di tutta la mia vita!*[3]

She was not long to survive him. A few months after her husband's death she was suddenly taken ill. It was on the seventeenth of
May 1943, about noon, as she was reading Bossuet's *Elevations*. She

[3] Angel of my whole life.

had that day chosen the Elevation on the Song of Zacharias:
"Blessed be the Lord God of Israel!"

I have looked up, in a copy of the *Elevations*—which my mother
also kept always by her—this commentary on the Hymn of
Zacharias. In the fifteenth week, dedicated to the forerunner's birth,
I read:

O Peace, dear object of my heart! O Jesus my Peace . . . when will it be
that . . . by a complete acquiescence, or rather by an attachment to, a
satisfaction in, thine eternal will in the events of life, I shall possess that
peace which is in thee, which comes from thee and which thou thyself art?

I do not know why, but when I read a biography (that of
Leonardo da Vinci, that of Goethe or of Teresa of Avila, for
instance), I wonder: *Who was their mother?* What was her
nature, what were her words, the depths of her silences? Racine was
thirteen when he lost his mother. Pascal was three. Genius, deprived
of early tenderness, sometimes has a timbre of desperate ardor.

The life of a son and his mother, above all of a son devoted to
study, what a strange adventure it is, from the time when he is but a
little thing of flesh in her arms to the final moment, a trifle melancholy, when he walks with her, old, yet still young, in some Concesio, in a long avenue, where she is like an elder sister, an angel—a
veiled image, enigmatic and prophetic, of him.

Finally comes the moment—if the mother dies before her time, or
when her child, having passed her age, is older than she was—
when he has had a longer experience of life. That is when I understand why a mother is ageless. Or rather that, away from the passage of time which consumes, she remains ever a young mother. It is
very difficult to imagine the Virgin old.

I do not know if I expressed in words to the Holy Father all these thoughts on his father and mother. Reserve may have held me back. But he told me that he had dreamed of Fournoux in the margins of my book, *A Mother in Her Valley*; that the valley had reminded him of Verolavecchia; that all mothers are alike, are one mother.

In truth, a writer is a paradox. To an invisible and unknown people, his readers, he dares to tell certain things about his own people, about himself, which he would never pass on to his intimate friends, which he will forget. But that gives him, perhaps more than anyone else, the right to keep himself to himself in a private interview.

Like Marcus Aurelius, Paul VI loves to recall those who gave him life. Seemingly, each of us, when he thinks of himself, sees himself as a diamond in which each facet brings to life in his memory some initiator, some exemplary friend, some person suddenly encountered who has opened a world. Reflecting thus, in the evening of life, the first thing one finds of oneself is one's father and mother.

"To my father," said the Holy Father, "I owe examples of courage, the idea of never acquiescing in evil, the vow never to prefer life to the reasons for living. Which may all be summed up in a single phrase: to be a witness. My father was without fear. And those who knew him, like Bonomelli, have kept something intrepid.

"To my mother, I owe the sense of recollection, of inner life, of prayerful pondering, of pondered prayer; she gave the example of a completely dedicated life.

"To my father and mother's love, and to their union—for a separation cannot be made between one's father and one's mother—I owe the love of God and the love of men. I should rather say that the love of God, which filled both their hearts, and which brought them together in their youth, in my father was translated into action, and in my mother into silence. Or again, I would say that the same obstinate will, the same absolute determination had in my father more of strength and in my mother more of sweetness. But a sweetness which reposed on strength."

"I remember," I told him, "having once heard Cardinal Mercier say, 'Sweetness is the fullness of strength.' "

"He was right!"

"We all more or less, as Renan himself said, live from what a woman has taught us in the realm of the sublime; sons are more aware of this than daughters because of the difference in their natures. And priest-sons more than other children, since they are dedicated to solitude."

J.G.

"The mother of a Pope is set apart from other mothers."

HIS HOLINESS

"The mother of a Pope never knew she was that, but her son knows it. And he suffers because he is not able to thank her or kneel before her to receive a blessing."

I

"Every mother is like Moses. She does not enter the Promised Land. She prepares a world she will not see."

HE

"I think that to understand destiny it is necessary to fathom that initial mystery: Why am I *here* and not *there?* Why did I appear at this moment in history? Why have I sprung from this man and that woman? Simone Weil said, with great truth, 'Meditation on the chance which brought my father and my mother together is even more salutary than meditation on death.'

"Yes, indeed! For there is a danger of meditation on death becoming enclosed in death; whereas meditation on the meeting of a father and a mother leads us to life and beyond the hazard of chance to the secret of our being, eternally foreseen."

If I have undertaken, O unknown reader, this book of memories and thoughts, it is not to make unpublished or secret revelations. I know almost nothing of the intimate Paul VI but my love for him. What I wish to make known in all tongues is that the mystery which we bear in ourselves, the mystery of "man come into the world" is lived in a deeper way by him who bears the name of Father and of Servant of Servants.

4

TRANSIT BY MILAN

It is said that Milan is to Rome what New York is to Washington. And Pius XI, who had known Milan as Archbishop before becoming Pope, had made the remark: "I assure you it is easier to be Pope in Rome than Archbishop in Milan." For Monsignor Montini his existence was totally changed. Nothing had prepared him for such a great mission; till then, in the work of the Curia, he was in the presence of signs, he handled symbols; worldly matters presented to him were already filtered and classified, evaluated by the channels of transmission. Here he was plunged into a sea of realities, at grips with things in themselves.

Milan is the dynamic capital of Italy, the city of industrial activity, of the future. The city of factories, of human labor, where there is very little room for reveries on the past or for contemplation. Monsignor Montini found almost a thousand parishes there, very diverse: urban, suburban, rural parishes; even almost inaccessible Alpine parishes; the whole range of Christian life in Europe, all periods of history; the immutable mingled with the changing, the old peasant civilization juxtaposed with the tentacled city, with skyscrapers; with the great spewing railroad terminals sucking in every morning, sending out every evening the workers from the countryside.

In Rome there is a populace. In Milan there is already the phenomenon of collective life, uniform, implacable, humanity packed together, uncertain, the very image of such times as Christ had never yet met on his way through history.

And certainly Monsignor Montini knew all that. Brescia is not far from Milan. But there is a vast difference between the picture, the idea one has of a town, a nation, a people, even of a village when one's thinking is confined in one's garden, one's library, and when this same picture, this same idea becomes flesh and blood. There is also quite another difference, almost limitless, when these realities are entrusted to you alone, when they are sheltered by your care and you are answerable for them.

Monsignor Montini, as I was saying, had not been prepared for this most redoubtable office either by his studies or by his early experience, nor yet by his health, which was delicate and had never become adapted to the rigorous northern climate. In that may be seen the truth of the saying of Thomas Carlyle: "The essence of great men is unique. And it is circumstance which imposes on them the role of king, of priest, or of thinker." Human nature is vast, flexible, malleable; too early specialization is a mistake. Open and attentive minds, generous hearts capable of ceaselessly listening to cries for help can come to know many types of existence in turn. And if this is true of every man, it is far more so of a priest by vocation—that is, of a pastor of other men. Monsignor Montini was swift to confront this unexpected task.

The day he entered Milan it was raining. When he arrived in front of his cathedral he was wet through. The day before, arriving at the boundary of his diocese, he had got out of his car. And, in the rain, had kissed the red, muddy clay.

For those who have tried, as I am doing here, to study not so much his life as the swing of his destiny, it was a moment of pathos, a pivot of destiny. Would he bear up under burdens so heavy for his fragile shoulders? Would he be at Milan for good? Was it only a transit in his life? No one could tell; in that moment of uncertainty everything was possible. Now that the adventure has been immutably recorded it is clear that, from the viewpoint of the Master of all fate, it was not just a matter of governing one of the greatest dioceses in Europe, but, as Goethe would have said, of a few years of apprenticeship.

I came to Milan almost every year to visit him, to receive light and counsel. I have found a page of my diary, which I reproduce as it is:

Rispetto singolare verso il mondo (A singular respect for the world). One cannot imagine he has reached his limit, and yet he is at the summit. "I seek positive good" (August 14, 1959). He seems riveted to his task.

—Mass. Purple liturgical vestments. Two peacocks, the birds of immortality, facing each other above a chalice. Triangular feet (Trinity?).

I do not know why, but my diary in that place has gathered these two thoughts of Joubert, which must have some relation to what I felt. Can a muse decipher them?

For the soul naturally scatters something of joy on what she has well understood.

What one has begun and has not concluded serves as a stepping stone for some other undertaking.

Visit to a great hall where are hung the portraits of the Archbishops of Milan. First, that of St. Bernard, who refused this charge (and with good reason, Monsignor Montini told me). Among the more recent ones, Monsignor Montini showed me that of Giovanni

Battista Capara, Nuncio at Paris at the moment of the Concordat.

It was at Milan, as I was saying, that Monsignor Montini had the revelation, in concrete terms, of the modern world. He spoke of it without optimism, in the accents of a prophet of Israel:

"It is not preconceived ideas which blind us," he declared in his Christmas 1962 message, "which mask the hopes of the world, its profane, temporal, and natural hopes. Today when a man hopes, he founds his hope on himself. A new humanism, which men dream of and which becomes a legend, sustains the hopes of the world. But parallel with this movement of hoping, often enough at the very heart of the movement itself, is born a kind of disillusionment, of pessimism, of despair characteristic of modern man. Literature and philosophy speak clearly; they are not afraid of the worst conclusions of absurdity and nihilism. A potent pragmatism sustains the forces of the world, and the world goes forward, advancing headlong like a blind giant unleashed."

"Our society," he also said, in a sermon given on Good Friday of 1959, "is becoming irreligious and atheistic.

"Yesterday's atheism, which if I may express it thus, was a rare illness that had little strength, has become an international malady, deliberate, organized, with its presses, its books and publications, its propagandists and parties. Our world calls itself Christian, because it is heir to the Catholic tradition, because for thousands of years our faith has built sacred monuments, established laws, customs, noble traditions, brought teaching in schools, a culture. And despite it all, the sin most characteristic of our times is apostasy, abandoned faith, incredulity, crisis of thought and conscience, the almost normal abandonment of holy and sacred religious traditions."

On August 8, 1963, he questioned: "Will social evolution prove to be the ruin or the hope of the Christian life? That is the problem."

It was to the world of the worker that he devoted himself. He appeared as the workers' bishop. This was an intimate dedication. It will never disappear. It explains many of his actions in the present and for the future.

In his first sermon he had promised the workers his solidarity with them, as shepherd, as father, in every case of suffering, injustice, legitimate aspiration toward social betterment. To the workers at the Pirelli tire factory he declared: "It is true, I have nothing to give you; my hands are empty. But I also know that you aspire, precisely because you are workingmen, to something beyond your work, beyond your wages, beyond matter—you aspire to a particle of true life, a particle of happiness. And in respect of that I have immense treasures to distribute: hope, the sense of human dignity, the immense horizons of light. You have a soul and I have treasures for that soul."

Monsignor Montini, passing from effects to causes, discerned the root of today's sickness: ignorance with its consequent indifference, then collective atheism, which no longer opposes Christian faith because it sees it as empty, vain, and, above all, historically an anachronism. He had the idea of having a general mission made simultaneously in the streets, the factories, the cinemas, the theaters, at the crossings, not omitting the churches. I have read that there were specified 1,289 meeting places. The strategy was to give a functional shock, as a Protestant mission had done in the City of New York, to shake up atheistic indifference. Then Monsignor Montini found a tone of voice rare in a Catholic bishop, of a moving humility, which was to be heard again from his lips in the Council. It has been said that they were the finest and the noblest words ever spoken by a religious leader in modern times:

"How empty the House of the Lord often is! If it were possible to shout loudly enough to reach you, sons who love us no longer, I would first ask your forgiveness. Yes, we ought to ask you to forgive us before you ask God to forgive you. For why has our brother separated himself from us? Because he was not loved enough. Because we have not watched over him enough, have not instructed him enough, have not initiated him into the joys of the faith. Because he has judged the faith on the basis of what we are, we who preach and represent it; because through our fault he is driven to boredom where it is a question of religion, to mistrust it, to hate it, because he has heard more reproaches than warnings or appeals. Since it is so, we ask you, our estranged brethren, to forgive us. If we have not understood you, if we have too easily rejected you, if we have been too little close to you, if we have not been adequate spiritual teachers, adequate doctors of souls, if we have been incapable of speaking to you of God as we should have done, if we have treated you with irony, with sarcasm, if we have indulged in polemics, today we implore your pardon. But at least, hear us. . . ."

The cathedral of Milan, the *Duomo*, is not really a church, it is a world, a self-sufficient universe. I know that that could be said of several European cathedrals. Here more than elsewhere, by the thrusting forms of its dome, the Duomo is a burning bush, an apocalypse of spires, columns, bells, a peaceful atomic explosion, motionless, complex, silent, and radiant. Chartres alone gives me such an impression of uplift. It is rather as though the plain had allowed a flower of thought, of prayer, to spring from its depths and its distance. The city of Milan seems not to exist, despite its factories and skyscrapers, but to serve as carpet or as monstrance, for this Duomo. The Duomo is not topped, like our cathedrals, by towers and a spire; nor does it display a dome. I would rather say that the whole cathedral is a burning spire, a puissant tower, a dome embracing the greatest space in the smallest volume. And it *germinates*, so to speak, like an immense Tree of Jesse, mother of the Saviour, the *nascent Virgin*.

When one enters the interior and the glare has died down, one finds oneself in obscurity comparing the brightness of the façade with the light and shade of this cavernous abyss; then what predominates is an emotion of beauty, of a tender, grand but sweet and even friendly beauty. I do not know to what this impression is due. Shelley, Stendhal, Taine, even Hemingway have felt it. The cathedral of Milan is suave, virgin, human. It is a symphony whose parts answer one another, a theme renewed a thousand times, a picture whose brushstrokes seem to remember one another. That is doubtless due to the multitude of statues, to the fact that these statues, which recall the presence of man at the heart of the inhuman stone, are not brought in like ornaments from outside, but seem to leap out of the stone, to express it, to crown it. Never have I, being only briefly Milanese, been able to enjoy the round of the seasons here. I imagine the Duomo in melancholy gold or springtime's blue; I should like to see it on a snowy day, in the sun, when the whiteness of the snow outlines the stone tracery. I would like then to climb to its top, stand upright among the stone angels, and finally see it as the pistil of an immense corolla of mountains, as the focus of the Alps whose summits were pointed out to me. Then I would compare the Duomo with the land of Italy, which it expresses in a language of beauty.

Monsignor Montini has often extolled to the Milanese the charms of their cathedral.

"It is," he has said, "a hive for souls (what a honeycomb!) a castle peopled with silent and mysterious characters, where the saints seem to reach up through the stone as though they had becomes flames in the blue. One enters: What a mystery! What silence! But it is the same call to the soul's ascent. . . . I never wearied of seeing this play of colors, these myriad forms and figures, these columns which were like strong, unshakable trees, and which yet took light. I really had the feeling of a victory of mind over matter. The stone was at prayer. Matter was at prayer."

I found myself on September 8, 1960, in the Duomo dedicated to *Mariae nascenti*.

The Archbishop was speaking from the pulpit. I had difficulty in recognizing him, staff in hand, crushed beneath his white miter, his hands gloved. These were not favorable conditions for a family sermon. What was he saying? He spoke of the mystery of the Virgin. I noted on my pad, as a summary, the words of Angelus Silesius referring to Mary, *Sie Ist ein' And're Welt.* (She is another world.) Did he quote him? I believe not, but it was the spirit of the sermon in which I discovered an unknown aspect of his being—he is an orator, a great orator when he lets himself go, but I did not note his words in detail. The crowd breathed at ease. People came and went during the sermon as if at home, in the Lord's hall, in God's marketplace. Monsignor Montini, who till then had only known small audiences of students, doubtless enjoyed addressing the whole populace in which "a chance may place in the presence of our words the heart awaiting you in loneliness, which perhaps bears a world." He constructed, with harmonious singing phrases, a sort of sonorous vault, into which he let pass his emotion, his zeal, his prayer. It was his soul in communion with Christian people, a moment of repose.

Silently I listened to the first lyrical words which he addressed to the people of Milan:

"I shall pray that the rattle of machinery may become music, that the smoke of the factory chimneys may become incense."

5

THE MYSTERY OF NEW BIRTH

I am curious about human nature, about what torments it, what exalts it, also what surprises it, in things both great and small; which are so alike. I have said that this book, which speaks of one alone, should speak for all as well, for our destinies are similar "save for the degrees of perfection."

Indeed, in every man's existence there are these moments of surprise when one is unexpectedly thrown into a world of new emotions, of new suffering; for example, when war suddenly bursts upon peace, as this generation has twice seen.

These states are like those which follow birth; they doubtless prefigure the astonishment which will follow death. Those sacraments too, like marriage or Holy Orders, which establish a state, give this impression of a beginning, of a new and irreversible time, of a consecration.

But among these metamorphoses whose theater is man's consciousness, how deep, how rare, is that of a Christian, a priest who suddenly becomes Peter's successor, who finds himself flung, precipitated to the summit of the pyramid, where the wind blows, where one sees the distance, where one is alone!

Nothing can prepare one for such a change. And even were one to be designated as adoptive heir, an immeasurable difference would remain between the old horizon and the new—as when scaling a mountain between the last step and the summit. However high may be a function which is not the highest, it is in nothing like that of the person solely responsible, who has nobody over him, who alone carries the whole weight. John XXIII told how, in the first days of his office, he caught himself thinking, "I will ask the Pope,"—then, "but that's me." An infinite difference, in that one can no longer obey and wash one's hands.

Toward five in the afternoon, the eighty cardinals passed through the Seven-Doored Hall, which Paul III had Sangallo build for royal visits, into the Pauline Chapel.

Cardinal Montini is said to have been the last to enter, with hasty step, like that of Peter and John running to the empty tomb.

Of the conclave's secret I will say nothing, having no information; but deductions can be made—an incontrovertible way of making history.

I enter his consciousness, divine what is passing there. Monsignor Montini cannot fail to be saying to himself that, in spite of what he calls his "infirmity," he is *papabile*. The choice of the cardinals is determined by necessities which, like diminishing concentric circles, encircle and designate him alone.

The choice is never as wide as one thinks!

Two conditions were essential. A Pope was needed who would not interrupt the Council already begun, whose views were compatible with those of John XXIII, who would not go into reverse, who would bring to a conclusion this vast assembly, on which public opinion had fixed its gaze, and on which the future of the Church rested. And already that limited the choice. Who knew the thoughts of John XXIII better than Cardinal Montini? The latter had lodged him during the Council within the confines of the Vatican in order to have him nearby. The decision of November 23, which oriented the Council toward openness, who could say if it was not he who had proposed it, recommended it? In any event, he had spoken but once in the Council, in December, and that to propose a method, a program, a structure for the Council.

Again, a Pope was needed capable of uniting Italy to Catholics everywhere, of assuring the bonds between the Italian majority and the entire world. Doubtless it is too soon to give the tiara to a bishop who is not an Italian, to impose on the City of Rome, and on Italy, a non-Italian western patriarch. But if the Italian bishop of Rome is, in addition, the universal Pontiff, he must himself be universal: knowing the world, known to the world, accepted and esteemed by the world. And if possible still young, for so vast an investiture. Who met these conditions in 1963? *Who?*

Lastly, it would be desirable that the new Pope be familiar with the wheels of the central administration, that he should have been associated with the pontificate of his predecessors, particularly with those of Pius XI and XII. Here Monsignor Montini's name was the only one heard. It was quite evident to many watchers and some prophets that far-reaching ways had prepared him for the Papacy. For the Papacy is a charisma, but also a profession. A Pope may play it by ear, and the Spirit will take care of everything, but it is perhaps preferable if he has mastered the art.

Monsignor Montini was not unaware of these reasons among others, and they had long weighed on him, a shadow over his future, a sort of cloud, sometimes a sword. It is certain that so elevated a future also foretells suffering. He had, against his will and by force of circumstance, to assume the weighty role of being, in the sight of many good judges, a possible Pope, a probable Pope, a Pope in store for the future. But it was impossible not to think of the dictum:

"Who enters the conclave a Pope, leaves it a Cardinal." I have noticed that the powers that be do not like public opinion, wisdom, or even necessity, to dictate their conduct, that they prove their freedom by choices which surprise everyone. Cardinal Montini, in the depths of his heart, shivering and calm like a garden of olives, was, I imagine, praying that *this* pass from him.

The simple fact of being apparently designated was also an argument against ever being chosen—the more so since a personality as strong as Monsignor Montini had only friends in Italy; above all in Rome, where no one is a prophet. His exceptional value could be an argument against him: Authority has often need of a certain apparent mediocrity. It is good to be undistinguished, talent is so prejudicial! Common sense and piety are enough. How many ordinary popes among the 262, thanks to whom the Church has triumphed! After John XXIII, who stirred things up so much, the tiara needs a rest. And then, who knows the leanings of this silent prelate? In particular, what are his views on world politics—European, Italian? Is he not too open-minded too soon? Can the reins be confided to a being who remains an enigma? Reasons, apprehensions of this kind might enter many heads, win over the hesitating, bring about a wise decision, the choice of a less exceptional Italian Cardinal; for example, Cardinal Lercaro, a mystic, open to the people, personally poor, who at Bologna had coexisted with the Communists; or again, Cardinal Agagianian, who would have symbolized the union of East and West; or some Curial cardinal, less in the public eye, but broken in to the business. Who had known the future Benedict XV or even the future Pius XI before their election not to mention St. Pius X? And again, what was still more important than the name of the Pope was his choice of a Secretary of State, as they used to think at Courts, especially in France. And Monsignor

Montini was precisely the ideal Secretary of State for a clear-headed Pope.

Such might have been what the opposition was whispering, without resentment or passion, with only the good of the Church in view. Also those who write history in afterward, who go about saying that they had "said so," that "it could not have been otherwise," are the fine-weather prophets. The true saying of Clio is: "One never knows; the unexpected always happens." The more so as in the Conclave a two-thirds majority is necessary, and this majority is impossible when a hard-core minority exists; even if the latter only has a one-third-plus-one vote, it blocks everything. Then a compromise must be envisaged. And he who may have come so close may, like Cardinal Rampolla, end his days in a certain silence; the silence which befogs broken and unaccomplished destinies.

Monsignor Montini knew all that when he entered the Conclave with rapid steps, through those halls he knew better than the next man, beneath the gaze of his peers whom he knew better than anyone else in the world, since the Sacred College contained many cardinals created in the time of Pius XII. One can imagine his controlled anguish, his mind veering between a quite probable hypothesis that he rejected, and the defeat of his name which he hoped to see accomplished. Each solution wounded him, but with a different wound. Only detachment was possible.

The Conclave began at 7:20 P.M. Shut away from the world and from contacts, as if in an abandoned ship, or a mountain refuge, or some Patmos of the Apocalypse, behind symbolic bars, were 170 persons in addition to the 80 Cardinals. Never in the history of the Conclave had the cardinals been so numerous. In this day of clandestine radios and miniature receivers, walls, keys, and bars are out of date. The day will come when the secrecy of the Conclave will rest solely on conscience; a consequence of that respect for the person defined by the last Council. But in this our transitional time, popes have increased the precautions. Reflecting after their election on "what should not have been done," they have added to the measures against the indiscreet. Pius XII decided that the voting papers should no longer be signed. John XXIII decided that the cardinals should give up the notes on which they had entered the number of votes. Historians of the future, your pastures are being taken from you! The lions are effacing their tracks in the sand. I remember these words of M. François-Poncet: "In Rome the bronze perspires, Heredia said, and the stones burn and sweat." Once again, and perhaps for the last time, was seen that custom of the Conclave which consists in shutting up—as if they were subtle cheats—these venerable fathers, clad in blood-red as a sign of their willingness to die for the truth.

So the cardinals voted on the twentieth of June. There were four counts of votes that day. Fifty-four votes were needed. That evening, I was at the French Embassy to the Holy See. It was whispered that the Pope had been chosen, but there would be one more deciding count tomorrow. It almost amounted to an announcement that Monsignor Montini would be elected.

I am sure that he relived in a few moments the essence of all he had lived through; that he saw Brescia again (the sanctuary of Our Lady of Grace of his first Mass) and perhaps the garden of Concesio. The faces of his mother and father; those of his masters; then in an intelligible, calm light, some other, still unexplained, events of his life; his youthful sicknesses, his coming to Rome, his exhausting occupations; his renunciation of apostolic for administrative work; patience, silence, his coming to Milan, his pastoral duties, his hasty journeys, his great friendships—all taking from that moment their full meaning: *justification*. Still more, certain acts of total sacrifice he had made, which nobody had ever known, that is, those secret moments, present in every generous, tempted life, in every dialogue of the soul alone with its lonely creator, where it is stricken, like St. Paul at Damascus, and speaks blindly: *Lord, what will thou have me do? Father, take away this cup from me!* Yes, these moments of the oblation of oneself, of pure love, surely shone in his night like points of light. And in one or another veiled form (perhaps even in no form, and in a way sensible to the spirit alone), the Lord reassured him in his heart: *It is I. Be not afraid.* Paul VI has always pointed to that passage from St. Luke's Gospel where Peter, sinking in the waves, is lifted up by Jesus; he had it engraved on a medal of the Council.

From then on, as in a sort of lucid and sweet agony, he could understand his past, his destiny, and himself; agreeable enough seen in the light of God. To see one's changing past and the divine immutability through so many situations momentarily disconcerting, through so much infirmity! And nevertheless that past exists substantially. Nobody can modify it. It must be accepted. This mediocre clay must be yet further kneaded. There is no choice: There is nothing else to knead. And this time not only for some but for all, to help the vast family of man.

Pope John had had a vision. That vision had to be changed into reality, into history.

He would be its continuator, but in another mode, another manner.

What had been, till then, a personal matter, without echoes, would be noised everywhere, subjected to criticism, to judgment. Private life is no longer possible, and with it go relaxation, rest, pause, suspense; *one must go on to the end.* And even old age, retirement, that interim time which everyone wishes for between active life and death, will not be given. *One must go on to the end;* the agony of a Pope (as just witnessed in the case of John XXIII) is the agony of a general wounded in battle who is still in command. One puts aside a function. One cannot put aside a state, such as that of son, husband, father any more than one can give up thinking, or being an artist.

In moral life I think more about level than choice. The choice between good and evil is rare. But at every moment I can rise to a higher degree, do what I was doing in a nobler way; speak with more precision, suffer with more acceptance, be joyful more happily. It is not so much a question of choosing as of growing. It seems to me that this exalting movement is evident in the last conversations of Jesus as St. John has reported them. Then Jesus lived his same life in a yet higher, more tender, stronger, and dare one say it, a more eternal way. To be called to final birth there must indeed be a last climb; to be identical in a higher key.

Is it so difficult, so superhuman? I do not know. A former President of the Council, whom I had known when he was my colleague, once made an admission. I had asked him how, as an academic, he had been able to face politics. "Read Tocqueville," he said. Tocqueville was a man of letters; for a time he was Minister of Foreign Affairs. He has told in his memoirs that the number and scale of his difficulties had made him tremble at first. "And," he added, "what made me most uneasy was myself. Then I observed that affairs do not always become more difficult as they grow, although it easily appears so from a distance. . . . It even happens that they become simpler. . . . Moreover he whose destiny is to influence the destiny of a people finds to his hand more men able to inform him, help him, execute details for him. . . . Finally the very greatness of the project arouses all the forces of the soul." If that is true for the statesman, how much more so for him whose forces are only those of the soul. Winston Churchill has told of his relief when he became responsible in 1940, that the first place is where one is most at ease, when one knows that one has been called to it. One sleeps with abandon. Nothing cradles like the storm.

I will shortly tell how at Brescia I knew Father Bevillacqua, who had been the master and friend of the Holy Father from his youth. One day, speaking to me of Paul VI, he said with such justice: "He has to do all at once what his predecessors did successively. But don't worry; I know how equipped he is for that. I have known and watched him more than forty years. If you knew his power of attention to everything! His capacity to feel, to suffer, to understand. Are these three very different?"

PART TWO

Portrait of a Mind

6

PORTRAIT OF A MAN BECOME POPE

O myself, I take leave of you forever, until my Lord orders me to take you back.

ST. FRANCIS OF SALES

It is said that Paul VI's personality is enigmatic. The comment most often heard about him is indeed true: He does not give himself away.

This is the more striking because John XXIII gave the impression of giving himself away every moment, to everyone: of saying to each person what he hid from all others, of living open-faced. He never burned the pages of his "intimate journal." I am sure that if Paul VI has kept such a journal, it is now ashes. And yet one cannot love a being without wishing to know, to penetrate to its depth. I could not be satisfied with a history of the Council; if one wishes to understand it in its movement, it is necessary to refer it to him who is its guide, who communicates to it its impulse or its restraint, its impatience or its patience; who, however invisible and even absent, remains. During the Council, Paul VI remained; he it was of whom one thought, although he was hardly ever mentioned, he to whom each morning one turned one's mind, as the peasant questions the sky, to know from which direction the wind will blow. He was an oracle: He represented the future, that which is not yet, that which could be. The causes of the future are confused, the winds do not tell what they prepare. At least one can look at the pilot, who is the only fixed point. One can try to read the signs on his face. In 1967, as at its beginning, the Church is linked to the character, the fate of a man. That is what makes its history so moving, so human. The Spirit works in it, acts invisibly on the mass of the faithful, on the elite of the shepherds. Visibly, it concentrates on the person of a single man become Pope.

I remember his first speech to the Council at the second session. Our era is not hierarchic. It likes simplicity. To the modest and majestic "We," it would prefer St. Paul's "I." Pope John had not dared to make that step. He had at least changed the style of papal speech, he had joviality, ease, and a little of that offhandedness which Raphael said was necessary in order to paint effortlessly and as though without taking thought. With Paul VI, this characteristic does not exist, at any rate not in his public utterances.

The difference between him and his predecessor could not but astonish. John XXIII seemed simple to the people, although he was much less so than his speech and his appearance indicated. But he had the gift of joviality like La Fontaine. Of Paul VI it is everywhere heard said that he is an enigma. Curiously, this was never said of Pius XII, who was not jovial, who was not familiar.

I have often heard it said that this pope cannot be classified, that he is a person impossible to categorize. Some have spoken of ambiguity. They have said that the Pope suffered from "world-sickness," that historically he is more acted upon than an actor. A sad and sorry person, wishing one day to sum up in a word what he found to criticize in Paul VI, said to me of him: "Actually he is a philosopher." If that is true, I should be able to find the key to him, as I know that strange species.

How to begin this discovery of a being at once so far and so near, since in a consciousness everything is connected, and all our attributes reflect an indecipherable essence? I take a tentative step. In the depths, I take a sounding, I write a word—*inwardness*—which the following pages will suffice to explain.

The heart should not have to be separated from the mind. The charm of Christianity as one sees it in St. Paul, St. John, the Gospels, is to unite mind and heart, thought and love. The doctors have human tenderness too. The mystics also are theologians. And piety always intervenes to mitigate what is dry in the intelligence. But this composition of heart and of spirit is not so easily made, it is not common. There are specialities. Although charity is the bond of perfection, it is rare that the Spirit, master of its gifts, associates opposite faculties—for example, that he creates a theologian quivering with sensitivity, or an abstract poet, or a leader capable of compassion. When we see one of these unlikely mixtures, we cannot but be surprised. Here is a first enigma.

With Giovanni Battista Montini, and no doubt since his adolescence, what astonished masters, witnesses, friends was his capacity for solitude and silence (inwardness already, always inwardness) and his possession of his body, of his word, even of his gestures; as if he were always watched, heard. Here is the union of an intuitive intelligence, artistic, penetrating, and I would also say musical, architectural, with the vibrant. He has a particularly receptive and sensitive soul; to him should be applied the epithet we give to certain flowers whose petals seem sense organs. Sensitive are his conscience, his way of listening, of understanding, of perceiving, of being silent. And this is a first charm, which acts magnetically.

That is why he is easily an orator, without ever being loquacious, while still being able to lend an ear at length, to look without saying a word. Orator he is when in a sermon he *gives rein* to those two coursers, the mind and the heart, one preceding the other, but quickly drawing close together in a joyous and jubilant race. Anyone who has not heard Paul VI preach impromptu at an early Mass before pilgrims, when he speaks without immediate preparation, does not know what a conversation of spirit to spirit and heart to heart a fatherly and motherly talk can be. He is a father still quite young who seems an elder brother, and a guide rather than a patriarch. Thought is not exterior to being. It is incarnated in its flesh and in its vibration. When one hears his dialogue praised, one guesses why. It is because in his way of being there coexist the search for some very intimate secret, the need to seek out the depths, as we shall see—but also (and this is the obverse) the desire not to be alone, to vibrate with other consciousnesses, to offer and to welcome—as though that which he feels inwardly in the intimate sanctuary could be shared by him to whom he speaks. As though he could enter into another's home not by the door nor even by the word but by—how describe it?—by reconciling two intimacies. And this brings me to a second point, closely allied. In my language I call it: *respect for each one's destiny.*

There exists in him a torment, a torment engendered by the idea of the perfect joined to a lively perception of the conditions in which this perfect should incarnate and integrate with the earth. He knows too well what are the circumstances, the conjunctures, the resistances, the duplications, the ambiguities. He knows too well that nothing is simple, which is very rare in a leader called upon to simplify, to see and decide from above. For example, he has said, "The burning questions are also complex. Simple honesty requires that they should not be dealt with in haste. We should respect complexity. . . ." Complexity of problems, complexity of people. . . . For each of us wears, it can be said, two faces.

Besides the visible personage which each one acts on and acts out, there exists a hidden essence of ourselves, the real person, deep, little known, badly known, unknown, the burning complexity of the person who has his troubles, his indecisions, and who does not really know who he is.

Paul VI is at ease among these complexities, these difficulties of being, which characterize the man of today.

His faculties of intuition, of divination, silently exercised, reach to the innermost point of the destiny of beings.

Generally he is silent. I have said that he has a tremendous capacity for silence. But when he has been with a person a long time, then his memory, which is exact and exquisite (I mean, it chooses the best, it singles out what deserves to be saved from the past), this memory reminds him of the still-unfinished symphony which is human destiny before death. In this symphony, he can do nothing to transform the theme or the modulation. It is already much to be silent and to listen. A silent father can do much to help a son's story to unfold. I have felt that when he is asked his opinion on a future, a project, an enterprise, his advice is that of the sage: "Be what you become; or rather, better still, become what you are. Continue. Be better. Be more. Be still better. That is to say, remain the same, remain the person I see in you, but at a higher level or at a greater depth. And may the polarity of the ascending spiral approach the point of unity." Actually to say this, to suggest it, is to bless.

Yes, to bless. And that is why this pontiff, young and thoughtful, still further refines the gesture of blessing, eternal, but so difficult if it is to be sincere and efficacious. He blesses by remembering. He blesses by the feeling he has of the individual, of what for each being is his own, his spiral, what Leonardo da Vinci called his "serpenting." And that too combined with an almost anxious sense of the difficulties of being, and even of the impossibility of counseling. Sometimes, during these almost twenty years that I have known him, when I have asked him for advice or for angles I have come away disappointed, as of old from M. Pouget's cell, because the two *odegetes* had not told me what course they advised, but said things like, "Do what you do. Be what you are. It is for you to see."

I have so often seen in him how intensely his mind respects beings and, even more, circumstances. He certainly does not move the pieces on the chessboard. Like a chess player who would take over from another in the middle of a game, he leaves the bishop, the castle, and even the knight, on their black or white squares. "He enters into the game." And he prefers, at first, to maneuver pawns rather than to move the queen, to lay siege rather than to conquer. Thus Jesus came to terms with circumstances. He neither arranged things nor disarranged them. He effected a renewal in all the beings whom he encountered, people or things. He eternalized circumstances. He "took bread," the bread that was there, as he took those men that were there, to make apostles of them, neither better nor worse.

In the same way Paul VI has not displaced many; hitherto he has made very few changes of personnel. He has kept the high functionaries of his predecessors.

In the same way, he auscultates, he listens: He accepts what is said; he enters into what is said; he is aware of obstacles; he has much adaptability and patience; he intervenes as little as possible. And does he perhaps not sometimes reproach himself for having tolerated too much, accepted too much, agreed too much?

Then he reassures himself: "If the past teaches us anything, it is that it is better to wait, at the risk of disappointing the impatient, than to improvise in haste. The higher the authority, the more it should accept to wait. It is easy to study, difficult to decide."

There is in his nature not so much concern for detail, as there often was with Pius XII, as for attention and exactness. The parallel has often been drawn. These three men will always be seen together: Pius XII, John XXIII, Paul VI. And to oppose John and Paul, who loved each other, will be an obvious gambit, one which is a warning not to repeat what has already been said so many times. What was the relationship with Pius XII, whom the young Montini daily saw many times, whose mouthpiece he so often was, and who resembled him? What was the difference between these men, so alike? I have asked myself this. As to the resemblances, I would say: a natural reserve, tact, a sense of subtleties, courtesy, the power to work hard, an approach at first hesitant, then, once the line of duty has been drawn, clear and unchangeable. And there are so many other more visible resemblances, such as the curve of his lifted arms in the breadth of his benedictions.

Inwardly I see deep differences. Pius XII's intelligence entered into details: That was his charm; he refined and cultivated it. He really learned new languages. He spoke of agriculture with agriculturalists, of atomic science with the atomic scientists, of obstetrics with midwives, of the law with solicitors. He made himself a child with children. And, inversely, as if to compensate for this incarnation in a technique, a profession, a circumstance, a case, he rose up to Tabor. He gazed at heaven. He *saw*.

He had early exercised the functions of secretary of state without having the title or the authority. Young, he had to give advice, orders, and transmit the Pope's wishes. While it could be thought that he had a part in the decision, he was the inferior. This was the time when his very rare gift, a sort of radar, which by putting yourself in another's place enables you to hear the echo, the immediate reflection, came to the fore, and increased. Here was a velvet patience in listening, a way of disappearing in the very moment of seeing, of not appearing to understand what one understands, of hearing what one knows. These dispositions were present in Monsignor Montini; they became habits.

A position where one is exposed to criticism and is doubtless solicited by clans and parties suggests a universal manner like that of a Pope, but more retiring, since nothing must appear, since nothing bears one's seal. Without a self-denying servant, such as the leaders of Church or State have sometimes conjured up, authority would often be misinformed or impotent. Besides him who is seen, there is he who hides and sacrifices himself in the sight of men and even for future history, who operates vestigially. The confidential escapes history and always will. It is said that Monsignor Montini received almost public affronts, that he suffered the more from them because he could not defend himself and reply, that he sometimes hid himself to weep: This is not improbable. Between him and Pius XII, there was the obstacle and the comfort of a similarity in their sensitivities. In this world's great friendships, sensitivities themselves cause suffering the more because they have been chosen because of their resemblance.

Paul VI's intelligence does not proceed in the same way. He is not attached to details, he does not rise into the clouds. He keeps himself on the human plane, on the plane he will so often call the dialogue. This word "dialogue" is in his mouth one of the key words, obscure because so clear, in which a thinker condenses many experiences, much significance. I shall revert to this. It cannot be taken in its banal, common, Socratic sense. And since I have given this work the title of *Dialogues*, it must be emphasized how this approach through the dialogue suits the Pope's character: It could be said to sum up his way of thinking, his life of relations with men, and, as Fra Angelico would have suggested, his "conversation." Here I am thinking of that rather well-known picture by the Dominican painter which reproduces the "conversation" of the Virgin with some doctors; as if the happiness of heaven could not exist apart from conversation. A very human idea! One also thinks of that phrase of St. Paul: *Our conversation is in heaven.* To my mind, much that is unexplored remains in these words "conversation" and "dialogue." These are acts of the mind where contact is immediately made with the other, like the very young Jesus with the doctors, listening, questioning. The Gospel is a summons, a divine conversation. The Greeks imagined the intelligence as not so much teaching as conversing, listening attentively to the echo of what has been said, as inviting questions.

And one could find in the case of Paul VI, in his life since his youth, many examples of this need to question, to hear the truth, to pierce the veil of timidity and of conventions, to go to the core, to the pith, to bring to light what is hidden in the heart of man, which was not known either by the other or by oneself. Then it is that the dialogue becomes the instrument of the second revelation, of the *human* revelation: It permits each conscience to reveal itself as it is. This revelation, which our modern technicians try to obtain by force—I am thinking of drugs, of torture, of psychoanalysis and even of polls and tests—there exists an ancient method of obtaining it, Hellenic, human, evangelical, much simpler, which is contained in this little phrase, "Shall we talk for a moment, if you will?"

I would like to give here some pencil sketches I have made of his features:

The eyes: gray-green, clear but at the same time unfathomable like a curtain drawn over the intimate. Sometimes they seem to stand out, they look like tiny marbles.

Prominent eyebrows, close together, those of a mountaineer, but which do not shadow his face.

Fine, mobile lips.

As to his voice, his accent, how to make them heard? A deep voice, a little rough, mountain style, I would say again, like the voice of our mountaineers who live in sunlit places, a simple, melodious voice. If I were to describe it in colors, I would say that I see it dark red with violet shades, or dark blue but sometimes shot through by a ray of light, like a stained-glass window.

A calm forehead, without wrinkles, even when seen full-face. But when seen in profile it is arched as though under the weight of thought.

All the features of the face are mobile, attentive, taut . . . cheerful. I look in the dictionary and find under *cheerfulness*: "gentle and habitual gaiety." The reverse, the dictionary tells me, is "grave, severe, somber." That's right.

Hard to say how this face, on the whole strained and attentive, exudes calm and not tension. It is sometimes clouded by worry, suffering, fatigue, but quickly overcome. There is peace in the depths. A secret hard to penetrate . . .

His bearing is discreet, lively, elastic, immobile even in movement, like a wingless victory. The head sometimes inclined to the left, even when walking.

The look once again: Something which does not just look at you, but which penetrates and fixes you.

> The angel does not argue. He gives with pleasure. What he gives is not proof but tidings.
>
> ALAIN

The look again. The arched eyebrows that shadow, but the look has an expression of surprise, like the voice which always seems to be astonished, seems to say, "Oh, how happy I am to hear, to see." He has, as it were, exclamation marks in the tone, a caress in the voice.

Another characteristic of his mind is the desire for *immersion* in the world, and by this I mean the modern world. Immersion—the word suggests a plunge into the waves, the current, even into the foam and flotsam of the sea.

In Monsignor Montini there was always something more than the wish to know, to apprehend, to enter into contact with ideas or people, something more than insertion into the world, more than this understanding of problems and ideas so remarkable in Pius XII, even something more than the generous and prophetic movement of John XXIII. It is audacious, candid, perhaps chimerical, which suggests the absolute engagement of intellectuals in situations far removed from their usual occupations—those of war, of work, and of factory—to compensate for the distance which the use of the intelligence increases, in the face of objects which it, however, pretends it knows.

There is a desire to commit himself, to dirty his hands if need be, to mold the clay, to share in grief, in sorrow, to plunge into man's problems; to go not to the periphery but to the heart of the battle where one cries out, where one weakens; where the future is created, is compelled, in the flowing, boiling whirlpool of being.

And it may be imagined that, as Pope, he suffers because he can never again throw himself into scrimmages, and that in his sleepless moments he meditates above all on some new way to enter into contact with people. No, he tells himself, it is not impossible; it should not be difficult to the successor of him who entered the water in a single bound, who was not afraid to wet himself to the waist, who indeed probably kept all his life the habits of his first calling, that bitter taste of the waves, that desire to plunge in or to cast his net not near the shore but into the high sea.

In collecting memories of his former life, I find this line of fate: the entry into movement in spite of the risks. Thus his former relations with students: their tumult, their deafening welcome. The mixture of ardor and fragility has always pleased the young, who decided that Don Giovanni Battista Montini was altogether too long a name. They called him Don Gibiemme. He must recall the day when, as he said, he was thrown into the lion's den.

He said, "It was a discovery. If I know anything, I owe it in great measure to the students of those far-off days. They were a stimulus for me, a living lesson which I could never have learned from books nor even, I daresay, from examples from the ecclesiastical world, however brilliant its other aspects."

Another time, he said again, "If there is one thing capable of rejoicing the heart of the Pope and the bishops, it is the fine sight of a poor priest, dressed in an old worn cassock, its buttons torn off, in the midst of a group of young boys who play with him, who study and reflect on life, who welcome him and believe in him."

This taste for confrontations, for plunging into the pool of Bethesda, has never left him. It is not so much the desire to enter the crowd, or to let himself be carried along by it, to mix with it. No; it is the desire to go and speak to a specialized group, like the workers in a factory, to conquer their initial indifference.

This account of the visit of Monsignor Montini to Falconi is worthy of the Golden Legend.

Falconi left the Church after having been a priest for eleven years because his faith had "dwindled to a belief in the insoluble mystery of God." Now we come to Christmas 1950. A knock. It is Montini. He enters the little dubious lodging, between the Piazza di Spagna and the Corso, "where he could see a suggestive divan bed covered with a dark damask." If Monsignor Montini, Falconi said, had come to see him this Christmas Eve, it was because he knew he was alone under circumstances where solitude is a burden. What passed during this interview between priest and priest? . . . Falconi does not reveal. But one senses the surprise, the movement, the gift; the gesture which consists in going forward to meet the other.

In our day and age, and I think rightly, fathers are close to their sons and daughters; they wish to be like elder brothers. And it is difficult, very difficult. That a Pope has a young face, manner, smile, and bearing, and that, in spite of his youth, he should be in the position of father, of "Universal Father, like the Ancient of Days, the desire of the eternal hills"; and that one sees his even look, his bright eye, and around the thoughtful skull a crown of still black hair, a forehead without wrinkles, then one has the feeling of having a Father-Brother. That is exciting, that is reassuring. That is how, on this difficult road, the human caravan advances with a single impulse, all ages mixed without much sense of hierarchy, under the crook of a young Abraham.

I have often noted in him what I call for want of a better word *elasticity*. Thus, when during a ceremony—something all the spectators can see for themselves—he goes from one place to another, from his throne to the altar, sometimes wearing the heavy liturgical garments frankly introduced into the liturgy to serve as a staff to the Pope. But all this does not make it easy to walk, the more so because one has to come forward while blessing, to see without seeing, to look at the Lord in front of one and at many faces diagonally. Well, he advances as though moved by the spirit, his vestments billowing. Looking at certain photographs I believe that he likes being in a wind, going against the wind, letting the wind sculpt pleats in his mantle like in the "Nike of Samothrace." The will goes against the winds, but the winds outline it. He is spirit. The gesture reveals his inmost being, always pressing forward: . . . *obliviscens, ad ea vero quae sunt priora extendens meipsum* (Forgetting what I have left behind, intent on what lies before me, I press on).[1] The expressions where St. Paul describes himself apply to Paul VI.

Finally, he needs to visualize.

Imagination sustains him. For a long time he suppressed it; he was not always able to express himself with the poetical part of himself. He has always allowed something of fantasy in his life—in the margins, the interstices, the grooves, wherever his so supervised nature could have a moment's respite. No doubt it is his maternal side: the source of poetry generally comes from that side, that is, pure poetry. For his father had another poetry, the poetry of action. It is said that when he was a child he played with puppets. Knowing him, I can imagine he has the gift of animating the marionettes, a gift not so far removed from love, insofar as loving is coinciding. The imagination, or what we clumsily call by this name, is the faculty of the dramatist that burst out in Shakespeare. It supposes a love of creatures.

I remember some of his escapades which are not generally known. Thus, one November day in 1965, when he went to the gypsy camp in the Roman campagna, to the *tziganes*, those nomads in whom he saluted the modern image of the pilgrim, and even of man himself insofar as he is a voyager upon earth. These gypsies were encamped; it was a nasty day of rain, of wind, of mud. I was stuck between gypsy men and women in an Oriental crowd where strange languages were spoken. Because of the rain, the Pope said his Mass on a place improvised in the midst of the babble. Everything was common, not to say vulgar—the umbrellas, the cries, the childish joy of this people without frontiers whose religion seemed to me a trifle

[1] Phil. 3:13.

indefinite. The gypsies had a king, who was not able to make them close their umbrellas or shut up their cheering. Paul VI was visibly happy.

Another time, at the Vatican, the Pope was receiving children at Epiphany, and a camel from the zoo arrived in solemn pomp with the three kings. This gay camel had crossed into the sacred premises, as doubtless had never happened before—not at any rate since the Renaissance popes, who had vivid imaginations.

One day two six-month-old lions, which an Indian governor had sent, and which the Pope gave to the town of Brescia, arrived by plane. The Pope was delighted to see these lion cubs; he put his fingers on their paws, scaring his entourage, but not the lions. The photo of this scene shows a happy man.

This is the imaginative side of the Holy Father, who likes to combine relaxation with animation. We have neglected imagination too much, rather, we have limited it to certain days, have assigned it to the theater, the radio, banished it from everyday life. But the real poets—I am thinking here of Jean Cocteau, of Girardoux—know how to integrate, as did Shakespeare, the dream with the midsummer night, dreaming with existence. Claudel could have added, as a scene to *L'Otage* (*The Hostage*), to *Le Père humilié*, the Pope with the camel, the Pope with gypsies and children.

It is also in this imaginative key that the unexpected journeys are set. When, on December 8, the Pope spoke on television to the intellectuals and the infirm, he wanted a blind man with his dog, an outsize dog, which delighted the viewers. In our French countryside, where I am writing these lines, what people remembered most were this dog and the blind man.

It is here that I must also talk of his quality of surprise, his quick mind, his unexpected gesture. Thus, at Milan, he was attending a conference of St. Vincent de Paul. A collection was taken up for the poor. He has no purse, he never carries cash on him. What to do? Casually, into the bag, he dropped his pastoral ring.

Or again, and I think this too was at Milan, at a time of great social crisis, he suggested to some industrialist friends certain measures he thought just. But they said, "Quite impossible. One cannot alter the fact that two and two make four." "But three and one also make four," the Archbishop said. This reminds me of Goethe's saying, "One can always behave more nobly."

A noble heart. Or, rather, a spirit capable of ennobling each thing and every creature raising them into another light, a higher sphere. Novalis said that democracy consisted in making of every citizen a noble, as science consists in raising the fact to the level of mystery, and mathematics in the elevating of the infinite. It could be said that love ennobles friends or that piety carries attention to the point of prayer.

I do not know if this disposition to rise higher is the result of his early education, of his delicate childhood, of his mother's influence, of the practice of recollection as an adolescent, of his reading: Everything must have contributed. They prepared. This disposition prepared him for this magistracy, where there is no question of saying anything novel, or of standing out, or of being extraordinary, but of ennobling whatever appears, even if only by a greeting, a grace, a smile, a blessing.

This capacity for deepening or raising (they are the same) particularly applies to language. The word for him, as for a prophet, is a constant preoccupation, the substance of his art. Without any doubt the consciousness he has of his gift for words, of the difficulty of words, make him so interested in the dialogue.

Words are in danger of becoming an algebra, a worn coinage, with the effigy effaced. In the mouth of the prophet or the artist, as in that of a very simple person, words are again what they never should cease to be: The designation of that which is. They approach the gift and initial meaning contained in what is so rightly called the root.

They are brought back to what Heidegger calls *die alte Bedeutung* (the classic significance).

This power over words shows itself when Paul VI speaks a language not his mother tongue, but one learned by effort and will. I have never heard him speak for long in German, English, or Spanish. I do not think he knows these languages as he knows French, which he worked on in his youth with delight, a little as we work at Greek. He pronounces French words with a slight preliminary hesitation, an imperceptible delay. It is as if Paul VI waits for a second to pick the words out of a basket, as if he hesitates among several words almost equally valid. Or rather, that, having already chosen and preferred the most suitable word, he savors it for an instant in silence. Is it the slight delay of the archer who draws his bowstring? Then in his look—always a trifle veiled by reserve and prudence—I see a rapid elliptical movement of the eyelids, which in a face evokes the spirit that will pass, the spark. The word has been pronounced. It is there, heard, vibrates, for Paul VI is a musician, even when he speaks: There is a fervor in his pronunciation. The consonants explode, the vowels sing. The hunting-horn sounds. Speaking one day of a certain kind of style necessary, he said, "It should be like a trumpet from the Apocalypse."

The word is spoken. Sometimes it pierces like an injection made by a good nurse, whose hand is gentle and sure. The word remains in the memory—rare, solitary, often seminal.

He almost never improvises. But when he does, his speech seems an inner reading. Already when he was at college, when he was examined, he seemed to be reading the answer. This takes away from the spontaneity of his speech, which is never familiar, but what a power it gives over language. And what an ascetic discipline! For every moment there is the choice either between two words, or between speech and silence.

Le mot que tu n'a pas dit est ton esclave,
Le mot que tu as dit est ton maître.[2]

I admire, I was saying, this anticipatory silence, then the explosion of the accent on the first syllable. Thus, when he says in the Ordinary of the Mass: "Lord, you will return to give us life," I remember his accenting of adjectives, which sing in my memory. It would take a musician to notate their rhythm and number. I can still hear, "A minimal difficulty." I remember hearing him pronounce, separating every syllable, the beautiful adverb, full of humble hope: gra-du-al-ly. I cannot hear it since without remembering that accent. That adverb in fact describes him well in his action: reticent, progressive, marked with delays.

He seems to like sequences of adverbs, such as the following, to describe the methods of ecumenical union: slowly, gradually, loyally, generously. That is his style.

And by style I mean something quite different from the art of writing, from human rhetoric or eloquence: I mean the gift of translating his spirit into language, and to express that spirit in all the crannies and details of a text. Victor Hugo said, "Style is the depth of a subject constantly brought to the surface." I add: It is the

[2] The word you have not said is your slave,
The word you have said is your master.

depth of his intimacy, of his being; the groaning, the rising, the murmuring of the Spirit.

Paul VI wished his first encylical to have a conversational tone. He renewed and deepened the literary form, which the Greek Fathers called the *homily*, a noble and serious conversation between a Christian and mankind. In this way, the Pope sets an example to all preachers. It can be said that television will kill rhetoric. A deep simplicity has to be relearned. But how difficult it is to be simple without being vulgar, to speak familiarly without being slovenly.

I had occasion to tell Paul VI how proud I had been to hear him speak in our language in New York to the assembled nations; and everyone heard him speak in his own tongue as at Pentecost, but I saw that most people did not use their earphones.

"At this time, when the French language is no longer that of diplomats and treaties, Your Holiness does it a great honor."

"But," he interrupted pleasantly, "it's quite natural. How communicate what one believes to be true with clarity, with depth, without unnecessary embellishment, except in French? You see in this library those books bound in red. They are Bossuet, whom Pius XII liked to read. I also often open a Bossuet volume, and I notice he has not become dated: The thought is expressed and shown with all its sparkle as though it were still alive. Still, I prefer your Pascal: how vigorous, how striking."

Then Paul VI spoke of the French language, and of its value for the communication of thought. He used it again for his recent messages of the eighth of December, at the end of the Council which he called Seven Trumpets of the Apocalypse.

If I had had my wits about me, I would have been able to say to this Pope, who has done so much to teach the dialogue again to the minds of our time, that the French language suits the dialogue, that it was formed at the beginning of the seventeenth century in order to make conversation possible.

In German, to know what the speaker wishes to say, one must wait for the end of the sentence, and sometimes the last word of the labyrinth changes the sense. In French, as the sentence is short and follows a natural order, one understands at once, one can interrupt at any point and add one's reserves, one's comments, one's reply. Thus did the Greeks, but lengthily and subtly. Plato makes Socrates speak, but did he use dialogue? I question it; Plato's dialogues are monologues.

Seeking what characterizes the French language, the Holy Father noted that it obliges one to find the exact shade of meaning, but also to emphasize what in a thought is the most important because intelligible to all. I recognized this spirit in his speech to the UN, which remains a model of this universal type of discourse, more "Socratic" even than "Pauline," although it ends with the evocation of St. Paul on the Areopagus. It seems to me that what Paul VI said then was, "French allows the mastery of the essential." In any case, that is what he thinks, and is the reason why, having to say naturally things simultaneously pure, simple, profound—in short, supernatural—before an intelligent audience, he chose French as his instrument.

Now I would like to make his voice, his style, his rhythm, his inflection known, first in the sustained and reflective tone in which he "homilizes" when he analyzes. Here is an old text, taken from a letter to Monsignor Veuillot.[3] Formerly I saw in it a shadow of coming events. I was only partly wrong.

"He is light. He is salt. That is to say, he is an active operative element. He penetrates souls with an infinite respect, to free them, to

[3] Now Cardinal.

liberate them, to gather them together in the unity of Christ. If he does not do this, what is he? That is why he must be extremely deft. Artist, specialized craftsman, indispensable doctor, versed in the subtleties and profound phenomenologies of the mind; a man of learning, a man of trust, of taste, of tact, of sensitivity, of delicacy, of strength. How a priest must have devoted himself to working on himself in order to be able to work upon others! And all this in the simplicity of truth, in the humility of love, without false artifices, without vile timidities. Fearful of ever being, or even appearing to be, an interested party, of receiving without giving, of commanding without serving. A difficult, very difficult, art, which suggests a mastery of numberless incomparable teachings. As often happens upon close examination of various aspects of Christianity, one will certainly have, in this analysis of the priesthood, the impression of the inaccessible. The ideal is too high; the man was too audacious; he will miss his goal. Yes, this is possible, and terrible; nothing is so close to perfection as the ridiculous, nothing corresponds to it, while counterfeiting it, so closely as the monstrous. And, unfortunately, to fall from on high, very little is enough. But this picture would be incomplete if the forces capable of producing the miracle that the priesthood is were not also indicated. One, humble and courageous, is called vocation, that is to say, an inner torment, a love without rest, assurance in weakness, a command that liberates."

And if now you would like a sample of his way of speaking, of talking when he "Socratizes" and lets himself go, here is one.

It is the memory of something read (perhaps a personal memory?) a pleasant way of saying how the search for truth has two aspects. It seems long, then suddenly delicious, as though it were given without merit, without search, and by grace. We have experienced that during our apprenticeship.

"Soloviev was one day guest at a monastery and had talked very late with a pious monk. Wishing to return to his cell, he went into the corridor onto which opened cell doors all exactly similar, and all shut. In the dark, he could not identify the door of his own cell. Impossible, on the other hand, in this dark, to return to the cell of the monk he had just left. Nor did he wish to disturb anyone at night during the strict monastic silence.

"So the philosopher resigned himself to spending the night walking slowly, absorbed in his thoughts, up and down the corridor of the monastery suddenly become inhospitable, mysterious.

"The night was long and tiring. But, finally, it was over. And the first rays of dawn allowed the philosopher to identify without difficulty the door of his cell, in front of which he had passed so many times without recognition. And Soloviev commented: 'It is often like this for those who seek truth. They pass quite close to her during their vigils without seeing her, until a ray of sunlight . . .'

"Had I a single critical remark to make, I would say that the philosophers who I have known believe they opened the door in their youth, and they by no means resign themselves to wait for the light."

But perhaps we will hear his intimate vibration better still in this unpublished letter written to a friend, Don Francesco Galloni, at a most important moment in his life: on the eve of his ordination.

Brescia, March 6, 1920

My dear Don Francesco,

I am very happy that you wish to share with me the delight and the solemn expectation of my first definite ordination, for by being shared the delight is increased and the expectation gives way to that feeling of confidence which is the mark of friendship in Jesus Christ. I am so permeated by my inability to understand and to contemplate the mysteries impressed on my poor intelligence by the Holy Spirit that I would be afraid of losing the sense of their transcendent grandeur did not the look and voice of my good friends take care to recall to me the grace I bear in myself. I feel strongly the extent of the Magnificat which Mary taught me to repeat with the Gospel from the earliest days when God's plan first became apparent to me, and when I understand to what extent I must praise him for wishing, in his excessive goodness, to raise an infirm man to become one of the elect. May the Lord, who has given me such a clear vision of my nothingness, give me also a clear vision of his strength and preserve me beyond the wily lies that germinate in us. May his strength alone prevail. I believe it is so great that it requires only our cooperation to bring, almost in spite of ourselves and in spite of our insufficiency, that which surrounds us of the world to heaven. But what application is necessary to enter into contact with ourselves and with the souls of our brothers! Or rather, to what a vast enterprise we are called! But what a hope always sustains it. I do not yet know how it will be given me to use my talent, but if some day you see me confound physical incapacity with the laziness of inactive criticism, and, under this elegant mask, live as a parasite in the House of the Lord, out of fraternal charity, transmit to me the flame that vivifies your apostolate, out of pity for the blind who would become the leader of the blind. Remind me of what, more than anyone else, I am in danger of forgetting, almost by a physical predisposition, the duty of increasing my energy and hope for the glory of God. I know that I am not addressing you in vain. Help me with this prayer next Sunday when, consecrated a brother of Saints Stephen and Lawrence, I will receive into my hands the Bread to bring to those who hunger and the Gospel to preach in a society that has invented and discovered everything except the Gospel.

I also commend to you my father who is tired and very sad.

When shall I see you? Don't forget that we wait for news of you here. Our news is good.

In osculo sancto.   G. BATTISTA MONTINI

Piety is a gift that is not equally distributed by the Spirit, even among priests. I use the word *piety* here in its fullest, most classical meaning, remembering with Maurice Blondel that "in Latin *pius* does not only mean the exterior signs of the habits of a practical devotion, but the tender gentleness, sympathetic and helpful, which, free from egoism and from proud harshness, is compassionate toward God and the neighbor." I would further add that the piety of which I speak here (which could be predicated of Vergil and of Goethe, as of the two Saints Francis) is a capacity for recollection which brings us into harmony with the peace of the universe. It is also a *sublimation* which seizes upon what in us is sensation, sentiment, which raises it, and brings it into the purer zone of the spirit. The verses in Goethe's "Marienbad Elegy" may be recalled, where, toward the end of his life, he tried to define this fundamental piety.

> *In unsers Busens Reine wogt ein Streben*
> *Sich einem Höhern, Reinern, Unbekannten*
> *Aus Dankbarkeit freiwillig hinzugeben,*
> *Enträtseln sich dem ewig Ungenannten;*
> *Wir heissens, fromm sein!*[4]

This gift of piety sometimes makes the soul too melodious, sometimes makes us mistake its movements for thoughts. How great the risk that this gift will evaporate into a certain vagueness we can observe in Fénelon. Here it is balanced by punctilious care, application, spiritual exercise, humane culture.

Paul VI has an architect's mind. It would seem that he long meditated on the Temple. Has he perhaps read Paul Valéry's *Eupalinos*? More than John XXIII, who was a prophetic type, an improviser, he has a sense of time and space. When he spoke at the Council in December 1962 as Cardinal, I understood his implicit

[4] In our hearts' purity dwells a desire
Freely to give itself to something higher,
Purer, less known, from gratitude alone,
Which will the eternally unnamed reveal;
Piety is our name for what we feel.

criticism: The Council lacked an overall program. The Council had to find its bearings; which were: the Church considered first in its intimate mystery, then in its missionary development in today's world. The Council also lacked method, rules. I thought then that the dialogue between John XXIII and the Cardinal of Milan must be like the conversation between a musician and an architect (yet Montini is also a musician; he loves Bach and Beethoven). But here I refer to what the intelligence can assimilate in the art of architecture, and which is also found in higher mathematics; and to the profound poetry which dwells in the depth of music itself: composition, proportion, measure, interval, a desire to put each thing in its place and time, to bring silences and pauses into order, to cause the disappearance of what does not matter or no longer matters in order to bring the essential to light. When this habit of architecture is applied to the government of men in the span of time, then we are in the presence of a spirit of hegemony and cybernetics, which calculates intervals, progress, maturity—so difficult an assignment. Architecture in time requires a much surer hand than that in space, of which it is no doubt only the image.

I write this for the reader of 1967. No one can foresee the future. But the Pope's age, his self-possession, his healthy way of life, his measured habits, make it seem that he has years before him. If it is a symphony, we know the first bars, the *leitmotivs*. These won't change. Of course, we perceive only dimly the whole rhythm of the song as it begins. What we know is that the conductor of the orchestra is thinking far ahead.

The Pope has always set the liturgy at the center of his life of prayer and thought. But the liturgy for him goes much farther than the official prayer, the public worship. It is present in his whole existence, in the details of his behavior. I find in his daily life the essence of the liturgy. Work, meals, rest are profane liturgical acts for those who, like Vergil, cannot live without submitting themselves to a sacred order.

What then is the liturgy? I would say, were I asked, that the liturgy seen at a distance is an elegance, a deliberation, a dignity in what one does. Many people need spotless raiment, a ring on their finger. The liturgy is also habits raised to the sacred: an order in the details of life, a solemnity in the path one takes from one's room to one's office. It is the tranquillity of things in good order, which is manifested in the abbeys of St. Benedict, where the word PAX shines over the things of common use as over unoccupied moments. It is also a fear of changes, a care to set up in this life, so fleeting, something lasting, and, for example, when one writes, to have a clean pen, shiny paper, and margins on that paper, and in one's writing some useless flourishes.

Paul VI has lively gestures, but when he writes, he writes attentively, like a schoolboy; each stroke is deliberate. To have a liturgical sense is to live in tensionless monastic time, where each moment, separated from the next, is valid for itself alone as if it enclosed a small eternity. It is a slow respiration, watched by smiling angels.

Now that the altars of the basilicas can easily be seen on all sides, every Roman, every pilgrim, has been able to see Pope Paul say Mass and hear him say the prayers with deliberation though with joy and tenderness. He raises the Host slowly, white as he is white. Order, certainty, peace, splendor, serenity, repose . . . Without this liturgy of existence, now sacred, now profane, the life of a Pope, subject to so many upsets and urgencies, would be inhuman. Here, as in many other realms, the means to prevent the human's becoming inhuman is to bring to it a rhythm, which is a remote resemblance to the peace of God.

His soul transforms the boring prose of his day into strophes, verses. From now on, it is in the mystery that he rests, reflects, remains.

And all this is in him enveloped in reserve. His simplicity contains no ostentation of poverty, but a shame of his wealth. He is silent, he locks doors. He does not "put on his sandals" like the bride in the Song of Songs. And this becomes more marked with the weight of responsibilities and solitudes. "Be active in your behavior, slow in words, ripe in silence."

He has in him, constantly ready to appear, a bold impulse. Everyone has to reconcile his contraries: That is everyone's fate, as is well known. The higher one goes, the harder such conciliation becomes. I have described how he was respectful, reserved, submissive to others, and how his past and his nature, indeed everything, inclined him to temporize. Careful in his pauses, he practiced the art of measured waiting. But whoever looks further into his character, who studies his acts during the last four years, sees something quite other than discretion or synthesis. Like his predecessor (and perhaps even more in spite of appearances), this Pope of modern times dares acts which he knows to be irrevocable, and that without warning. Father Bevillacqua spoke of a clear orientation, courageous toward new ways of feeling, willing, behaving. I weigh these words, for here words must be weighed. Precision, boldness, novelty of sensitivity, of decision, of conduct. How much mystery there is in him now and for the future!

The frailty is in his body; the vulnerability is in his spirit. But

under these coverings he hides a strong will which manfests itself
and drives forward when a cause he considers sacred is at stake.
Then his faculty, to which I have referred, of immersing himself in
the waves, comes into play.

"Professional quiet-livers," Silvio Negro wrote, "were often horri-
fied, even frightened, by so much tranquil audacity." *Ma chi glielo fa
fare, a questo Bresciano?* (Whatever has come over that man from
Brescia?) they asked each other with stupefaction.

A Pope's life has no respite: Each hour presents him with equally
essential duties between which he must choose, as a doctor has to
choose among several urgencies. But the urgency in which he is
enmeshed demands a concentration of attention, a flowing speech, or
there is total, absolute unfissured silence, which is another way of
willing.

He is said to be changeable, undecided, acting in several directions, either too soon, or too late, suddenly putting on the brakes,
sometimes too elastic, sometimes too heedless of warning. I believe
that whoever reads what I have written will judge him quite differ-
ently. For he will enter into the mystery of the *chief,* and by that I
mean, of him who has the care of the *capital* and who bears on his
shoulders the weight of the whole, not only for the ecumenical
interlude, but for a long ecclesiastical period.

The present Pope, by vocation, by physical makeup, by his
nervous system, his former way of life, is not made to rule, as were
without a doubt Pius IX, Leo XIII, or those who bore the name of
Gregory. He belongs to another kind of which no doubt there will be
many more examples in the new times. One will be able to rule from
a sickbed, to speak to the world on television up to one's last
moment, and amplified, the weakest murmur will reach, will fill
millions of hearts. There will be no further need of strength to be

strong. Formerly, certain qualities of fragility, of reflection, of delicacy, of scruples and tenderness which are indispensable to those who are in charge of others, automatically set one apart from such responsibilities. Since Alexander and Caesar it is the sanguinary and the choleric who have run the world. And hitherto there have been few fragile saints. In spite of appearance, for those who endure in goodness, health has been a necessity. I am sure that a future that will allow ninety-year-olds to rule will also be favorable to the sensitive. And it will be to the general good when the sensitives are sublimated by love.

In this age of journalists, of television, of total information, no one can hide. And, for the discretion of the Pope, the Council is a trial: He is watched by the vigilant gaze of ten thousand eyes. To Pope Paul VI's projects could be applied what Newman says about the great ideas of the Church; I have always loved the following passage:

Her beginnings are not the measure either of her capacities or of their extent. In principle no one knows who she is, or what she is worth. She remains for a time in repose, she tries out her limbs, she gropes her way, she makes beginnings that fail, she seems uncertain of the road she sees before her. She vacillates before finally throwing herself in a definite direction.

Newman, who was by nature anxious, here drew a portrait of his own mind. May one not think that what happens over a length of time for the whole Church (this anxiety about the choice, finally overcome) is reproduced in miniature in the conscience of certain popes, who find themselves living in foreshortened form the drama of the Church?

But if one examines his conduct not at the moment, but over a long period of time, one sees something quite different from hesitation. The seismograph's needle may tremble, he may himself act with fear and trembling, he may feel his carcass shudder like Turenne's, but that has no effect on the forward axis, on the line of combat, on the trajectory of his conduct. The great works of human art, when they are studied deeply and in their history in the depth of consciousness, we know what they conceal: the fear of being mistaken, the dislike of not being liked, a hesitation between several possible courses, a disgust for what is planned, a fear of not knowing how to finish, a regret for the alternatives. St. Paul has well described this contrast between the certitude of the visible front and the constant uncertainty within: *Foris pugnae, intus timores* (Conflict without, anxiety within.) [5]

Here once more I find in Paul VI the human condition: What we all are, he is too. His office, at the same time as his nature, causes him perhaps more than any of us to tremble. Who will reproach him with this? I even say, Who could pity him?

Is this the place to reveal a facet of his character often noted by those who approach him? It is the complete absence of resentment, even perhaps the presence of a contrary motion, a wish to please those who have displeased him. I happened one day to ask one of his oldest friends and comrades: "But why on earth has he so much delicacy, so much consideration for one who has been opposed to him, even sometimes an adversary?" I recall that this observer of human nature replied, suddenly taking me by the arm, "Don Battista, to accomplish his tasks, needs all his strength. And he does not want to deprive himself of this joy, this calm, the strength that is given by the exercise of nobility of soul." I thought of the phrase of

[5] II Cor. 7:5.

the *Imitation*: *"Amor Jesu nobilis."* Above civility, there is goodness; above goodness, there is what Aristotle already called mag-
nanimity.

Now a last question must be asked about this character: How, in
spite of all the contrasts and constraints I have mentioned, is he so
all of a piece? Here is a tormented spirit that remains calm; with
wide views, yet a perfectionist in details; an active, lively man who is
slow to choose; a bold man very patient; a reformer who wishes all
things perfect yet is in no hurry to reform, but "endureth all things";
a prince among friends, but also reserved, lonely; an interrogator, a
listener to so many counsels and so much advice, but who leans
upon himself alone; transparent, direct, simple, at the same time as
enigmatic and doubtless an enigma to himself also? The *in-spite-ofs*
are *because-ofs* unaware of themselves. And one must not say:
"Although I run scared, I am bold enough at times; although I am so
worried, I am quite calm. It is because my nature is timid that I leap,
because anxiety throttles me I dominate it better than someone who
has never known it." Neither apply in this case. Paul VI finds his rest
in overwork like the plane that is kept up by its speed. For such
natures, their mental hygiene requires them to multiply occupations
and worries, then nothing takes up more of their attention than it
should; no work gives them hallucinations.

And to overcome contradictions is peace. It is a matter of building
our own intimate council, of emphasizing the so different pillars that
constitute us—opposite qualities, contrary tendencies, old weaknesses and their traces still in us—of pushing them, I say, upward
until they curve like an ogive and then under this key arch we can
rest. This, then, is the secret of our inner unity. In maturity this
struggle for the unity of the spirit is doubtless harder, for the parts

to be brought together are more resistant and more dispersed. *Factus sum mihi magna quaestio* (I am become a great problem for myself), St. Augustine said. Everyone has his minicouncil, more difficult than another's.

One of his childhood friends, an excellent judge, said to me, "He is stratified," a profoundly true remark. I also had the feeling that in his mind there were levels like geological strata, superimposed horizons, perspectives seen from different heights, differing decisions which correspond to different designs. It is this that deceives those who judge his conduct superficially, those who only observe one layer, one level, one appearance. In him resounds that deep spiritual word, the word pronounced by Polyeucte in Corneille's play: *Je considére plus* (I consider more). That is the ultimate sense of his maxim: to deepen, to penetrate to the deepest fold, to the fountain, to the source, there where is felt *la meravigliosa freschezza delle cose sempre vive, e non mai abbastanza esplorata e comprese* (the marvelous freshness of everliving things, never sufficiently explored or understood).

But who will say, who will ever know if there truly is the *ultimate* which is reached in this search and in this quest? With a mind so fascinated by the ultimate there is always the possibility of going deeper yet, of saying *non satis!* (not enough), of having an impulse to go on still farther.

All that I have said on the character of Paul VI indicates this calm anxiety, this blend of effort and tranquillity. This exists in each one of us and perhaps more than ever in this age. It is the tone of life. But how all this is magnified in the Pope by the greatness of his office! At every moment in history a Pope should carry in his blood, in his sinews, and in his moods as much as in his thoughts the same *"difficulté d'être* (difficulty of being) as his contemporaries.

When one has inherited a sensitivity which increases the intelligence, then the bitter sweet of life, of which I am speaking, is at the same time more delicious and more cruel—the source of joy being also that of sorrow. And this mixture has to be drunk daily. Paul VI does not generally have the resources of confidence, not even of confidence in crowds, which made John XXIII such an attractive figure. But with John XXIII, too, a natural joy, the happiness of being alive, served to mask the sting inherent in his difficult, solitary function.

In spite of his orderliness and his prevailing reserve, which prevents him from ever talking about what touches him, one sometimes hears a cry in the dark. So, on February 17, 1965. "The Pope also needs refreshment. He who only sees his outward appearance and his activity could imagine that he lives in an atmosphere of lofty serenity, where everything is beautiful, easy, and admired. . . . But in spite of the spiritual refreshments God gives him, the Pope has his troubles, arising above all from his human inadequacy which at every moment has to face and almost to enter into conflict with the enormous and disproportionate weight of his duties, of his problems, of his responsibilities. This is sometimes agonizing." This word "agonizing" is very understandable; its etymology explains it: an undecided battle, a solitary battle, the earth being far, the sky seeming far. Friends asleep. A sweat.

And then there are the troubles which arise from his ministry. . . . Among the most acute is the infidelity of certain good folk who forget the beauty, the gravity of the commitments which unite them to Christ and the Church. This is a phenomenon which the evolution of modern life accentuates and renders more painful, as much on the level of doctrine as on that of moral living and practical cowardice! How would we not suffer from the abandonment of some formed in the school of Christ, and so loved by him, so necessary to the good of the ecclesiastical community and society!

"And what to say of the pain that We feel daily from seeing the thought of the Church misunderstood and her love rejected? The ineffectiveness of apostolic labor and the perversity with which sometimes her intentions are distorted and her offers rejected are deep and daily thorns in the hearts of the pastors of the Church and are felt also by Us."

In Paul VI modern man presents himself. That is extraordinary. For the popes, as guides and leaders of humanity, do not themselves have to resemble the man of their times, especially this distracted man who is the man of our times. The Pope is called the Holy Father to emphasize that he should not be of the same clay, of the same composition, as the mass of vacillating men.

Recent popes could love and help modern man but their deep sensibility was not in step with contemporary sensitiveness. Pius XI was solid, square, a mountaineer; Pius XII had Roman firmness, mystical ardor, humanist genius; did he feel these things as a modern man? I do not know. As for John XXIII, so modern in his aims, he was not modern in his nerves and substance. His spiritual *Journal* makes this clear. This rugged priest, without hesitations or misgivings about himself, without interior contradictions, who developed along ageless ways of thought and piety, was the opposite of modern man. Certainly a simple man can be adopted by modern man as a remedy, as a reproach, as a regret; but he is not of the same race. The same does not apply to Paul VI. We are here in the presence of a man of contemporary disposition. His is the style of several of our thinkers, and above all of our artists; this Pope is not satisfied with thinking as we do, which is comparatively easy for an intelligent man, but he feels, he worries, he suffers like us. From this point of view his resemblance to St. Paul is striking. St. Paul had many characteristics of what I call "modernity": He rejoiced in his weaknesses, he said he was torn, tempted, feeble, hesitant. Paul VI bears in his nature this resemblance to contemporary man—in his aspirations and also in his torments.

And by this he restores, he already rehabilitates certain ways of thinking and feeling which had been held suspect. He gives happiness and strength to those pioneering spirits who in the last two centuries have suffered in the Church above all not because of differences between their spirit and the true spirit of the Church, but because their type of sensitivity, their method of search, their *difficulté d'être* were not represented among the high echelons of the Church, and thus they found themselves "misfelt," which is for some people perhaps harder than being misunderstood.

But the *ecumenicity* of the Catholic Church implies that she should permit all temperaments to live and to fulfill themselves in her, just as she must assemble "all peoples" together, as she will one day, perhaps, assemble all churches. Every personality is the image of a people.

It must be admitted that, with very rare exceptions, the saints who are put forward as models bear no resemblance to modern man; they are rougher and simpler; their strength does not come to terms with weakness. To use the language of character-readers, they are sanguine, phlegmatic, but they are not nervous. They are sometimes sentimental or converts from the flesh. They are not sensitive. They lived in a universe harsher than ours, but also more rounded and simpler; the sprightliness of their blood sufficed. Even the women were "lusty." How we would like to know that the complexity, the nervousness, the anguish and fatigue of being, bathed in the life-giving Spirit, that what we call weakness, disquietude, ambivalence —and also overwork, trepidation, haste—are not an obstacle to the divine life in us, but, on the contrary, an unexpected aid. That our nerves, our analyses, and our subtleties bring us nearer to the good-

ness of the Father, to the sensitivity of the Son, to the vibrance of the
Spirit, than did the placidity or the vigor of our fathers in the
faith.

I offer these sketches of a soul to the record of the Council, to its
history in depth. This should attempt a true "analysis" of the "soul"
which would not be content to note the eddies, the undercurrents,
the substructures. After the death of the last living witness, when
writing alone will hand on the Tradition, the historian, removed
from the carnal, will be more free to see the Spirit at work in the
Council, to write the history of its deeps. Then he will not fail to be
astonished at the sequence Pope John, Pope Paul. There are double
stars.

The Council was the common work of John and of Paul. Perhaps
at certain moments of blurred prescience, did Pope John not conceive it thus? Once more the names of John and Paul (recited in the
Roman Canon of the Mass) will find themselves forever united.

This is how I imagine the conjunction of their successive roles. I
see a Caravelle in which Pope John takes off and breaks away. But,
in infinite space, all directions are possible. The Caravelle rises, rises.
How to return to earth? Here the original pilot disappears. The man
behind takes his place. He would not have had the strength to take
off. But he has the strength to come back to earth, to choose a
landing strip, to trim the wings, to put on the air brakes, finally to
make a smooth landing, the passengers forming a single unit. There
is no doubt both these differing characters were necessary.

"When I think about Pope John," Paul VI said one day, "I
remember something Father Bevillacqua used to quote. He had taken
it from a book by André Schwarz-Bart called *The Last of the Just*,

which came out in 1959. A Jewish child asks an old man what the just should do. And the old man, without hesitation, replied:

"Do you ask the sun to do anything?
It rises, it sets, its soul rejoices.

"Pope John rose, set, rejoiced souls. Thus he set in motion a current of love and this current of love was irreversible. I only had to ride in his wake, to follow his trace."

How the methods of these two popes resemble each other and how they differ!

Where John XXIII made a practice of going from the center to the periphery, of setting in movement waves which expanded and increased, Paul VI preferred a complementary way, that which goes from the circumference to its focus. Nevertheless he starts from Christ to arrive at the Church, which, with St. Augustine, he calls "the total Christ."

While John XXIII solved obstacles by leaving them behind, he prefers to incarnate himself in the refractory element; he makes straight for the difficulty. From his long years of study he has kept the idea that man is a creature who searches in order to know more, who is tormented by not knowing. The mystery is never fully grasped, but it is divined, embraced in the shadow. This light and shade invite a search which does not end. With Paul VI the Council has taken on a new sense, having become the instrument and the image of the religious conscience at work, which seeks what it has already found in order the better to discover it, to give it covering more to the measure and more adequate to the needs of our time. To "bring oneself up to date," as John XXIII expressed it, the church of Paul VI turns and *plunges deeply* into herself.

The characteristic of the Spirit is to unite, but through difference.

7

DIALOGUES ON SOME PREFERENCES

He has always kept some moments, in the interstices of his days and nights, for reading alone.

Speech can only relate us to our contemporaries; there is no guarantee it will be with the wisest, with those who represent humanity's highest point. To cull and conserve that most precious fruit called culture, the spoken and written word must associate. It might be said that the best of the books called profane are a diffused Scripture, a secondary and dispersed revelation; this is especially the case when the books have been written by spiritual men, not on their own initiative but because they were inspired, were called.

I had noted, in looking at his library, the variety of Monsignor Montini's reading. At the Vatican this personal library has been enlarged and enriched; it occupies a floor underneath his private apartment, while a little staircase allows quiet access. It is a city of books, another mirror of the world, a mute, innumerable audience, complementing his audiences. A sort of walled garden in which the Holy Father can inhale thought, and thoughts; for a book is like a flower. And, just as in the West the very name of a flower is a poem of some syllables, so the very title of a work of the mind—a title so long sought by the author, with hope and despair—reveals an aroma, an *essence* of thought or beauty or prayer. And for people of a certain age or for those who lack time, it is enough to run the eye over the shelves of a bookshop, the stacks of a library, to receive instant nourishment from the titles alone, of the whole substance of the books. While I await a stranger in a room where his books are, a single glance at the titles reveals what in a moment he will doubtless hide from me; perhaps what he does not know about himself.

I have noted among the Pope's books a number of modern authors —English, German, Spanish, French. I noticed novels, essays plays. A man who wishes to know the world's secrets cannot be content even with confidences. He must extend them by those public confessions which have become our modern literary forms—more metaphysical, more interior than those of classical writers—for in them we shamelessly unveil our anxieties, our scars; in short, all the ills which precede or follow our sins, which we no longer acknowledge. It is with good reason that Baudelaire, Dostoevsky, Bernanos, and other living authors I will not name, doorkeepers of twilight realms, are to be found on the Holy Father's shelves.

I shall be forgiven for making some observations on certain preferences. Perhaps the reader will say that St. Augustine or Newman are also my own preferences. But a description such as that I am attempting will only be an empty, static work if it does not issue from interrogation, from encounter; and that can only be clearly heard which resounds in you yourself.

On French Literature

(Casual Conversation)

"I owe much to your literature," the Pope said. "In 1926 I spent some months in Paris, living with the Benedictines in the rue Monsieur. I said Mass in the chapel, to which came on Sundays a number of your writers and converts. I am told that it has since disappeared. It was a place of recollection, of inner renewal, in the midst of Paris, Benedictine peace in this world's tumult. I remember meeting the Abbé Maurice Zundel: mystic, poet, philosopher, theologian, liturgist—have you read his book on the *Poem of the Holy Liturgy*, which has been translated into Italian?—he had moments of illumination, one might even say, lightning flashes.[1] What a lot of strange folk in Paris then frequented this monastery! But my chief occupation was perfecting my knowledge of your culture, literature, language and—I would even add—syntax and pronunciation. You know that for us certain of your vowels and diphthongs are hard to pronounce; for example, the very simple word: *coeur* (heart). But the North Italians are Celts like you; the Celts know how to pronounce *u!* So I was attending the Alliance Française on boulevard Raspail; I well remember how the Paris streets were always so clean, blue, and cool in summer. I still smell that Paris asphalt.

"What a peaceful, tucked-away corner . . . what an ecclesiastical oasis in Paris! There are so many sacred buildings there, and those three domes which remind a Roman of the Roman skyline, but set in the gray-blue of Paris: the Val de Grâce, the Carmelite Chapel, and the soaring dome of the Invalides, so near my rue Monsieur. I remember visiting the Chapel of the Sisters of St. Vincent de Paul in rue du Bac, where the apparitions were seen by Catherine Labouret in 1830. The Church of St. Sulpice, which also recalls the Roman churches, is the cathedral of this peaceful quarter. And in

[1] I asked Abbé Zundel if he remembered his companion of rue Monsieur. "Indeed," he replied, "the first year I remember having heard Abbé Montini speak of his suffering when faced with the petty-official mentality of certain priests. I answered him: 'Any priest of twice our age has had to face difficulties we do not know of: behind a mediocre exterior his constancy may be more heroic than we think.' The next year, Monsignor Montini spoke to me of the Apocalypse, of God's judgments, and that it was opportune to present this awesome aspect, to awaken sleeping consciences. He had during the interval, I believe, had occasion to conduct retreats which had brought him to this conviction."

front of that church there is, if I remember right, a fountain on which are depicted the masters of the French Church; let me see if I can remember them: Bossuet, Fénelon, then . . ."

"Massillon and Fléchier," I told him, "the four Gallicans who were not honored with the purple."

"I know," he went on, "you call them the four *points cardinaux*.

"But I did not waste my limited time, only three months, in France.

"Let me repeat, I did not waste it paying visits. I devoted my time to your language. The Alliance Française offered exceptional teachers, a completely admirable French teaching staff. I had learned your tongue by closely reading one of your books: the *Jeanne d'Arc* of Gabriel Hanotaux. But I did not find M. Hanotaux in Paris. I was the assiduous pupil of René Doumic, who had great authority and a gift for teaching. I shall never forget, as long as I live, the course he gave us on Baudelaire, Flaubert, and de Maupassant. Speaking of this, I remember that he read us a de Maupassant short story called 'The Little Tub,' which was not at all edifying, as I recall. You have some remarkable storytellers in France, who know how to evoke a whole drama in a few pages. In *Lettres de mon Moulin* I liked 'The Pope's Mule,' and 'Father Gauchet's Elixir.' . . . Before coming to France I knew Verlaine well. M. Doumic encouraged me to deepen my acquaintance with Verlaine. I also liked him on Victor Hugo, particularly on the *Contemplations*.

"Are the novelists to whom M. Doumic introduced us still spoken about in France: Loti, Bourget?"

"Not much."

"And yet they had talent. But tastes change with you as with us.

"There is one author whom I liked very much; I do not have the impression he is very well known in France; that is Malègue, and his novel *Augustine*, or *The Master Is Here*. What a remarkable work,

in which modern man encounters himself, just as classical man did in
the *Confessions* of St. Augustine! And how well Malègue puts the
problem of the difficulties of faith, just as in that unfinished novel
Pierres Noires he also raised the question of the difficulty of holiness!
Monsignor Colombo, the theologian, told me that one evening,
having opened Malègue's book, he spent all night reading it till
dawn. He could not put it down. I also liked Huysmans *La
Cathédrale* and *Saint Lydwine*, for example. I remember also having
read *Un Prêtre marié* by Barbey d'Aurevilly. Since that time I have
kept up with your literature.

"Tell me about André Maurois; is he still writing? What a gift he
has of making himself clear, what lucidity! And Jules Romains; is he
still writing? I need not ask if François Mauriac is writing; what a
gift for style! What sincerity! As for M. Carcopino, whom our
Italian archaeologists like so much, I have a passion for his books; I
say a passion because he brings enthusiasm to learning. He carries
one away.

"Doubtless some day it will be said that in the twentieth century,
your country gave the sky a new Pléiade. And what strikes me is
that several of your great writers have been, more so than in the
sixteenth century, more so than in the nineteenth, authentic Catholics, among them converts.

"What do the French think of Simone Weil? I consider her out-
standing. She writes your language in a way I find admirable. And
what unforgettable mystical intuition! I shall always remember what
she wrote on the Cross."

The Holy Father spoke about well-known women writers. He
gave his preferences: Sigrid Undset, Selma Lagerlöf, Gertrude von
Le Fort. "I remember Selma Lagerlöf's book on Jerusalem. It gave
one a sense of the holy."

"In your opinion," he asked me, "who is the greatest French poet?"

"Some say Racine; others claim that one must go back to Ronsard, Villon, and Maurice Scève in the sixteenth century; others that one has to wait till Victor Hugo, others that one starts with Baudelaire; others that poetry begins with Mallarmé (*finally* there is Mallarmé!) ; others that it begins with Rimbaud."

"They tell me," said the Pope, "that for you to produce the equivalent of Dante, Corneille and Racine must be rolled into one. Is that true? Would that be enough?"

"I do not know if we have the equivalent of Dante; for Dante is the universe of nature and of grace in a single work of poetry. And such a combination is not suited to the French genius. There are many poets in France. Is there one poet in which poetry is concentrated, summed up? I do not think so. I even wonder if France is not the country above all of abstract music; that is, of prose."

On St. Augustine

THE POPE

"Father Bevillacqua very early transmitted to me his admiration for St. Augustine, which was constantly on his lips. I remember what he said of St. Augustine's style: 'It is the union of form and content. There is such a fullness in St. Augustine that already the formulation is in itself a lesson. It is the Latin genius at its most perfect. What in Cicero would be rhetoric, here becomes style itself.' And Father Bevillacqua made me notice the beauty of the plays on words in St. Augustine. For example, he says that the soul is present more where it loves than where it lives: *ubi amat plus quam ubi animat.* Well, who could ever reproduce that! How colorless that is in every language, even when something of the alliteration is kept! In the

Latin of St. Augustine it resounds, is registered not only in the audiomemory but *in mind and in truth.* And other examples could be cited. For example, that *Ama et fac quod vis* (Love, and do what thou wilt), which when translated so easily becomes vulgar and ambiguous; here rings high and pure. *Love God and then whatever you will will be good!* And, in the *Confessions* the famous untranslatable prayer: *Da quod jubes et jube quod vis.* (That which thou ordainest give me. And then ordain what thou wilt.) Or again: *Deus qui interior es intimo meo et superior summo meo!* (O God closer than my most intimate self, higher than my highest!) Father Bevillacqua used to say to me: 'That's untranslatable, it's untranslatable!' That's it! It's absolutely that!

"He also said that St. Augustine is the poet in essence, if it is true that poetry, like the Eucharist, is whole in itself and whole in every one of its particles. And with St. Augustine the poetry is that of truth, of the doctrine. It gives the doctrine its savor, its depth. Consider the *Commentary on the Gospel of St. John:* How difficult it is to add anything to that sublime Gospel. Well, St. Augustine found the means to give it a new splendor, another radiance.

"The ideal for him who expresses, comments, preaches is that the truth should also nourish life. And this St. Augustine almost always managed to do. I go back often, as I was saying, to his *Commentary on the Gospel of St. John,* which is, like your Bossuet's *Elevations on the Gospel,* one of the works I like best; for perhaps the best of our works are those which flow from us without effort, without our thinking too much about them, and if you ever wish to write again, I would advise you to write as Bossuet wrote the *Elevations on the Mysteries* for his nuns, by—as they say—'letting your pen run.' With St. Augustine the link between form and content, between beauty of word with depth of idea, and, too, the link with the hearts of the faithful, is more found than sought. The reader has the illusion that this has been written, thought only yesterday, that it is fresh, distilled from the earth every night like dew.

"Do you know the new Archbishop of Turin—Monsignor Pellegrino? He was a professor at the State University of Turin, professor of ancient Christian Literature, when he had to obey the Pope and accept the duties of bishop of Turin. In the first days of his episcopate, he even went on teaching his courses at the University and giving examinations. In that I find an example of the bond between thought and action; between the University and the Church; I would even say, between patristic and modern times.

"Monsignor Pellegrino says that St. Augustine is his master, his adviser for his pastoral initiatives in the wake of the Council. . . . And what teachings, you ask me? . . . This: the sense of synthesis which brings together into a higher unity the diverse aspects of reality. Attention focused on man concretely, on his problems, his crises. The sense of history, so important in contemporary culture. The sense of the Church considered as a mystery, without neglecting its existential reality, and, too, without forgetting its hierarchic structure, which St. Augustine illustrates so brilliantly—for example, in his controversies with the Donatists.

"Finally the sense of the inward: 'Do not go out. Enter into yourself.'

"In my youth I was familiar with an Italian writer you do not know called Vito Fornari. He was of the school of St. Augustine: that is, he broadened his subjects exhaustively. Fornari lived from 1821 to 1900. He had taken inspiration from the *City of God* to write his chief work, *Vita di Gesū Cristo*. It is a philosophic life of Jesus, that is, written by a philosopher who situates Jesus in Salvation history. The first volume deals with the creation of matter and spirit, then the design of God for humanity, Israel, all the preparations. The second volume throws light on the life of Jesus through these preparations, and also on the consummation to come in the universe. He throws upon the Gospel the light of the glory to come, of the Resurrection, of Jerusalem on high. Thus all is understood because all is placed, that is, situated within the whole of history, which emanates from and returns to God, and not within that which the moderns call *the situation*, which is only our relationship with space at a given moment. The life of Jesus for Fornari is not the passing of Jesus through history, which was so swift."

J.G.

"One moment, as my master Pouget said, and four snapshots: the four Gospels . . ."

THE POPE

"It is all history from the beginning, to the end of history. Hegel and Vico felt this, which is the idea of Isaiah, of the prophets, the idea of St. Paul. The Gospel is then illuminated by reflection from what preceded or follows it. It is, as we would say today, exegetical and the most profound exegesis.

"I am well aware of Fornari's faults. Although the style is simple and ardent, the book is dated. But I am not aware that Fornari's work has been followed up.

"How many mysteries Fornari brought to light by that intelligent method of trying to see everything at once, to show the harmonies of history! For example, this constant phenomenon of expansion and compression, of extension and recapitulation, which results in a whole people being summed up in one man or in a single individual's story presaging that of a whole people, by which biography is the image of history; that of Abraham, that of St. Paul.

"Fornari was a mathematician of the infinite. And he demonstrated the laws of the infinite in the finite, the rhythm of opposites, like creation and redemption, reason and faith, or again the dichotomy of Jerusalem-Rome, or that of Peter and Paul. He does not limit himself to the visible Jesus; he shows Jesus as continuing to act in the Church, in the beginnings of the Church; for example, the first Council of Jerusalem Fornari explains as a first presence of Jesus in his family which is the Church. . . . Fornari brings invisible harmonies to light; he does not oppose beings, persons, events; he shows how all forms a harmonious whole; how, for example, Peter the head and Paul the preacher buttress and illuminate one another, as Paul and John complement each other in their writings.

"He shows the migrations of peoples, the exchanges between continents, for example the links between Asia and Africa and Europe; and he sees these links reflected and explained in the journeys of St. Paul. This is what he calls *il concerto dei moti nella storia* (the concerted movement in history). In short, he rises always to the highest point of vision, of view.

"I remember those admirable pages on the journeys of St. Paul of which he gave me profound understanding. He says in parenthesis that the supreme moment of St. Paul's life, before his martyrdom, was his speech to the Greek philosophers. There, by a sublimely elegant theorem, summing up the maximum of doctrine in the minimum of words, St. Paul exposed faith to reason, that reason to Greek philosophy whose language he spoke.

"Fornari always sought for what he called the *respiration* of Christ in history. He was in advance of his time; he had strongly felt the value of myths, which he called fables. He said that Homer was the image of the coming of the West to the East, that of Vergil was its return, that Aeneas, more priest than layman, was the son of Shem. He spoke of *l'Ufficio delle favelle*, which might be translated as 'the significance of myths.'

"One day all these views will have to be taken up again, suffused by our greater knowledge, to show, as did St. Augustine in the *City of God*, that when history is complete it shows Christ at work in time. Then all histories, all literatures, all poetic presentiments will conspire together in one immense poem. Then will be heard what St. Augustine called the voice of the ineffable modulator.

"I do not remember all the discoveries in this book written by a mystical logician. I will send it to you. Read it. You will see there the method of research in depth he advises. And if you have any leisure in your old age, go to school with Fornari. Give us a *Philosophy of Jesus*."

On Dante and the Divine Comedy

I suppose that Dante is to the Holy Father what Goethe is to a German, or Shakespeare to an Englishman, Cervantes to a Spaniard, what Pascal is to us: He who summarizes and signifies the mind of a whole people; more still, he who carries this mysterious essence to its universality yet without robbing it of its earthy savor, the charm of an individual, carnal language.

The Italian earth, Vergil's earth which has bred so many geniuses in the arts of volume, form, and color, has no artist to compare with Dante. And Dante, too, is without question the sole poet who merits the name "catholic" in the full meaning of the word. "I do not see," I said to Paul VI, "how the same unlikely combination of chances which produced Dante and his poem could occur again in Europe."

"It is true," he answered gravely, "that the laurel wreath on his brow has never withered. And in some sense, in various ways, that laurel is still in flower. It is because the *Divine Comedy* includes everything that is possible for intelligence to conceive and for human love to love: heaven and earth; eternity and time; the mystery

hidden in God and the historical events of this world; theology and
the sciences—such as they were in the period when Dante wrote. In
short, I would say that all that had been thought before Dante
existed was carried to its highest degree of simplicity, of depth, and
of connection with everything by Dante. For instance, the ideas of
Plato, the synthesis made by Aristotle, the astounding intuition
St. Augustine had of history insofar as it is the flow of time,
the synthesis made by St. Thomas, angelic mind full of courage
and balance; and I must not forget the fervor of St. Bonaventure,
the ardor of St. Dominic, the pure spring of St. Francis of Assisi, the
tender and royal asceticism of St. Bernard. I think too of the boldness of a Joachim of Floris, whose weird prophecies helped Dante
to pierce the mystery of the future.

"Thus to unite all that had been of value before; to arrange these
lights in your own light, in your intimate unity; not to be uneasy or
dazzled or overwhelmed—what ingenuity, what genius, what a
quality of innocence, initially present, then acquired, that implies!"

"And one might perhaps add," I interrupted, "that the *Divine
Comedy* is simultaneously a continuing song, a quasi-theatrical work
by its ceaseless action, and at the same time, by its adventures, a
sort of medieval and modern novel. And one must add that sorrow
and joy are there united, and even, I daresay, that Dante always has
a certain smile. I remember this line of the *Paradiso: O dolce amor,
che di riso t'ammanti"* (O sweet love that clothest thyself in a
smile).

THE POPE

"Which demands two qualities rarely found together: fullness
and conciseness. Apart from that, have you not noticed in reading
the *Divine Comedy* that mutual interpenetration of intelligence and

love carried to an extreme degree and apparently effortless (the effort of Dante is, as with the saints, dissimulated) but in a peace; a joy which transcends all pain . . .

> *"Luce intellectual, piena d'amore*
> *Amor di vero ben, pien di letizia;*
> *Letizia che trascende ogni dolore.*[2]

"It seems to me," Paul VI continued, "that the *Divine Comedy* is the very song of PEACE, and that in its triple form: when it is lost forever; when it is removed for a time, in *Purgatory* linked to hope; and finally when that peace reposes in its fullness.

"And all that in a language which is not only *sweet and lovely*, as Horace counseled, but one in which the enthusiasm, and, one might say, the abandon of the inspiration are governed by number, rhythm, and euphony; and in discretion of simplicity, that art possessed by God alone. Do you know these words of Papini: *il poema di Dante è poema teologico ma tradotto in idioma stellare, agreste, sanguigno e terragno?*[3]

"Note further that Dante achieved this as though playing, for he played in the manner of creative *Wisdom* in all styles: epic, lyric, didactic, satiric, dramatic. He says so himself when speaking of his nature: *Transmutabile son per tutte guise!* Transmutable they are in every guise.[4]

"But I have not yet said everything. I have not yet spoken of Dante's project, which was to make a great journey, to pass with us

---

[2] Light intellectual full of love,
  Love of true good full of joy,
  Joy that surpasses every sweetness.
        Paradiso, Canto XXX, 40–42.
        Translated by John D. Sinclair.
[3] Dante's poem is a theological poem but translated into the language of the stars, of the fields, of blood and earth.
[4] *Paradiso*, Canto V, 99.

through a great adventure—the only one which is a drama, a real drama. It was not as in the case of Homer, as with Vergil, an existence bound beforehand by destiny. Here if one goes forward, it is toward heaven, toward happiness, toward divine justice and its demands. And as you have no doubt observed, the farther one goes forward, the slower time moves, but also the greater is its span. That is the experience of life. At our age one feels it. The horizon, as one climbs, becomes continually more vast. Time, as one grows, becomes increasingly intense, more dense, more collected together. All conspires together. Everything seems to rush upward, toward a mysterious moment. That, I repeat, is human life; Christian and Catholic life; it is the real journey, the real voyage, the true movement from below upward. One starts from here. One is going there, near God.

"And in that ascent, as in existence, guides, initiatory loves are given us one by one, some vanishing when they are no longer useful, to give place to others; when it is a question of climbing still one step higher, to mend one's ways and to teach us to do, to be, to suffer in a nobler way. After Vergil it is Beatrice, after Beatrice, Bernard. After Bernard it is the final initiator, the Virgin and her Beauty, which can be joyfully read in the eyes of all the other saints.

"Finally we reach the ultimate inaccessible end. You remember? Dante sees three circles, of three colors. And the second circle seems to him to be inscribed with our likeness: *parve pinta della nostra effigie* (appears painted with our likeness).

"How can the human likeness be included in the cycle of the Trinity? That is the supreme mystery. *Kyrie Eleison, CHRISTE ELEISON, Kyrie Eleison.*

"Note well. Contemplate. This shining face is not that of humanity in general, is not Christ eternal, is not humanity projected in the absolute, is not a divinity who merely has a human appearance; no, this poet Dante rejects the myths. To maintain this historicity of Jesus of Nazareth, who died under Pontius Pilate, Guardini rightly noted, is 'the grave task of Christian laymen concerned for the world, and it is expressed in the *Divine Comedy.*'

"We are here," went on Paul VI, "at its highest point; where poetry and mysticism coincide. And one understands that literature can be, as Bremond thought, the mute prayer of those who seek beauty in the light."

THE HOLY FATHER

"I do not know if you have read what Romano Guardini says about Dante; he tells us that, though he knew Italian well and was a theologian, he had never understood Dante. The *Divine Comedy* remained a closed book, till the day when it was revealed to him by a friend. From then on it accompanied him everywhere. And do you know what most struck Guardini in reading Dante? It was that for Dante the finite is not annihilated in the infinite. In the *Paradiso* the whole of history is still there, the whole earth, raised to the state of reconquered purity and glory. There is the basis of the mystery of Christian hope.

"If Dante is the Christian poet par excellence, it is because of his assumption that even in the eternal peace is man, all we have loved, history, events, encounters—in short, the whole of existence. The *rose* for Dante descends from God at the same time that it blossoms from the world."

The Pope continued: "And I would again say that for a layman of the twentieth century, that layman's work is exemplary.

"Dante carried the weight of the whole world. Dante looked for an ordered world where every being would have his place, his situation, his vocation; where each, based on his predecessor or his neighbor, sets the base in his turn for him who will follow him in history; where power rests on justice; where obedience, being the presence in us of the All, is not different from true freedom.

"Dante remained with me for the whole duration of the Council. The Council's end coincided with the seventh centenary of his birth in Florence.

"And when the fourth session was ended I presented to the bishops, the observers, the auditors a copy printed for them, light and portable, illustrated with a few miniatures taken from a fifteenth-century codex preserved in the Vatican—as a memorial of the Council and a breviary of poetry. I even ventured to compose for that edition a dedication in monumental Latin, trying to interpret what Dante might bring to our ecumenical ideal:

> *"Divini poematis vatis summi vereque oecumenici*
> *quod veritatem nos tam extollentem*
> *mirus mire concinit."*[5]

On Shakespeare

THE POPE

"I remember paying a visit some thirty years ago to Shakespeare's cottage at Stratford-on-Avon. The lessons I received in my early youth and my personal reading have increased my admiration for Shakespeare. He is such a great poet, such an extraordinary writer, and, like Dante with us, he represents the culture, tradition, and artistic genius of a whole people.

"Perhaps what has struck me most in Shakespeare is—how shall I put it?—the coming together of a deep humanity with poetic invention and exploration. But there is another coming together, more admirable and better concealed, in Shakespeare.

[5] In this divine poem by a supreme, and truly ecumenical poet,
This marvelous man marvelously sings
That Truth we also were extolling.

"This is when that humanity and that poetry, equally inimitable, lead Shakespeare, without any moralistic intention to the *rediscovery* of the sacred laws of the world of morality which give human life its sublime dimensions. For this reason the Shakespearian theater introduces us to a religious understanding of the universe.

"Yes, his forceful genius, his vast vocabulary, so full of overtones and of power, help man to listen with respect to the truths which Shakespeare incessantly presents, which are the substance of his dramas: the truth of death, the truth of the Judgment, and the truth of heaven and hell.

"The weaving of his tragedies is in itself a teaching. It reminds modern man of God's existence; it reminds him constantly that there is a life after this life, that the author of evil is punished, that the good receive their reward.

"In this context I should like to add a word about the significance of the theater.

"Shakespeare is so great that by reading alone he satisfies. And I remember my feelings when I would read Shakespeare by myself, trying to find for myself a personal, intimate, imaginative, vibrant conception filling out everything, so necessary for stage representation. But the stage adds a personal communication between interpreter and spectator. It could be said that the actor creates the piece over again. The actor acts through eyes and ears on the heart and mind. The shades of vocal intonation, unlimited in their subtlety and variety, the gesture, movement, and posture of the whole figure, the look above all, and the slightest quiver of the features communicate emotion from mind to mind.

"In that the theater differs essentially from the cinema. The cinema has its own resources, which are great, very great; but they are different. On stage the actor is there, and while his soul communes with the whole audience or better with each person forming part of it, he on his side can read in them the feelings he has brought to life, is moved by them in his turn, and the reciprocal communication becomes ever more intimate and potent.

"Excuse my speaking to you of the cinema and the theater in the context of Shakespeare! I do not think I am digressing from the true Christian tradition, which St. Francis of Assisi rediscovered in the figures of the Crib and which represented the mysteries with such intensity and acted them with such sincerity that one had the impression of *seeing* them. It was the wish of the Apostle Thomas: "Except I shall see . . . and put my finger . . . I will not believe."[6]

"It seems to me that the theater of Paul Claudel has rediscovered that simple and royal road, that he has created *mysteries* suited to the spirit of these times, with epic and lyric power, which recalls the great Greek tragedies. That is the theater's triumph. Your French art of the seventeenth century reached its height with *Polyeucte, Esther,* and *Athalie.* But already at the end of the sixteenth century, the plays of Lope de Vega and especially of Calderón de la Barca stirred enthusiasm throughout Spain. Our own times, far from bringing about the disappearance of the Christian theater, as was rumored, have made it shine."

On Cardinal Newman

I know he likes Newman. He has often told me with conviction that Newman had done something heroic: a conversion in the midst of life, such as Newman's, was more than losing one's life. He abandoned his own people; he separated himself from his country,

[6] John 20:25.

his Church, his family. And for what? For an idea, for the Truth, for wholeness.

"That is a good example," I said, "of religious liberty."

"It is the highest example and reminds one of the martyrs; one immolates oneself, one sacrifices oneself, not for some interest or other, but to obey the voice of conscience. That conscience which Newman placed higher than everything when he told Gladstone: 'If they asked me to propose a toast to the Pope, as they toast the Queen at our banquets, I would lift my glass first to Conscience and then to the Pope.'

"It is clear that conscience is for us the highest authority, which allows us to recognize the authority of God. That has always been understood in the Church. 'The truth can only be imposed by the strength of the truth, with as much gentleness as force. It is through the mediation of his conscience that man receives the injunctions of the divine law.' "

At Pentecost 1964 a Newman Congress was held. Paul VI had sent a telegram: BY THE LUCIDITY OF HIS INTUITION AS WELL AS BY THE ARDENT DESIRE OF RENDERING CHRISTIAN BELIEF MORE ACCESSIBLE TO THE MEN OF HIS TIME, NEWMAN SHOWED HIMSELF A PIONEER OF GENIUS, WHOSE TEACHINGS THROW A PRECIOUS LIGHT ON THE CHURCH TODAY.

One day he said to me, "Since you passed your youth studying Newman, tell me what you have gleaned of actual value."

I think that I answered something like this: "Conscience and science were discoveries made outside the Church. Then humanity saw a new world arising. Nietzsche and Marx, in the realm of unbelief, took over conscience and the science of becoming in order to create, in an atheist climate, those two opposite philosophies: *atheistic existentialism* and *atheistic dialectic*. The nineteenth-century Church lacked leaders.

"Newman was perhaps the only one to have understood in the nineteenth century that *conscience* could be explored and the *duration* of historical time interpreted in such a way that conscience would not lead us to the void but to The Supreme Being; that the science of becoming would not lead us to dissolve Christianity, but to understand its depths, and in addition to justify that *structure* called Catholicism, which extends from Abraham to Christ, from Christ to Paul VI through the line of Roman pontiffs.

"Newman is present at the Council in several ways: by his idea of the laity, of Tradition and its relation to Scripture, of the organic episcopate, of the mystical Church. One might even say the idea of the Council is Newmanian: The Church must reform herself constantly to preserve her identity in time, to adapt herself. Tomorrow the Church will be still more Newmanian, for she will have to become aware of the profound identity between the Church after the Council and the Church before the Council and of all time."

The Holy Father seemed to approve these thoughts. He added:

"In Newman it is the personality which attracts, which charms, which is unforgettable. Newman is—how can one express it?—an autobiographical author. When he speaks of himself he speaks to us of ourselves. He touches the entire being, both mind and heart: All becomes vibrant, all awakens at the same moment.

"Consider the Council. Read the *Acts* of the Council, forgetting the circumstances in which these different texts were composed, discussed, voted. Look at them in their construction and their result, in their harmony; they are a cathedral, a symphony. And one could also say they are a new style, corresponding to the sensibility, the needs of a new epoch—our own, in which we are, which carries us along. Read especially Schema XIII, which is like a fountain from which will draw those whose concern is to reach the men of our time, to speak their language, to enter into their problems. This is an emphasis both new and old, a kind of union of light and heat.

"Formerly the Councils were the work of theologians who were chiefly preoccupied with giving a doctrinal lesson, which lesson was summed up in definitions; the definitions were themselves defined in anathemas. Such was their method, and nothing tells us that this method is out of date when it is a question of defining religious truths. But this Council had a different objective: first a pastoral one, cordial and communicative, seeking a dialogue of the Church with the world, seeking applications, resonance more than reasoning, and I would say, *ministry* rather than *magistracy*. And, to return to St. Augustine and Newman, one might say that the Council, although speaking with a sovereign authority, speaks to the *heart*, to that heart which your Pascal considered to be the source of mind, because it is concrete, human, and incarnates truth in charity. In short, the Council obeyed the counsel on the 'order of love' which consists, if I remember rightly, in point-by-point digression referred to the end, keeping it constantly in view. And that end is Christ."

I remember then having told Paul VI that near the end of the pontificate of Pius XII, speaking with him about Newman, telling him of my wish to see him better known and approved by the Catholic Church, I spoke to him of a possible future canonization. Then Pius XII, in an almost inaudible, but very sure, very sweet way, in a prophetic tone, said: "Do not doubt it, sir; Newman will one day be a Doctor of the Church."

Paul VI confined himself to observing that Leo XIII, in making Newman a Cardinal, wished to indicate that the Church saw herself in his mind and his writing. He added: "At the beginning of my pontificate, I had occasion to canonize the Passionist who received Newman into the Roman Church, Father Dominic of the Mother of God. The story of this new saint is very strange. He was a monk of an order founded in the eighteenth century by St. Paul of the Cross. He was a philosopher, a theologian, a mystic, a Mariologist. His unspoken and compelling vocation was to work for the renaissance of English Catholicism. But he was totally unprepared for it. He did not know English. In 1841, he was posted to England, where he was met with insults. Newman recognized his value and sent for him because he did not try to make converts. Father Dominic received Newman into the Church in October 1845.

"Then he died in 1849, as it chanced in the waiting room of a wayside station during a journey. His task was done. He had fulfilled his wish."

The Pope went on, "Newman is a great man. To go the length of what he judged to be the Truth, that is, absolute truth, undivided truth Newman renounced, in the midst of his life what is more than life: He renounced the Church of England not in order to separate himself from it, but to fulfill it. He said that he did not cease believing what he had believed, but that he believed yet more, that he had carried his Anglican faith to its fullness."

J.G.

"But he also said that he had remained, he would not have felt secure."

THE POPE

"Newman followed the light according to his light. He asked the light to guide his every step.

"Lead, kindly Light . . .
. . . I do not ask to see
The distant scene—one step enough for me."

I

"In the perspective of the Council, does not Newman's step become less exemplary? Has not the idea of conversion to the Church been replaced by the idea of a convergence of all churches toward the Eternal Christ? In these conditions, why become a convert?"

HE

"There is only one Church, axis of the convergence, one only Church in which all churches should reunite. It is our duty to recall continually this basic truth. One flock, one shepherd. Ecumenism presupposes that. But charity impels us to respect every liberty, every conscience, every delay, every ripening. Conscience impelled Newman to the absolute witness, very near martyrdom. And sometimes martyrdom is asked of us. I would even say that martyrdom, that form of witness, is always virtually demanded of us; that we should all, whoever we are and even if we have no belief, be ready to give our blood in order not to lose our reasons for living. As a pagan poet has said:

*"Summum crede nefas vitam praeferre pudori
Et propter vitam vitae perdere causas."*[8]

"We should always be prepared to climb upward. It is here that Newman's example speaks to each one of us.

"A conversion is a prophetic act. Abraham ushered in a nation. Luther lived in solitude the tragedy of separation. Newman lived the story of future reunion, of that recapitulation in Christ Jesus whose time is hidden from us, but to which we all aspire."

[8] Believe that the worst thing is to prefer life to honour. And to keep life at the cost of the reason for living.

8

FACE OF A FRIEND AND FATHER

Toward the end of the second session of the Council, Paul VI said to me one evening: "I would like you to know an extraordinary man, such as M. Pouget was for you; there are unknown geniuses, hidden splendors."

And the Pope described to me this man, in his way unique and the only one of his kind. He spoke to me of his universal culture, his poverty, his independence of mind, his zeal. Saying this he frequently smiled; I gathered that his extraordinary friend must also be a joyful, a surprising person. "He is an Oratorian," the Holy Father had said, "you know the Oratorians?" The Pope cited Berulle, Newman, Father Faber, Father Samson. He remarked that the Oratory often has produced exceptions to the general rule, intelligences in advance of their times.

The door opened and I saw Father Bevillacqua for the first time. He introduced himself simply; priest of the small working-class parish of St. Anthony at Brescia. He was a mountaineer, broad-shouldered with a natural dignity, peasant, warrior, mystic, and that in a simple way. He gave himself no airs, did not make much of himself, he accepted himself and went his own way, somewhat in the manner of John XXIII, about whom he has written so well. I noticed the well-known white unstarched neckband by which the Oratorian priests, who have retained the seventeenth-century fashion, may be recognized.

His conversation erupted ideas, memories, quotations (always very exact), prophetic views, and all with great happiness and joy of being. He liked to discover, innovate, set out for new shores. What I especially noticed in this first meeting was that between the Pope and him there were indefinable affinities such as history rarely presents to such a degree: of a mutual fatherliness. Each honored the other and respected his preeminence. They played, so to speak, at *hide-father*, as one plays at hide-and-seek. To watch and listen to them conversing so freely was as pure a spectacle of friendship as this world can conceive of. *"Maestro incomparable ed amico singolare"* (incomparable master and unique friend), the Pope said when the Father had left, and he recalled in speaking of him the mysterious motto of another son[1] of St. Philip Neri: *Cor ad cor loquitur* (heart speaks to heart).

At our next meeting, one autumn day, Father Bevillacqua suggested we visit the relics of St. Philip at the Chiesa Nuova. He showed me first of all the most striking of all the remains, the death mask, as our so clumsy expression goes, which is one of the most lovely sleeping faces which there could be. Michelangelo, I know, carved several faces buried in sleep, seized at that moment of eclipse and beauty which transforms every human face, at death's touch, into an object of contemplation. No single one of Michelangelo's sculptures has the delicacy of that mask. Is it a man still in his strength or one grown old? Is it a layman, a family man, or an ascetic? Impossible to say. Is it a mystic his eyes half closed the better to see, to savor what he has just glimpsed?

[1] Newman

Giovenale Ancina, who had been close to Philip at the end of his days, described him as "white as ermine," with a girl's complexion. When he held up his hand to the sun, it had, it seems, alabaster transparence. As Sainte-Beuve stresses in speaking of St. Francis of Sales, a sort of brightness emanated from his face when at rest. It is known how particular St. Philip was about the things he used, that he did not like to celebrate Mass in a borrowed chalice, drank from a glass of his own. That may be guessed from that face fixed in ineluctable sleep. I said to Father Bevillacqua, "It is a mask which does not mask, but on the contrary unmasks the intimate, as a look does with the living. There are three masks which I put in a class absolutely by themselves: that of Pascal, that of Napoleon, and that of M. Pouget, my blind teacher. I find this one superior in its humanity."

We were seated at that moment in the chapel on the second floor, where other relics of Philip are kept. The Father took my hand; I felt the rough skin, his irregular pulse, his heart had beaten too long; the weariness of evening. He said:

"This Philip was a unique character among the saints. He had the joy, the pride, the independence of the Florentines and that ability to laugh at himself, which is the essence of humor. But he was Roman to the very roots; he was human in the way the good Roman people are. He had the sense of the *buona vita* (the good life), so different from the *dolce vita* (the agreeable life), an international import. Philip himself was the master of the joyous, of the true *sweetness of life*.

"Never, I believe, were the natural and the supernatural united more exquisitely. You know the trouble we have to take in concentration; he had to take it for distraction, so much did ecstasy carry him away; he did absurd or extravagant things, such as reading a novel before Mass, so as to be able to resist the mystical force which lifted him, at times, off the ground. He was so imaginative and so reasonable in everything. You know how one of his gestures was to touch the center of his forehead with three fingers together, saying that perfection resided in that one small point of the brain.

"With all that he could not do without people! He made no great projects, his only passion being contact with mankind: in inns, in public places, in the market, on Roman holidays. He wished to be with the people in their sufferings but also in their songs. On these occasions where everything is done in common, both thought and song cease being methodical and solitary. That is the *Oratory*, so different from the *Exercises* of St. Ignatius. It was not a question of dialectic, still less of preaching. Philip conversed, sang, *was*. He did not know how to preach; it was prayer and dialogue in the pure state. It was fire. It was the unforeseeable, the Pentecost of love. It was music itself."

I said to myself, "How happy Abbé Bremond would have been to hear Father Bevillacqua!"

I remember that at that moment I interrupted the Father to say to him: "I will give you a definition of eloquence which I once read, I don't know where, but which has been a great help to me in life. To be eloquent is to say something to someone."

"Oh," he said, "how that fits Philip!"

"That," I answered, "would also have fitted Montaigne, who, if I am not mistaken, wrote an essay on the art of public speaking."

"You know that Philip had an exceptional mystical life, yet not morbid. So far as it is possible to know, there was an intense ardor at the center of the breast, a sort of inner fire, a joy which he could not contain, which made his heart, his sides; his whole body tremble. He made every effort to conceal it. For example, he said the Mass, in public, very fast, in a hurry. But when his time was his own (in this Oratory where we are) he went so slowly that the altar boy put the key in his pocket and went peacefully off to lunch."

Then he told me his opinions of the Italian saints. Philip headed the list of honor. He told me that Francis of Assisi was favored with mystical graces, but these set him rather apart from ordinary humanity. He could not conceal them, and did he perhaps not wish to? Don Bosco had little critical faculty and was very capable in business, while Philip understood nothing about it. He praised Philip as a mystic whom Bergson would have called complete, because while he was apparently like others, independent and serene, with no system, he had brilliant intuitions, was without narcissism, without special devotion. "And nevertheless," he added, "Philip had great authority over St. Charles Borromeo—whom he often criticized— and even over Pope Clement VIII, with whom he was close friends. For example, the Pope had just lunched. Philip entered, and without the slightest genuflection took his biretta and said, 'Good morning, Holy Father, I cover my head.' The Pope, doubtless with a touch of irony, said, 'Monsieur Philip, you are the master here.' Then Philip put his hands on the Pope's face and caressed his beard with respect. The Pope never stopped smiling."

I remember I repeated this homily, and the last anecdote in particular, to Paul VI, who was very amused by it. He said to me: "Father Bevillacqua does not imitate his patron saint in all respects. What is sure is that in describing Philip Neri he has somewhat portrayed himself, excepting for the jokes. It is already over thirty years that I have known him, and I have always seen him over-flowing with zeal, gay, enterprising, and of a most unbelievable curiosity. He used to devour several books a day. I know that at any hour of the day or night he was available for anything and everything. Like St. Philip, he had a holiday air which, for the problems I brought to him, was already a solution. No dramatizations. Like Pascal: *Joy, joy, tears of joy.* The open door. Unpredictable, yet always the same. Familiarity with what is great and what is little. What one loved in Cardinal Mercier, whose pupil he had been at Louvain, was also in him. *Direzione Cristo!*

"He was also a man of great courage. Few men have thought, have suffered the two World Wars as he.

"Christ was for him the sole object of culture. He discovered Him through everything, even in the darkness of those who denied Him. You remember what he said in your presence the other day about atheist existentialism: In it he saw an experience proving by the absurd the reality of God. And how he celebrated the liturgy! It led him through beauty, through poetry, to the most inward center of mystery."

Certainly Paul VI knew this anecdote: Philip said one day to one of his visitors, "Would you believe it, the Pope wishes to make me Cardinal? What do you think about it?" Then, raising his eyes to heaven, "Paradise, Paradise!"

One could imagine a similar dialogue when Paul VI manifested a desire to make his old teacher a Cardinal. The Father argued about poverty, which was the soul of his life. Paul VI answered him, "That doesn't mean a thing; I have purple robes and a hat, which are no more use to me; I give them to you." Then Father Bevillacqua fell back on the necessity of Roman residence. He could not leave his poor and peripheric parish. Paul VI said to him, "You will remain parish priest of St. Antony. A Cardinal cannot be parish priest, but a parish priest can be a Cardinal." The Father drew attention to his great age, his tastes, his horror of those ceremonies which were not liturgical. It was all resolved by obedience. I am sure there was also a question of his eventual intervention in the last session of the Council, in particular on Schema XIII, which he had so much wished to see appear. Was that perhaps the motive which won him over and which made him pass over the rest? He doubted, too, feeling in his body and heart a great accumulated weariness, that it would be for long.

The Pope said to me, "Doubtless you know how Philip died? Joyfully, and not without jesting, on May 26. On the twenty-fifth he had been believed dead, but on the twenty-sixth, Cardinal Cisano saw him climbing briskly up the little wooden stairway which led to his chapel." Cardinal Bevillacqua was ill for longer. He fell ill from fatigue, on Holy Saturday. He had time to receive all his friends and to say to each a word of farewell.

I telephoned him. I heard his broken voice giving me his last benediction. I will read you his last letter to his parishioners, dated April 26, 1965. He was to die on May 6.

Carissimi,

Quante volte ho benedetto il viaggio dei vostri cari dicendovi in mille forme o stesso pensiero: piangete perché è umano ma guardate a Cristo, che è risurrezion e vita!

Ve lo ricordo ora salutandovi con tanto affetto. Vi ringrazio perché mi avete sopportato, vi chiedo perdono se le mie durezze vi hanno reso i nostri contatti più rari, ma vi ho amato e per questo benedico ogni anima: vecchi e giovani, appartenenti a tutte le situazioni della vita.

Che Dio vi bénedica, che la Madonna via sia vicina, che lo spirito di Cristo vi renda membra vive di questa piccola "ecclesia"!

*Un addio, una benedizione, un augurio di incontrarci e di ricono-
scerci nella casa del Padre.*

26 *Aprile* 1965[2]

The Holy Father also said to me, "Cardinal Bevillacqua looked at
the present situation in a penetrating manner. He made this remark
on the subject of contemporary atheism: 'The position of atheism
and of the faith have changed. Atheism is more radical, no longer
triumphant. It has become tragic and problematic; the horror of a
total absence of God makes us feel by its emptiness His presence. At
the present time it is clear to all that the more knowledge grows, the
more anguish increases; the more technical means are augmented, the
more the chances of death and suffering are increased. More than
ever before the image of the servant of Yahweh described by Isaiah
in Chapter 54 is present to us. The *man of grief* is contemporary
man. Christianity is more actual than ever. It must then increasingly
unveil its true face. It must again become essential, logical, heroic;
essenziale, logico, eroico." There still echoes in my memory the
sound of his fine voice, so powerful and youthful, when he pronounced these three words in Italian.

"As for me," I told the Holy Father, "I remember some of his last

[2] Dearly beloved,

How often have I blessed the voyages of your loved ones; telling them, in a thousand different ways, the same thought; weep, of course, because that is but human, but
look to Christ, who is the Resurrection and the life.

I remind you of that now, greeting you with great affection. I thank you for having
put up with me, I ask your pardon if my harshness has made our contacts more rare,
but I have loved you, and thus bless every soul, young and old, from all walks of life.

God bless you, the Virgin be near to you, the spirit of Christ make you a living
part of this little "church."

A good-bye, a blessing, a wish that we meet and know one another again in the
house of the Father.

April 26. 1965.

words: 'What! You don't know Venice! I won't tell you it is the most beautiful city in the world, for there is Verona. I was born in Verona. But I will tell you Venice's secret—in a word, Venice is a little bit of the Orient set in the West. It is also the innocent city, the prelapsarian city, and also the city found guilty by the judgment. It is the city of color, of color dissolved in air and color refracted in the water, passed into motion like sound. It is often said that one must choose between salvation and beauty; it is your Cartesians, your Jansenists who said it. Go to Venice and you will understand what light is.' "

9

DIALOGUE ON ST. PAUL

THE POPE
"I remember how, during the first session of the Council, you sent me an essay you had written (referring to Pascal, I believe) on the definition of genius. You distinguished between genius and talent. I approved of what you said about genius. I think I wrote and told you."

J.G.
"I keep your letter and value it. Genius seems to me to have to do with unity, that ultimate mystery. It is a matter of uniting in oneself, by thought, the maximum of things, but of uniting them without confusion or discord, leaving each to itself. I would say that in this sense genius is Catholic, or, as people prefer to say these days, ecumenical; these two words evoke unity in diversity, multiplicity in unity."

HE
"If that is the case, St. Paul deserves to be called a genius, and perhaps the greatest, because of the depth, the opposition of the things to be united. He wished to unite in Christ all that presented itself to his intelligence and love. He wished to unite the religion of

Adam, Abraham, and Moses with the grace of Christ Jesus. He wished to unite the pagans, the Gentiles, with the Jews and Christians. And that while respecting beings, persons, beliefs, inheritances, hopes. Thus he wished, if I may put it so, the Jews to be more Jewish, better Jews. The Gentiles he wished to be more themselves, free only from vice and superstition."

I

". . . not because we would be stripped of something; rather, we would clothe ourselves afresh; our mortal nature must be swallowed up in life."[1]

HE

". . . *ut absorbeatur quod mortale est a vita.* That is it. St. Paul, it might be said, did not wish the unbelievers—or those not yet Christians—to be naked; he wished whatever was honorable, just, substantial, presaging, and prospective in their belief to be freed from what might restrain or corrupt it, that it might be further clad by truth, might be *absorbed* by life."

I

"It seems that St. Paul—although he believed he was in the last phase of history—foresaw development in time, and the continuity of history."

HE

"To make known the Gospel will always be to act as though the moment of speaking were the last as well as the first. One never knows what is end and what is beginning. With death it is like that."

[1] II Cor. 5:4.

I

"The last time is always the first time. Nothing dies. Everything is reborn."

HE

"St. Paul announced the good tidings in a way which was genius. He spoke to small audiences, he wrote a few letters in haste (he dictated very fast) ; for a time he thought everything was going to end. And nevertheless he had in view the whole universe, all history."

I

"He spoke to all time and all space."

HE

"There is nothing in man he did not use. What did I say—use? Better: raise, exalt, and, if necessary, ransom, repair, restore, raise to its highest power. That is what light does; it recreates.

"Reread his letters from this point of view. You will see how close he is to modern man.

"In the work Ricciotti wrote on St. Paul, he says, I recall, that St. Paul took advantage even of obstacles, jealousies, shabby things inspired by sectarian sentiments; he used them to further the spread of his Gospel. 'For that,' he said, 'I rejoice and shall always rejoice.' In that *Castro Pretorio* where he was chained by the wrist (and who is not chained?) Paul talked with his guard, who remained three days with him, who was sometimes an Italian, sometimes a soldier from Pannonia or Macedonia. St. Paul talked; I might say he dialogued; with intent, without intent; in season, out of season; with success, without success. That is the true constant dialogue, the uninterrupted dialogue, the dialogue with the man next to you, with the taxi driver, the chance neighbor. Sometimes a banal exchange. Sometimes just a word, summing up the Gospel."

I

"The two words with that difficult prefix *dia* sum up St. Paul's method: dialogue, dialectic."

HE

"St. Paul joined thesis and antithesis, but of the synthesis Christ was the living link."

I

"How many antitheses: law and faith; Jews and Gentiles; old and new, death and life; slavery and freedom. It seems as though the need to unite contraries was so strong in St. Paul that it dictated even his itineraries. St. Paul shuttled between contrasting cities: Jerusalem and Rome. The intermediate towns, such as Ephesus, Corinth, or Athens, were only wayside halts."

HE

"What says the philosopher?"

I

"That these dialectics were not like modern dialectics, which are without end or exit, since the antithesis always begins again."

THE POPE

"The communities founded by Paul have vanished. Islam occupied all the lands he evangelized. Only Rome remains—which Paul did not found. In short, of what he did, not one stone remains on another, which is again, if I remember rightly, a remark of Ricciotti's. But, from the spiritual viewpoint, St. Paul is more actual, more living, than ever."

I

"His head rolled three times after his execution. Three times it has engendered a source of thought: with St. Augustine, with the Reformation, and in our day with the theology of Salvation History."

THE POPE

"It might be said that in our day we throw light on him, and that he bears up well under the innovations of our time, as though he had foreseen them. One might say he had written for the age of cosmonauts and atomic scientists, for this moment in history when everything is expanding, but also when everything might end."

I

"When everything explodes, as in a new beginning."

HE

"When everything could start over and begin again."

I

"When one does not know if tomorrow God will be outside of all, or all in all."

HE

"When one should divest oneself of all, to be clothed again in all."

I

"When one approaches a cataclysm or a Pentecost."

HE

"When we strive more than ever toward Him who possesses and propels us, when faith is more than ever the substance of things hoped for, when the events of visible history reveal, more than ever, the eternal invisible. The key ideas of St. Paul on the 'mystical body,' on the cosmos, on the meaning of history and time, on collegial government and on the authority of Peter, on marriage, on the Eucharist, on contacts, on zeal, on the apostolate of the laity, on the historical witness; all these reappeared at the last Council, and that by the very force of events, in obedience to the signs of the times! And, too, what one might call his apostolic strategy, his concern for striking at the nuclear centers, for pressing to the ends of the earth. In going to Bombay and New York, I was thinking of that."

I

"When Paul was called Saul, he was already an able strategist. Before he went up to Jerusalem, the Sanhedrin was content to arrest the Christians publicly in the squares and on the streets. The house was sacred, an inviolable place; those eastern houses with a wooden bolt, asylum for women and children, places of prayer. . . . Paul went into the houses like the police."

HE

"He dispersed the Christians. He forced them, by persecution, to disperse, that is to say, to be sown. What a strange affair! To drive the Christians out of one place was to force them to evangelize others. The seeds were separated. Too close together, they might perish.

"He was called Saul, and he changed this name, doubtless too Jewish, into Paul, like the Evangelist John Mark, who in fact was called Mark. But this change of name did not change his methods. Paul did what Saul did in him, before him. He continued to strike at the center. He established himself in the cities and the capitals. Ephesus, Philippi, Corinth, finally Rome, to which everything converges. He directed himself to the leaders in opinion and power; to the elite. In short, he dialogued always and with everyone. Thought and action, so often disunited and opposed, were very close together in him. What you call his dialectic today was also his mystique and his strategy. I had once read the books of Father Prat, which are still very readable; he well shows how in St. Paul thought and action were allied and marvelously simplified, because Jesus Christ summed up everything in him."

I

"His method, perpetually to return to the center."

HE

"The center is Christ, Christ alone. Remember: Christ is the image of the invisible world. 'He is the true likeness of the God we cannot see . . . all . . . things . . . were created through him and in him.'[2] You remember Dante:

> "In his profundity I see contained
> Into a single whole by love united
> What in the universe is manifested.
> The cosmos itself participates in man's redemption."

I

"Schweitzer has compared this method to the spider's. He says that the spider's genius is to spin his web round a center. The more

[2] Col. 1:15–16.

the threads are stretched, the more lovely the shape. If they are released, everything becomes confused."

HE

"The center is Jesus, and JESUS CRUCIFIED.

"After having sacrificed all, St. Paul meditates a more perfect self-immolation, with the idea that one must go continually forward tormenting him. You recall what he wrote to the Philippians. 'Not that I have already won the prize, already reached fulfillment. I only press on, in hope of winning the mastery, as Christ Jesus has won the mastery over me.' "[3]

I

"I wonder, as does one of my friends, a mystic deeply versed in Pascal, whether the latter, who wrote very rapidly, and made many slips of the pen, intended to write, not as our reading is: *Thou wouldst not have sought me if thou hadst not already found me*—a profound phrase indeed, but Augustinian—but rather the phrase even more profound and truly Pauline: *Thou wouldst not have sought me, if I had not already found thee.*"

HIS HOLINESS

"In any case that is the thought of St. Paul. The apostle—stretching his body and muscles, like a runner at the tape, tries to reach and touch Him who long since has always been ahead, He who first touched him.

"No, my brothers," he continued, "I do not think I have arrived. I aim at but one thing which I will tell you: to forget what is behind and tense all my efforts toward what is before; I run straight for the

[3] Phil. 3:12.

goal. Toward the palm where God calls me in Christ Jesus. Before
He was pursued; now He pursues.

"And when we have come to the end of our life, having finished
the race, *having kept the faith*, if we throw a glance behind, it brings
that same experience; we have the impression of having been chosen,
of having been preceded."

I

"One difficulty; I often heard it raised in the corridors of the
Council, frequently by our Protestant colleagues. 'Would St. Paul,'
they ask, 'have approved the Schema of the Council on the relations
of the Church to the world, which became the constitution *Gaudium
et Spes*? What would he have said?' The solution proposed here is a
purely human one: The Church of Jesus Christ cannot align itself
with international organizations which reflect earthly wisdom alone.
These organizations know neither man's sin nor Christ's salvation.
What is the aim, in short, for these wise men of the world? To
increase culture, to develop science or technology, to share out the
goods of this world, to augment comforts, making a terrestrial
paradise here on earth. In our day, after such bitter disappointments,
faith can no longer be put in reason's optimism, although lip service
is still paid to it. And the Church, which up till now had the
privilege of telling the cruel truth and the strength to displease, keeps
silence about evil. St. Paul never veiled or minimized the tragedy of
the human condition. And only the tragedy of sin makes the
madness of the Cross comprehensible.

"I remember what Professor Skydsgaard said at the Council:
'This Conciliar text (he was speaking of the chapter consecrated to
peace in Schema XIII) confides solely in God's grace, faced with a

constantly threatening cataclysm.' A cataclysm at the level of human history, which will be taken as a Judgment of God. 'That is what true prophets preach,' he added, 'while the false say all is well.' "

HE

"The Council never wished to say everything, or to present an organic synthesis of truth, as a single doctor might. Do not forget that it is a Council: It is the Church interrogating herself on a single point, corresponding to a historical need. It would be quite wrong to take the Council's decrees as a complete exposition of the Faith."

I

"The Council is like a single epistle and not the whole roster of the epistles."

HE

"The word of God remains unequivocal and eternal, an inextinguishable light for the comfort of our souls. In listening to the frank, solemn voice of the Council, we see the charge confided by Christ to the living magisterium of the Church to keep, defend, and interpret the 'deposit of faith.' We ought not to separate the teachings of the Council from the doctrinal patrimony of the Church, but see how they fit into it, how coherent they are with it, how they bring to it witness, development, explanation, application. Then the 'novelties,' doctrinal and legislative, of the Council appear in their true perspective."

I

"It might be said that an assembly has never the power of synthesis which the thought of one person has."

HE

"An assembly which deliberates and decides during a limited period (and what is four years?) has not the fullness that has individual thought, which sets forth not only one point of view but the whole. So that is my answer. The task of the Council was already a very heavy one; it brought a pastoral way and method, and these, as we have seen, in a spirit of optimism and confidence. This confidence too was truly that of St. Paul; you will remember how he spoke to the Greeks in passing through Athens.

"But that did not exclude his acute awareness of the extent of evil, of the work of evil powers, of humanity's tragic state, of the Last Judgment. As I said, never in St. Paul does one truth exclude another; they are propounded together."

I

"He was torn apart."

HE

"It is the rending of the truth, of the Cross. Indeed St. Paul himself says it elsewhere: *I am pulled from both sides at the same time*. The Cross always rends."

I

"Has not the Council drawn a veil over the Cross?"

HE

"Cross and Resurrection, the two linked truths summed up by St. Paul, must not be separated. The Council has rather stressed the joy of the Resurrection. This joy has been somewhat overshadowed in the West. The Council answered those who accuse us of not loving man, or man's time. It frequently underlined that God is also God of this world, which He has created, loved, and restored. The Word has truly come down, into the flesh of history, but the Christ of the Resurrection is the crucified Christ. The mysterious hour of which Christ spoke to his mother at the marriage of Cana is the hour of His death on the Cross.

"I reply to your misgivings. If the Church, in the first moments of the Council, went toward the world, it is not to sidestep the scandal of the Cross. I would say that it is to present the Cross in its truth, in its bare essential, in its naked splendor. For the Cross to appear thus in its truth and not only as the 'sign of victory'—as was the case with the labarum of Constantine—that effort of deprivation had to come from the Council; yes, to deprive the Church of all that she is not essentially, to deprive the Church of what during the course of centuries expressed her, of what corresponded to the signs and needs of those times, but by which she cannot forever be expressed. To deprive the Church of what is adventitious that she may appear with her authentic face. It is then that the Cross is seen in a more real and simple way, more human and more true. It appears to me that if the Council did not insist on that, it was because it was not its task, its particular duty, its aim. But here one can reverse the famous maxim and say that the Cross stands, while Councils turn, *STAT CRUX DUM VOLVUNTUR CONCILIA.* It is for souls to see the Cross of Jesus in the light of the Council. The Council wished to unite, and union is obtained by the Cross alone. St. Paul said it."

I remember that at this moment we compared once again those two pillars, St. Paul and St. John. Their diptych is figured on the threshold of time. And for theological thought, for Christian intelligence in depth, the constant comparison of St. Paul and St. John is an unceasing and dual light, light within light. I always find it hard to say which of them—if I had to choose, which God forbid—I would take with me to the desert. I do not know. It seems to me the Holy Father would choose the one whose name he bears.

I

"As for me, when all is said and done, if I absolutely, and sadly, were forced to choose between the scroll of St. Paul and that of St. John, I believe I would prefer St. John."

HE

"St. Paul did not know Jesus in the flesh. But even before the Gospels had been written, he had gone straight to the essential: He had deduced the theology of Christ before the data had been assembled. He had given the end before the beginning."

I

"St. John knew Christ in the flesh, better than any other, the historical Christ. He had his vibrant memory. This memory, even more spiritualized, reached the deep essence, without ceasing to be a memory of the flesh. For myself, loving portraits as I do, that speaks more to me. It is still more difficult. St. John was not a strategist. The end is *already* assumed. Victory is *already* won. In St. John God is, so to speak, *already* all in all."

The Holy Father did not reply. And I had the impression that, if he had to choose and live with prisoners in a work camp, as St. John had done on Patmos, he would take with him the Epistles of St. Paul.

PART THREE

The Pope and the Universe

10

DIALOGUE ON DIALOGUE

There should be a dialogue on dialogue. Dialogue should be applied, a thing Socrates did not do, to dialogue, that means of understanding everything. It is what I often said to myself when Paul VI was meditating an encyclical on the theme of the "Dialogue." Already at Milan I had a presentiment of what his *Discours de la méthode*[1] might be, were he ever to write one. I said to myself (and I was mistaken), "It will be a 'Search for Truth' taught to the modern world." I saw him as drawing inspiration from Malebranche or Pascal, rereading Gratry's *Logic*, or the "logic" of Balmes,[2] taking up again ideas of Sertillanges, Papini, Guardini, to point out in what spirit, with what zeal, and with what precautions one could, one must, go forward to the "Search for Truth" in every sphere. With the conviction that if there were discordances between truths—for example, between the affirmations of faith and science—then there must be a hope against hope, like Abraham's; that one must avoid, at every level, the snares, mists, and subjectivities, so that truth may finally accord with truth.

In fact, I do not think it would be wrong to say that he has in the back of his mind a project for a directory for the search for truth

[1] Descartes.
[2] *El criterio* is known as Balmes' logic.

(*regulae ad directionem ingenii*). Already one could outline its design with extracts from his talks. I see it prefigured in his address to intellectuals made on the last day of the Council. But let us not anticipate the unexpressed! The Holy Father has expressed himself in his encyclical on the *Dialogue* with clarity, insistently, fervently, delicately.

The dialogue of Paul VI is much more than dialogue! This word becomes with him a universal mirror-word, a sun, a pivot, a hinge, a spring, a focus, a mystery, a summation of thoughts, a world of possibilities. His pontificate has already been labeled for history; whatever comes, failure or success, the pontificate of Paul VI will be that of a pontiff who tried to dialogue with all men.

The dialogue of Paul VI is not that more or less artificial one, inaugurated by Plato among the learned, which is basically a method of exposition. Now is it that art of conversation of which our seventeenth-century moralists spoke so well. I reread La Roche-foucauld and La Bruyère; they are exquisite; they put their finger on the substantial failing of all dialogue, which is that it is nothing but a pretext for placing one's thought, for showing off one's brilliance, without listening to the other. It is almost impossible really to listen, and the French, who have carried conversation to such perfection, listen more to what they are about to answer than to the other man.

The dialogue of Paul VI is not a medium for showing off his brilliance or the self-effacement counseled by the cunning, which suggests we help our neighbor to be brilliant, or make him think he is. It is a matter of seeking truth in the other and in oneself, of ceaselessly entering into contact with another mind, but one equally in love with truth, in its precision, its purity, I would say in its supreme subtlety. This sort of dialogue is rarely practiced to resolve ultimate questions. It exists in the realm of taste, of art; so, when the French Academy every Thursday discusses the meaning of words, this is a truly convergent dialogue. It is a question of thinking in common, always ready to correct oneself by another's view; it is a question of being helped by one's adversary in the search for what *is*. This honest and modest way of thinking, if applied, would have no need of eloquence; it would contain within itself, by its very example, the force of persuasion.

I had submitted to the Holy Father an article which had appeared in *La Croix*[3] in which I had tried to contrast the spirit of dialogue with that of dialectic, so much spoken of these days. This is it:

There was a man called Socrates who invented the dialogue. And in doing so he gave rise to that form of thought which is called western philosophy. Plato did not retain all Socrates' ideas; perhaps he even generously, intelligently, lent him subtle conceptions which the good Socrates might have lacked. But Plato did not cease to dialogue, and we still dialogue. And I have often said that John XXIII, in his joviality, resembled Socrates. Paul VI is in Plato's situation; he teaches us "the dialogue." I would like to say in what dialogue consists.

To tell the truth, it is very difficult to carry on a dialogue: Many dialogues, even of Plato, are fictitious, juxtapositions of monologues. Each stays where they were. This is what so often happens in assemblies and congresses. The true dialogue demands an effort which is continual and almost heroic, which consists first in trying to see from the other's viewpoint. Leibniz, that mind so open and elastic, said that the position of the other is the true viewpoint in politics and morals, and this going out of oneself to adopt—if only for a moment—the point of view of one's interlocutor he called quite simply: *love*.

The dialogue then supposes that one listens to the other, and in the divine sense of this word *listen*, the sense in which Jesus the child *listened* to the doctors, or the risen Christ *listened* to the pilgrims at Emmaus, or that man *listens* to Revelation, or God *listens* to man's prayer. Let yourself listen, I

[3] French Catholic daily newspaper.

say, with the hope that the other's point of view will teach you something new, will complete your thought, or will allow you to expand it, to purify, sublimate, deepen it. An objector, contradictor, critic are unsuspected aids, for in every objection there is a part of the truth, which allows us better to express what we think, to forestall confusion, to give relief and contour to our opinions. St. Thomas began by presenting what went *against* his thesis. He leaned on the obstacle, on the apparent negation he built his discreet affirmation, filtered, tested, simple and sure. And Lacordaire, in the same spirit, said: "I do not try to convince my adversary of error, but to join him in a higher truth."

Perhaps dialogue permits us rather to enrich our thought than to bring that same thought to others. It is a joint exercise in truth and welcome. In this sense the dialogue is very different from what is known in our day as dialectic; it is even often its complete opposite. And I am not sure if the great Plato is not somewhat responsible for this confusion, whether he was always faithful to the spirit of the dialoguing Socrates, in changing dialogue into dialectic. . . .

In dialectic—of which Marx and Hegel in our times offer the model— there is no contact between the two minds, nor interplay between the two perspectives, nor search for a truth conceived as transcending individual minds, enveloped in a certain mystery. Dialectic is an articulated system of concepts which are necessarily engendered one by the next, as in a syllogism or mathematical reasoning. It may proceed by deduction, or by the Hegelian system of thesis—antithesis—synthesis, apparently more dramatic. But whenever dialectic appears, *there is no longer the other!* The creative intelligence is solitary and, like the spider, weaves its web. Or, if there is a dialogue, it is fictitious, the interlocutor enunciating what one is waiting for him to say, like the slave in *Meno*. The preference that the moderns have for dialectic, and their incapacity for dialogue, indicate a deficiency of true liberty. For dialogue, being the confrontation by two friends of eternal truth, is a free exercise in which each swears to the other not to give way, except to the light.

Such were my thoughts on dialogue.

One day Paul VI, aware of these thoughts, and knowing my desire to go bald-headed at burning and difficult questions and to say out loud what some people were thinking to themselves without daring to speak up, said to me point-blank:

"You have a liking for raising objections, I know, of which I do not disapprove. You have often sung the praises of the dialogue. I invite you today to sing the antistrophe, as in the classical chorus. Your duty is clear. I ask you to argue against the dialogue."

"Very well, Holy Father," I answered, "if you order me to, I shall obey. However, I will confine myself to commenting on the passage in the encyclical where it is said that the dialogue should not be a weakness, an ambiguous compromise. It is a fact that when one dialogues, there is always a fear of letting oneself be persuaded by the other instead of persuading him, that seeing his reasons, his sincerity, his virtues, one will say to oneself, 'But is he not right perhaps?' I felt that very strongly when I was young, and I still feel it. My parents had sent me to the state school; my companions often came from unbelieving families. I do not think I have many teachers who were Christian; if they were, they did not show it. And I could not help admiring my masters. Sometimes there was a dialogue, but I well remember how it made my young head whirl."

HIS HOLINESS

"You could have thought of St. Luke's account of the child Jesus in the midst of the doctors. A child can dialogue with his masters. Jesus listened, St. Luke tells us. Jesus asked questions. Often a profitable dialogue consists in listening and putting questions. Love does that: It listens, interrogates. That suffices it."

J. G.

"I listened. I questioned myself. Later, as a philosophy student, the opposing doctrines of the great sages were presented to me. It was a perpetual dialogue, a dialogue of the dead. I felt the dizziness returning. I said to myself that if these supreme thinkers are in disagreement, the truth must be outside man's reach. And for the adolescent the discovery is a happy one. 'What do I know?' asked Montaigne, that master of dialogue who so loved it that he discovered and illustrated a new kind: the eternal dialogue with oneself."

THE POPE

"That shows that the dialogue is not an end but a means. It does not give the truth, but seeks it. It is a method and not a system. The encyclical said: 'The apostle's art is full of risks.' "

I

"And it also said: 'Our dialogue cannot be a weakness in the face of the commitments of our faith.' Leibniz noted that in conferences, he who had most passion had the advantage; so he preferred writing to speaking."

HE

"And yet Pascal constantly crossed swords. He stirred up an adversary for himself. He listened. He answered him. Pascal's strength is in this constant dialogue."

I

"Pascal was the exemplary man of dialogue. But he was all fire too. I have seen in a French gallery a painting showing him in dialogue with his opponents. And I understood what a contemporary said, that he always spoke with anger. Is that the entry of fire into the dialogue?"

HE

"There is the fire of anger. There is also the fire of love, the fire of indignation, the fire of zeal. And all these kinds of flame enter into dialogue."

I

"I am not equal to that."

HE

"And yet we are in dialogue."

I

"But unequally."

HE

"It is true that dialogue presupposes equality. . . . According to you then, no dialogue is possible between son and father, disciple and master; and, especially, between a layman and the Pope."

I

"How to achieve that equality which never exists among men?"

HE

"Quite simply; certainly not by situation, information, authority, age, talent, not even by genius, but by an equal love of truth.

"It is that common love of truth which is the only reason for the existence of the sincere dialogue of which I am speaking, and which has little in common with worldly dialogues, which only seek a display of one's wit and, if one is able, that of others, as I think it was La Bruyère said.

"You speak of equality as a condition of the dialogue and—what a Sophist—you say that this equality is not possible between men. But if there is always inequality of situation, there is always equality of intention; an act of pure love, for example, makes the sinner and the just instantly equal. In the same way the absolute love of truth immediately makes equal those who sincerely seek it together."

I

"But when a believer has a dialogue with an atheist, where is the equality? One possesses, the other is dispossessed. Formerly my unbelieving teachers told me that a Christian philosopher cannot be truly a philosopher, because he no longer searches but professes to have found."

HE

"Those possessing the truth of faith are simultaneously dispossessed, as it were, by the torment of each day's possessing it more deeply and more purely. Those not possessing it but seeking it with their whole heart, as your Pascal said, have already found it in some measure. With both alike the spirit groans, as St. Paul would say.

"I think I expressed that at the end of the Council on December 8; but it was very late and the ceremony had been very long."

When a crowd assembles, waits, listens, and disperses in the open air, without being beneath a vaulted roof lighted by stained-glass windows, it does not have the fervor of people gathered in a church. The chanting melts into the atmosphere. And attention turns to the Roman winter sky, calm and solemn. I was distracted by the unexpected liturgy of the clouds; I followed their convolutions, the threats of that stormy light which Claude Lorrain could depict so well.

The messages read in French by cardinals, which the Holy Father had prepared as a general message, had not the required resonance.

As so often happens in the beginning of things, owing to the insignificance of the seeds, and at the end because of weariness and impatience to have done with what is already finished, the last ceremony of the Council left few memories.

There is a limit to emotions, to surprise. Human nature adapts quickly. It gets bored with what moves it too much or too often. I took the text of the messages. I read through the passage which the Pope had mentioned where he quoted a thought of St. Augustine.

For you, also, we have a message, and it is this: Continue to search, tirelessly, never despairing of the truth! Recall the words of one of your great friends, St. Augustine: "We seek with a desire to find, and we find with a desire to seek further." Happy are those who, possessing truth, seek it, in order to renew it, to deepen it, to give it to others. Happy are those who, not having found it, go toward it sincere in heart; may they seek tomorrow's light in today's, till they come to the fullness of light.

Then the Holy Father said:
"Have you finished your criticism, or should I expect more?"

I

"They are not criticisms, but marginal annotations."

HE

"To criticize does not mean to destroy, but to state precisely."

I

"I think that it is useful to distinguish between private dialogue and dialogue before an audience which has the fatal appearance of a match, because a third party takes part, the spectator. Then the dialogue becomes like the tourneys of old. There is something agreeable in not knowing who will prove the victor. Now I think it is dangerous for a Christian to expose his cause to these hazards. I know that it is a fine thing to give an air of conviction. But it can happen that the believer seems to be in a trance and may be victim of a greater talent, or more ability or prestige. For the believer is not free to appear diminished before men. He may be condemned, paralyzed, but not refuted."

HE

"What you say takes up what the encyclical calls the virtue of prudence in reference to dialogue. Is that all, you tiresome philosopher?"

I

"I hold that confusion of ideas is one of the evils of our time. Words no longer have the same sense for everyone; for instance, the strongest words like *liberty, faith, man, truth, love.* We rarely speak the same language. Or rather, there is something more disagreeable than speaking different languages, and that is speaking the same language but attaching different meanings to the same words."

HE

"The French Academicians, if I am not mistaken, have the task of fixing the sense of words; perhaps they are failing in that duty."

I

"I would go further. I want to show the danger of confusion, which is implicit in all dialogue whatsoever, in the very fact of dialogue."

HE

"We have reached the heart of the problem, if I have followed you rightly."

I

"When two men, of different convictions, dialogue with the idea of finally coming to an understanding, their procedure is first to delimit the zones of agreement, then to extend them as much as possible. That is what Socrates did. That is what diplomats, arbitrators, conciliators, and mediators do. The ecumenical method consists in such dialogues."

HE

"The encyclical shows that there are concentric circles and, as you say, different zones of adhesion.

"A first circle, the widest, doubtless includes all men; men of goodwill, those who have no other rule than that of conscience, who, as they declare, do not believe.

"There exists a second concentric circle, but narrower, while still immense; that is the circle of all those who believe in the transcendence of one sole God, all the children of the first revelation made to Abraham. Then there is the circle of all those who have heard the call of Christ and who recognize him as God. And within the circle of Christians there are also circles. The Orthodox are very near to us. Our brothers of the Reform form a larger and more differentiated circle. Between those who inhabit these different circles of thought and sincere conviction, there can be dialogue."

I

"Herein lies the error. For the dialogue presupposes a set of principles accepted by both sides. On the other hand, the dialogue aims at enlarging the field which is common ground.

"But the element of common consent is the starting point, not the finishing line. The minimum one starts with cannot be confused with the maximum at which one should arrive.

"If we discuss with our Jewish or Muslim friends, nobody must believe that faith in one God alone should be the maximum of the religion of the future, or that the Christians should abandon, like ornaments or superfluous growth, what they add to the simple faith in God. If that were so, the base would be the summit. What you call the *minimum* would become the *maximum*. It would be creating— how shall I express it?—a 'pan-monotheistic' community which would absorb Christianity, Judaism, and Islam in a unity of confusion.

"In the same way, in ecumenical encounters the dialogue between the churches could give birth to an expanded Christianity which would consist in giving secondary importance to differences of dogma; which would unite Catholic, Orthodox, and Protestants, through the sole bond they all admit, in a common body of simplified religion.

"This temptation is tempting. And certainly it came to people's minds after the Council, and was sometimes attributed to good Pope John. There is a general idea that we have practically renounced our dogmas and that we commune in a certain evangelism, like Rousseau or Tolstoy before us."

HE

"If the dialogue ended up as you say, it would abolish the very object of dialogue. Unless religious truth is defined a priori as the least common multiple of all religions."

I

"That is the limit it tends toward."

HE

"But that would mean the destruction, in their highest aspirations, of all religions, or at least their replacement."

I

"Their replacement by something quite different. And whoever would win such a dialogue on points would be the least exigent of the protagonists. Atheists and believers can be united in their common affirmations, such as the ideas of justice, respect for man, etc. But if this humanism were looked at as absolute and definitive truth, dialogue would have the effect of dissolving the highest and richest verities and aligning them with lower and poorer verities; that is to say, with truths less dense in content."

THE POPE

"It is quite evident that it would not be a dialogue of truth, but one which would empty truth of its essential character. The Catholics know that they have received the deposit of the highest truth, the deepest, and, I would add, the most difficult; that is to say, which demands the greatest effort from the whole man, from his thought, his will; that which demands he attach himself to it with 'all his heart and mind and strength.' "

I

"The world cannot understand, can perhaps admire, but cannot forgive this. Yet, moreover, judging us by the yardstick of this un-realizable ideal, it condemns us."

HE

"We have been given a rule which compels us forever forward. *Be perfect even as your Father who is in Heaven is perfect.* Our moral code is severe. It obliges heart and mind to lift and tense themselves. We must always fear lowering our ideal. The dialogue does not consist in giving in to him who has less. To be all things to all men is not to renounce *all things* in order to be *all men.* I revert to the image of concentric circles; we at the center have a duty which is crucify-ing, overwhelming, gentle—to be worthy of that central focus. Which demands in particular never to mistake human obligations for divine exigencies, as did the Jewish Pharisees in the time of our Lord, or again the earliest Judaizing disciples at the time of St. Paul.

"But those in the wider circles also have the duty of asking them-selves whether their faith is sufficiently developed, whether, in order to remain itself, it must not rise, *go up higher.* It is our conviction that they are not yet in their fullness. You may tell me that one can be satisfied with proclaiming the message, which today is called the kerygma. But for a fully conscious humanity, adult and often adverse, preaching, which is a monologue, is not enough. The other must be heard, one must put oneself in his place, as did St. Paul long ago in the Greek world, the image of our own."

I

"In the dialogue of two minds which judge themselves with absolute truth, each says to himself that the other is, fundamentally, an invisible friend. The believer thinks the atheist is a believer who does not yet know himself; the atheist thinks that the Christian's base is a belief in man, in his infinite capacity for progress, that everything else is symbolic. Then I hear this unspoken dialogue:

THE ATHIEST: You do not, basically, believe what you believe you believe.

THE BELIEVER: You do not, basically, believe what you believe you believe.

THE ATHIEST: Fundamentally, you are secretly with me and, if you were consistent with yourself . . .

THE BELIEVER: Fundamentally, you are with me, and I will make you see it. Be logical all the way!"

HE

"On the Areopagus St. Paul said to the Greeks: 'What you honor without knowing it is the very thing I have come to tell you.' But I do not believe the inverse was true, as you seemed to be saying. I cannot see the Stoics saying to Paul: 'Fundamentally, you are with us.' "

I

"The farther history goes forward, the more the opposing camps draw together, the more they draw apart. The twentieth-century atheist is both farther away and nearer than ever."

We had reached the point which one always reaches when one opens, in one of its many aspects, the unfathomable question which is summed up in two words: truth and charity.

When one envisages the mystery of God, it is already hard to say where the operation begins by which God *sees* the "eternal verities" and that by which He chooses between the possibilities, He *wills* them. And how hard it is to trace the frontier which divides the love of the Being from the love of beings! Or again, that which separates, in the Judgment of God, His justice and His mercy! And in the most daily of rounds, how to discern the moment when love counsels yielding, conceding, and the moment when one must not yield on the justice of one's cause?

And always and everywhere will remain hidden from us the point where conflicting essentials, attributes, duties are reconciled and bound together.

Let us not be deceived by inflations! It is easy to say, for example: Charity for those who are erring, but not for the error. That would evidently be so only if there were errors that were disincarnate. But error is mingled with truth, error takes its power only from the truth it is mixed with. And reciprocally, truth is only deficient and sterile by the encumbrance of accompanying errors which it has not been able to shed.

The dialogue which Paul VI recommends is not the somewhat abstract dialogue of philosophers, who are only preoccupied with themselves, but the real, concrete dialogue of man in search for truth in its deepest, most intimately incarnated purity.

Dialogue with concrete error must be carried on, truths it bears must be separated from the poisons which prevent those truths from spreading, like lights from the pitfalls.

But reciprocally, dialogue must be held with the concrete truth we bear, to purify it yet further, by painful effort, from the hidden errors which paralyze it.

The Holy Father raised the question to a still higher level, or rather, he said, to bring the question of the true dialogue and the apparent dialogue back to the Church-world perspective of the

Council. He said, "It is necessary to insist on a thing which, though obvious, is forgotten by the majority. A little experience distracts us from the essential. Much experience leads us back to it."

And he developed an idea, dear to him, on the two aspects of evangelization:

"I should like to say that there have always been two ways of looking at reform, or, if you prefer, two movements of the mind in relation to the world it should evangelize.

"The first movement is from the world to the Church, from the periphery to the center.

"The second goes from the Church to the world, from the center to the periphery.

"These two ways are like the two movements of breathing. We should always employ them together, but in a certain order.

"The first movement is animated by the just desire to understand the contemporary world, to accept its ways of living and feeling, to draw from life's experience a more human theology, to give Christianity new expression."

I

"That is the very method which has inspired so many modern seekers, which inspires so many Christian thinkers."

HE

"That is true, that is good. I am strongly aware of it in my own heart, of the desire to go toward the world, to be 'all things to all men,' as St. Paul said, in order to give light to all, if that is possible. But you know how hard it is to keep oneself within the right limits, especially when one is on the periphery. Then it happens that, when we compare the world to the Church, as also happens when we compare daily life, professional and family life, with the marvelous vision one has of what is going on elsewhere than at home, the world outside the Church decks itself in the most seductive colors. And the Catholic world seems small, mean, and colorless. One sees all its deficiencies. And then, instead of making common cause with one's own people, it is on the contrary with strangers to Catholicism that one allies oneself, to criticize what goes on at home. And by a strange though tempting reversal, one is closer to those outside than those within, one fraternizes with strangers, while cutting oneself off from one's brethren.

"That is a pity. That is not the Church's way. For to give the Church to the world, the Church must first of all be a living Church; that is, a united, fraternal community where each is joined to the others—those with pastoral duties, those who make up the faithful. I do not wish to utter the words discipline, obedience. I know that they are not liked in our time because of their former connotation. But equivalent words must be found, for what the word *obedience*, or better, the word *fidelity* designates is something no living community can dispense with. I mean an obedience full of respect, an active, joyous, intelligent, open fidelity, a fidelity which can be a state of dialogue.

"Religious liberty is related to dialogue. We cannot propose religion to an adult conscience as we propose it to a childish one. It is true that with regard to revelation we shall always be as children. But twenty centuries of Christianity have nevertheless left their mark on consciences; humanity no longer wishes a state of childhood. It feels itself as adolescent, capable of understanding. And for that it must receive instruction freely; that is, it should be allowed to ask questions. You will tell me that is new.

"*Yes* and *no*—as with everything renewed in the Church. And in one sense that is new. In another it is and has always been. Take St. Paul; visualize him on the Areopagus. He dialogues and speaks at the level of his learned or simply his heathen hearers. He says: 'I have seen one of your altars where is inscribed *Deo ignoto*—to the unknown God.' That is dialogue with the people. Soon afterward he quotes an ancient philosopher *IPSIUS ENIM ET GENUS SUMUS*, we are of his race. *In him we live and move*. Again it is dialogue; he puts himself in the other's place. He enters his perspective. He adopts a language. He does not impose on it more than it can bear at the moment. He does not give everything at once. He applies the *agape*, charity, as he has defined it: he is patient, gentle, not puffed up. Hoping all things, enduring all things. Jesus dialogued in the same way; the Gospel is a dialogue in the same sense. I mean by this: Our canonical Gospels answer the questions of the young Churches.

"The second method follows the inverse, or rather, the complementary way. It starts from the values deposited among the Church's treasure. It rejoices in actively loving them—in daily discovering them with new vision better than yesterday, less well than tomorrow. They are not only treasures; like diamonds they have many facets. They are rather, as Jesus said, seeds buried in the ground. Nourished by that vital substance with which he works and which works on him, the modern apostle finds superabundant joy, light and life, which allows him to go toward the world with a sense of responsibility. For he has more, far more, than the world.

"Then, trusting in God, in himself, in the Word of Truth which resounds within him at the center of his darkness, and despite his unworthiness, he goes toward the world. He sees continually how much of the divine truth the world can bear; then he shares, adapts himself, as God does; he becomes an educator.

"But where there were aspirations in the classical world, in the modern, besides aspirations, there are so many gospel truths imprisoned or confused . . . following the example of St. Paul the Apostle, who, at the same time he teaches, rediscovers and assimilates all that is right and good. And, indeed, he carries what is true to a higher degree of truth by integrating it with the fullness of truth. What is human he feels is still more human when it is raised to the sphere of holiness."

I

"But these two movements are not opposed."

HE

"Nothing is opposed in the plenary sense. All collaborate."

I

"But, Holy Father, if we absolutely had to choose between these two currents of missionary aspiration, to which would you reserve the quality of love, or at least, of greater love?"

HE

"By all appearances it is the method which moves from the periphery to the center which seems to reveal more love; it puts itself in modern man's place, it adopts his viewpoint, including, for example, his criticisms and disappointments with Christians, with Catholics. We know that today many of our sons have moments of weakness in the certainty of their faith. Is it a matter of temptation, weakness, unease, inner suffering, or—for some—of an inner emptiness, of blindness, going astray? *When the Son of Man returns, will he find faith on earth?* Those disquieting words of Jesus are deep.

Deep also were those he said to St. Peter: *Strengthen the brethren.*
The truth of faith demands an entire, frank adhesion, no less today
than yesterday and always. Truth, his truth, is firm and sure. It is
the exact reflection, even if for us an enigmatic one, of objective,
wholesome reality. Time does not change or distort this truth, but
commends and deepens it. History does not impair or destroy it; it
changes neither its significance nor its value, but it develops it and
applies it with wisdom to new conditions. Science, far from rendering it empty, seeks, implores it, in a sense. The Church keeps it, is
worthy of it. The Church defends it, professes it, possesses it.

"That explains why, of those two movements about which you
are speaking, that of the Apostle is first. For it reproduces the very
action of Jesus. You remember the last scene of St. John's Gospel."

I

"That where Jesus tells St. Peter and St. John what will be their
fate: for the former, death by torture; for the latter, prolonged old
age."

HE

"What is surprising is that indiscreet question of Jesus to Peter.
Jesus asks to know *whether Peter loves him more.* The word *more* is
a simple one, but as one ponders it one sees it contains a fearful
demand."

I

"Every time the word *more* is used in any context, there is a
further, an increasing appetite for growth, the call of the infinite to
the finite."

HE

"One has to be in the Pope's place to understand how that little phrase *Lovest thou me more?* is, like the word of which the Epistle to the Hebrews speaks, a knife which penetrates the joints, the nerves, the marrow; how that little word *more* becomes at the same time a source of comfort and a cause of torment: Does one ever know if one loves him *more?* That demand to love *more* is hard, to be branded on the forehead and on the shoulders with a love which must be limitless, which is disquieted by the uncertainty of loving *more.* What comforts, in that torment, is the power to love universally. And I mean by universally, not only to cast a look of love toward all, but also toward all situations, all states of human life. To recapitulate: No one is a stranger, no one is excluded, no one, however distant or faraway. Each loved one is present. And a Pope's heart, expanded by this so sweet duty, has perhaps the right to say to each one he actually loves, that he loves him more."

11

ECUMENICAL VISIONS

First Vision: A Meeting at St. Paul-Without-the-Walls

It was dark enough for the ceremony to look like a vigil: that is, an Easter vigil, that Passover of shadows and prefigurations, which Christ renews, which Christ fulfills. For the ecumenical mystery is not completed. We still celebrate it in the night of hope, like that Jewish Passover, which was marked with melancholy. But it was an ecumenical Passover prefiguring the day of total union, a day which will never perhaps be on earth, a day which will never perhaps enter the course of history, but which it is good to announce by a symbol.

It was dark enough. It was a December evening, around that day of the Immaculate Conception, which is the feast of the very first beginning, and, one might say, of the light before dawn: the feast of the origin of the redemption, of the time of the marriage of Anne and Joachim. In this major basilica it also was a sort of beginning. It was celebrated in the place of the martyrdom of St. Paul, the apostle of the "recapitulation" in Christ Jesus of all our differences.

It was dark enough for the brightness to be the brightness of the catacombs and not of daylight, for the lights to be those of the liturgical flames and not the sun's light as it is in the basilica of St. Peter. The Bishops were seated: They were crowded on poor backless benches. One could have believed oneself in some synagogue, or in some Cistercian abbey, anywhere where the architecture, the rites, the ceremony had rediscovered the essential and original poverty.

It was dark enough so that the Pope's white cassock appeared like a light, but a nocturnal, quasilunar light.

It was dark enough for the voices which were about to rise under this vaultless roof to be enveloped in silence. The liturgy of waiting, invented for this unique occasion, had united the most significant songs from each ecclesiastical community. It was a chant composed of *essences* in both senses of the word, which can be applied to flowers as to beings. It was a presage of the Resurrection, an announcement of that day of glory when, after the "accidents" will have evaporated, only "essences" will be breathed.

It was dark enough. It was also light enough. And this composition of chants and silences reproduced the marriage of dark and light. It was a sober spectacle, enigmatic, tender, and so new, so intimate that one could not help being moved, but with a taciturn emotion which checked every expression and every sign. It was, I have said, a *prophecy*, still very obscure, which respected that which remains unspoken among these as among those. Thus the Congress ended with a plunge into the inexpressible.

I was thinking of that first meeting of John XXIII with the Observers when he had given rein to his hope, yet without saying anything that could wound anyone's conscience, without appearing to wish to hurry the *hour* of reunion. He said, as the Anglican hymn puts it, that *one step was enough for today*, that one should not want to know *how*, that one should, each following his own itinerary, go forward into the night.

And now, after the Council, where *so many steps* had been taken, where so many acts of love, and, above all, of intelligence in love, had been taken, where so many possible ways had been opened, so many locks unbolted, now that advance through the night was translated by this ceremony at St. Paul-Without-the-Walls. John XXIII, however audacious he was, might not have had the audacity to project, to govern, and discreetly to accomplish this.

My thought went back to a still very recent past, yet which (I don't know why) appeared to me faraway, so much had time rushed headlong since 1959, as if the last days were already upon us. I was thinking of that time when John XXIII, one fine January day, and without notice, on a "celestial signal" as he said, driven by a celestial instinct, had categorically announced that he intended to convoke a Council. It was three months after his election, on January 25, a Sunday morning after Mass, in the parlor of the monastery and in front of the eighteen cardinals who had taken part in the ceremony. "My venerable brothers and my dear sons, while trembling with emotion, We are obliged to admit it, but also and at the same time with the humble will to carry on to the end, We inform you We have established the plan of holding two consultations, a double consultation, which will receive the two names of Diocesan Synod of Rome and of . . ."

Was there a pause? Was there a moment's silence? I do not know, I do not think so, for John XXIII spoke fast and without a break, though that would have been the place and the moment for one. . . .

". . . and of Ecumenical Council for the Universal Church."

The next day, the *Osservatore Romano* spelled out the Pope's thought, which was a second revelation of his intention, which he had not dared make publicly at St. Paul-Without-the-Walls. By the symbolic choice of the Feast of the Conversion of St. Paul, by the choice of the ancient basilica, "in the thought of the Holy Father," said the *Osservatore Romano*, "the Council should not only have as its objective the spiritual good of Christians, but, at Pope John's wish, be an invitation to the separated communities to search for unity."

It is impossible to overemphasize what a surprise this proposition was, coming from such a mouth in such a place. At the beginning, no one believed in it very much. And it was believed even less after the Roman Synod to which it seemed attached, which one must admit was more apparent than real in its results. There is no doubt that announcing this Roman Synod was for John XXIII a way of hiding the essential, which would have been hard to bear had it not appeared a trifle harmless because utterly fantastic. But this Pope, humble revolutionary, so decided and so sensitive, triumphed over all resistance. When John XXIII said *humble*, it was necessary to keep in mind that under the commonplace appearance, there was in him something tenacious like a peasant's will, like the curbstone of a road, like a wayside cross, like a root that buries itself in the ground and stays there.

I remembered the words of this very recent past in the silence of this Pauline basilica, where the shadows of bishops and observers glided furtively, while waiting to see, without much idea of it, what would happen: For no publicity had been made on the subject of this meeting, which retains something enigmatic. The memory of St. Paul was present.

I do not think I ever before understood so well the meaning of that dyad Peter-and-Paul, of the very old association of these ancient names, which is like a résumé of the Acts of the Apostles and of the history of the origins of the Church. I would gladly associate the third apostle, St. John, but he is not visible in the foundation.

Peter-and-Paul represents the two aspects of the visible Unity, whereas John is the prophet of the intimate and eternal Unity, he who gave ecumenism its charter in the Parable of the Good Shepherd, in Jesus' prayer for Unity. Actually John is not absent from this basilica, since the Pope of the Council was called John. In all these matters concerning salvation history, men are not aware of the whole significance of what they do. God, the author of history, assures the correspondence between visible and invisible. God inspires initiatives, of which everyone understands the immediate, but not the deeper, sense; the actual incidence, but not the extent.

We are near the place on the road to Ostia where Paul, beyond the daily, offered the supreme sacrifice. When we came into the basilica, we were surrounded by emptiness: It is a basilica dedicated to solitude, to fire, to destruction. It would seem that the devils gathered together around St. Paul, who was always a man to attract contraries and contradictions. The pavement is in marble; it exhales a vague phosphorescence. The columns are reflected in it as in a lake. But in this rarely visited space (for Paul has never been a popular saint; it is Peter who draws pilgrims and prayers) the great mosaic is not visible: Paul, his torso rising from the tomb, with his heart and his forehead, seems to dominate time and space. Paul was not thrown to the wild beasts; he was a Roman citizen. And, according to the Roman custom, he was led outside the city, *ne ipsa urbe conspectior mors foret* (so that his death should not be as conspicuous as in the town itself), as Tacitus says about condemned men of high rank. This man, so well known, was secretly put to death, an execution without hate and without witnesses. Stripped, then tied to a stake, he received his last flagellation. *Outside of the Law!* Outside of all law. Condemned by the Jewish law, rejected by that other law, the civilized law, the Civil Law, the law which had first saved him from the Law. His old, nervous, thin body, zebra-striped with blood, was bent double. And the sword cut off his head. It was done quickly, silently, correctly.

I thought of all this while hastily entering the basilica which was connected with the alpha and omega of the Council, with its mysterious origin, with its discreet achievement. I think of the ecumenical idea, to which so many had consecrated so many hours, so many pages of work, without much immediate hope.

Although the church of St. Paul is one of the major basilicas of Rome, it was to be chosen as the place where the Archbishop of Canterbury would receive the visit which the Pope hoped to make him. That was because St. Paul-Without-the-Walls had been placed under the protection of the kings of England up to the time of Henry VIII, the king who broke with Rome.

Second Vision: A Lecture by Professor Cullmann

THE POPE

"How can one not be full of gratitude for Dr. Cullmann, who is so fine a scholar? I saw him several times during the Council. And, during the first session, I was edified by the attention he paid to our deliberations, still more, by his attentive manner during the prayers. He deserved to be there, because for us he is the example of a man of the ecumenical dialogue. His study of St. Peter has, I think, reopened the vexed question—so important for us—of the personality, of the charge of St. Peter, of the relationship of St. Peter with Christ, with the nascent Church. Obviously, we would have deeply wished that his conclusions should coincide with what the Church of Rome believes and affirms. But to ask that this coincidence should appear is to ask that union be realized this very day. And one must not tempt God, who is patient. We can, we must, implore the Father of lights

with supplication, with insistence, with hope, with the impatience of
love. While we await the hour He has mysteriously fixed by His
power, divergences are inevitable. I need not emphasize them. You
have shown them well, if I remember rightly, in your book on *The
Church and the Gospel.*"

J.G.

"To my mind the nuclear divergence is in the conception my
colleague has of time in the Church. For him, when the Lord says
Peter, He says *Peter*, period. With what happens after *Peter*, Jesus
does not concern Himself. For us, when Jesus says *Peter*, He sees in
Peter the whole succession of the popes. And when He confers on
Peter His privilege of building the Church, it is the whole Church
until the end of time, it is all *Peter's* successors who are involved."

THE POPE

"I think that indeed is Dr. Cullmann's thesis. But our dialogue
implies that we should put between quotes that which still divides
us. I had noted in his fine book on Peter this passage which I will
read you. It is the last passage in the book:

'The rock, the foundation of all Churches of all time, remains the historical
Peter, the man whom Jesus had chosen, and singled out especially among
the Twelve, as witness of his life, of his death, and as the first witness of
his Resurrection. It is on Peter that Christ, who is himself the cornerstone,
will forever build his Church, as long as there is one on earth.' "

I

"It is true that that is the last organ chord. But if Dr. Cullmann
thus sets Peter as the hearthstone, it is because he rejects every idea
of a succession which would make Peter depend on an episcopal see.

Peter is a rock above time or space, above historical circumstance; he is the keystone of the vault of the Churches."

HE

"I do not say that Dr. Cullmann's conception is ours. But how good it is, how comforting, how honorable, the criticism that a seeker who does not belong to our Catholic world, driven only by his respect for what is said in Scripture, for what is expressed in the first origins—and that against many exegesists of his own Church who still hold that the passages too favorable to Peter in the Gospel are an interpolation—I repeat: How comforting it is for the honor of the human spirit, for the mutual respect of convictions, for the future of the ecumenical dialogue, to see that without any influence on our part, or desire to please us, a critic like Dr. Cullmann gives Peter this role of rock, of the first witness of the faith. You have remarked that for this author Peter's office dies with Peter. Perhaps. I do not know. One would have to ask him about this, know what is now the state of his inquiry, what is his perspective; but he opens up ways and views. And the final passage, which I just quoted to you, allows for a supposition, a presage, a possibility, a conjecture, rather different from those of the Council, I know, but perhaps even more remarkable, that by which a successor of the Rock would find himself obliged by the force of circumstance to assume the charge and the dignity of the cornerstone, of the keystone of the vault—this Rock being (it is Dr. Cullmann speaking), 'the foundation of the Churches, of all the Churches of all time.' Whatever the truth may be on this point, I appreciate his method, his intention, his discreet shades of meaning, his subtlety, his reserve on controversial points, the unfailing care taken by this wise and prudent author, to distinguish different levels of assent in what he affirms. If I remember rightly, he sometimes says, 'I am almost sure.' Sometimes, 'That will always remain hypothetical.' Sometimes, with a touch of humor, for he has humor, 'This is an idea personal to the exegesist and obliges no one but him.' I like that. It shows a respect for the half-light in which the intelligence has to work on many matters.

"At the end of the Council, one Sunday morning in December, when I had a little free time, I wished to hear Dr. Cullmann give me his views on the excavations in St. Peter's, and on the problems of the Apostle's relics, on his death and burial. Naturally you can imagine that I was not going to take sides; this is an entirely open matter where competence is the only authority. It is possible that one will never get farther than the area of probability, which leaves a certain freedom of choice. If there exists an arena natural to liberty, a terrain where this liberty remains total, where it is only limited (as everywhere else) by truth, the truth of experience, of historical or archaeological fact, it is here. And Pope Pius XII realized this very well when he took the courageous initiative of allowing these researches, when he published their results, when he offered these results for discussion among the knowledgeable. No one can be afraid of truth: We seek for it alone in great as in little things. No one denies that the Roman pontiffs are the successors of Peter, that from the beginning they have been regarded as the successors of Peter."

I

"It may be imagined that historical science will one day consider it very likely that we do not possess the works of Peter here; on the other hand, it may be imagined that this same historical science will regard it as very likely that we possess his skeleton and his dust . . . To my mind this problem is not essentially important."

HE

"I repeat, that the liberty of research and of coming to conclusions remains absolute. This openness toward the spirit of investigation, toward the freedom of investigation, in this basilica of ours, on a matter about which we care so much, but where we have entire freedom of thought, is like a surety given of the solicitude popes have for the honor of science. Dr. Cullmann understood this. And I am sure he will weigh carefully, as he always has, the pros and cons, the uncertain and the likely. And we will always be grateful for what he has to say and for his insights."

Third Vision: A Meeting in the Sistine Chapel

Dr. Ramsey, Anglican Archbishop of Canterbury, was received by Paul VI not privately, as his predecessor, Dr. Fisher, was, but as the head of a Church, in his dual capacity of Primate of all England and spiritual chief of the Anglican Community. Since this last title— which he holds in virtue of his presidency of the Lambeth Conference—is an honorary one, the Archbishop wished to consult all the metropolitan archbishops of the Anglican Community on the expediency of his visit. All approved. Thus the Archbishop of Canterbury went to Rome as the representative of fifty million Anglicans, divided into nineteen provinces.

Some remembered Paul VI's meeting with the patriarch Athenagoras at Jerusalem, in the drawing room of an old country house among the olive trees. This was far from the same setting. There Bethany, here the Vatican. The white cassock linked them. But it was covered with a red and gold stole.

Dr. Ramsey was draped in a mauve and purple cape, he wore the dark velvet bonnet indicative of a doctor of the Reformation, the same one that brings a grave, lay note into Renaissance pictures. Above them, the fresco the "Last Judgment." Some have affirmed that Michelangelo was a Lutheran, that this somber Christ, avenger of crimes, was a lesson given by the spirit of the Reformation to the Renaissance Vatican. It is quite possible that this idea came to the taciturn one's mind, filled as it was by so much anger, so many forms.

And perhaps the sorrow, the exacerbation which run through Michelangelo's work have as their cause his painful and profound awareness that he was not a saint.

I study once more these enormous bodies which dissolve in a sulfurous, bluish light, like that of a world's last day; it seems to me that since Hiroshima, one cannot see the famous scene in quite the same way. There is in this Judgment a sad splendor, a strange mixture of gravity and pity and so many contrasts: Michelangelo remarked that he was born under the sign of Capricorn. More than any other artist he felt the sweetness, the bitterness, the difficulty of being; compassionate and cruel, suspicious and confiding, conservative and revolutionary, living in palaces and a friend of the poor, full of anguish but also of certainty. The "Last Judgment" is his whole soul projected onto an old wall by a creative hand that never knew hesitation.

I do not know if any son of man has penetrated more deeply into this third dimension of depth and of volume; more than the Greek statues which served him for inspiration and model, his own occupy space absolutely. I have read that he admired the torso more than the face because the torso, the place of torsion, transition, and poise, retains the mark of the creator on his handiwork.

Into painting, a static art, Michelangelo put movement. To archi-

tecture, which hides the skies from view, as the grotto and the cave
do, he has brought heaven's light. And all that without apparent
fatigue, like an impetuous, hurrying and pitying angel, a trifle
morose, basically very tender. The theme of the "Pietà" which
haunted him all his life, well expresses the depth of unexpressed love
present in this taciturn soul.

How many times during the Council I visited this first "Pietà" of
his twenty-fifth year, which seemed to recapitulate the experiences
of a whole lifetime, when actually it is only a promise. I never tired of
seeing it. Each time I glimpsed some secret hitherto hidden; it is the
privilege of great works of art never to cease revealing themselves,
like a silent Scripture. One day I noticed that the beauty of the
Christ came from its suppleness: Jesus, on His Mother's knees, sleeps
in a divine sleep and will awake into life. It is a body broken but
incorrupt, a body still subject to a slight torsion. As for the Virgin,
how light she too is in her marble, and despite so many folds to her
dress. Another day, the Virgin seemed to me to have much too small
a head for her body's mass. She supports the corpse with only one
hand. She does not look so unhappy. The "Pietà" announces Easter:
The Resurrection is already present there. And this Christ, barely
dead, whom the Virgin holds like an elongated Host, seems ready to
leap out of her arms.

Michelangelo dialogued with everyone, but in order to sublimate
everything to the unique dialogue: that of art and prayer, where one
is alone with God. Like every genius, he was a genius truly ecumenical, and more so than Goethe or Shakespeare, because he
composed everything anew in the splendor of the Incarnation. It was
the Incarnation which was his inspiration, his model, his hope, his
despair as an artist, his horizon.

And it was because he wished to attain, to express, to translate

into terrestrial matter and form and into human shape the inaccessible mystery that his art, although supreme, although so sure of
itself, exploded, so to speak; that his work retains, in a perfect
measure, something exaggerated; that it almost always bears the
divine scar of failure, of a sublime defeat, and the kind of wound
which pierces beauty, since God was made man with neither form
nor comeliness.

How many times have I heard Lord Halifax say, summing up all
his hopes:

"What is needed above all is that the heads of our two Churches
should meet at the summit, alone together in the cloud beyond all
hierarchy, beyond all customs, all conventions; that they treat from
on high the problems of dogma and especially of practice, problems
of a union so greatly desired."

The noble lord's method was always based on conversations
between those ultimately responsible: His son, when he was Viceroy
of India, had talked with Gandhi. And today I remember that he
said to me: "Oh, how joyfully I would leave this world if the
primate of England and the Holy Father could see each other."

In a notebook where formerly I set down his advice, his sayings,
his confidences too, I found notes on what was behind the famous
Malines conversations. It will be remembered that from 1921 to 1925
Cardinal Mercier, approved by Benedict XV and Pius XI, had
received Anglican Church delegates in loyal dialogue. The surprise
at these conversations was the reading of a memorandum by Dom
Beaudouin on the manner in which an English Church united to the
See of Rome could remain herself.

Lord Halifax put on his thick glasses and in a glowing voice read
me these bold passages from the Benedictine's memorandum:

"The Anglican Church has had, since its origins, a strong attachment to the See of Peter. Vested with the symbolical cloak of the Prince of the apostles, the Archbishop of Canterbury shares in the apostolic jurisdiction, not only over the faithful, but also over the pastors. The truth is that an Anglican Church separated from Rome is above all a historical heresy. In short, *an Anglican Church absorbed by Rome* and *an Anglican Church separated from Rome* are two equally inadmissible premises. The true formula must be found in the *via media*, the only historical way: an Anglican Church *united* with Rome.

"There exists a catholic formula of union between churches, which is not an absorption, but which saves and respects the interior, autonomous organization of the great historic churches, while maintaining their perfect dependence with regard to the universal Church. Indeed, if there is one Church which by its origins, its history, the habits of the nation, has a right to concessions of autonomy, it certainly is the Anglican Church. Practically, the Archbishop of Canterbury would be reestablished in his traditional and effective rights as the patriarch of the Anglican Church. After having received his investiture from Peter's successor, by the historic imposition of the pallium, he would enjoy his patriarchal rights over the whole Church of England.

"The Canon Law of the Latin Church would not be imposed on the Anglican Church, but the latter, in an interprovincial synod, would determine its own ecclesiastical law.

"It would also have its own liturgy, the Roman litury of the seventh and eighth centuries, as was in use at the time.

"Obviously, all the ancient historic sees of the Anglican Church would be maintained and all the new Catholic sees created since 1851 would be suppressed."

Halifax said, "You cannot imagine the silence which followed this reading in front of the Cardinal, who approved it with a joyful smile. We were staggered. My Anglican neighbor said to me, 'It took my breath away.' I voiced the question whether, in view of reunion, the Roman authority would give Anglicans the liberty of not *immediately* having to adhere to dogmas defined by the Church since the separation. It seemed to me possible to foresee a period of maturation, during which a distinction could be made between the fundamental and the nonfundamental. Great things happen little by little. . . ."

Beneath a great Judgment scene, the Pope and the Anglican Archbishop are seated in armchairs backing on the altar. The Roman Church and the Anglican exchanged a kiss of hope. Then, next day in the basilica of St. Paul-Without-the-Walls, the Pope gave his pastoral ring to his guest. "I remembered then," he told me, "Cardinal Mercier's gesture before his death." "Let us forget the past," Lord Halifax repeated. Nothing is impossible to faith. *Let us put out to sea.*

12

DIALOGUE ON BEAUTY:
DESCRIPTION OF A PAPAL CHAPEL

What struck me at first glance in the papal chapel was the play of light. There light is at home, radiant. And yet there is no visible source of light. A stained-glass ceiling diffuses the daylight.

"We are here," said the Holy Father, "at the summit. Above us there is only the sky." I had, indeed, the impression of being in a place remote from the Vatican's architecture, of having reached an aerie of solitude and prayer.

The stained-glass ceiling looks down upon the earth it represents, up to the sky it captures. Far more than a painting, which has no transparency and depth, it allows the representation of what a creature would be if suffused by the Spirit while remaining itself. That is why stained glass is so suitable for depicting the Resurrection. Yet it is no accident that this stained-glass window of the Resurrection, done by Filocamo, is the center of attention; it serves as ceiling to the chapel; through it comes all the light.

I have always been fond of isolated chapels, which are churches reduced to human scale.

I envy Jean Cocteau's having been able to paint the chapel of Villefranche in fresco; dedicated to St. Peter, it is a sort of abandoned shell which one might imagine had come from Rome to

Provence. One day Cocteau explained to me the symbolism of his chapel. Perched on the ladder, trowel in hand, he said:

"A chapel is an altar toward which all lines and lights converge. Look at my altar; you will see that I have conceived the whole so that the slanting rays of the sun come to rest at the center of the altar, on the Crucifix, the tablecloth, the bread, the chalice, and the bowed priest. I had in mind that phrase of one of the Gospels, that of Luke, who, incidentally, was himself a painter, 'He was known of them in the breaking of the bread.'"

Jean Cocteau would have liked to decorate a papal chapel like a shield of Achilles. He would have made it too fantastic. This chapel was the concept of Paul VI. I describe it because it gives, perhaps without his knowing it, a picture of his mind.

Paul VI has had the style of the Vatican's halls and reception rooms modified, which Pius XII had not dared to do, and which John XXIII had not done, being resigned to "his golden cage," thinking that poverty should consist in enduring the worn hangings, the out-of-date paraphernalia of greatness. Paul VI, who has so many artist friends, put a program of renovation and beautifying into operation. And because all elegance consists in a selection and all selection is, basically, poverty, renunciation of the superfluous in decoration, the Pope got rid of the unnecessary, everything that counterfeited beauty by addition, scintillation, luxury, or profusion, with the aim of obtaining Beauty alone (like the Greeks or Florentines) by movement, by pure line alone.

I do not think I am mistaken in using the word elegance, because the best definition of Paul VI's taste in art is elegance. Gone are the curtains, the hangings; certain paintings have been returned to the museums. Tawny coverings, almost transparent; reflective, cloud-colored curtains. In that empty space statues were to appear, of his taste and choice. A statue, a sculpture, a desk should be isolated in space, wrapped in emptiness. Nothing is more luxurious than the poverty of emptiness, pure space, in these times which crowd and contrast. Nothing is rarer than rarefaction. And when the atom is almost empty and the stars so faraway, our earthly museums are cluttered up with beauties which are ruined by being crowded. The Pope is one of those rare beings to arrange *fullness* and *emptiness* together in the house where he is master. He has allocated them harmoniously. The new disposition of the audience halls on the second floor is already a silent teaching, a hygiene of the uncluttered soul, a call to the life of detachment. This rarefied splendor evokes the divine simplicity.

This risen Christ who is placed between the Roman daylight and the diaphanous half-light of the chapel is a symbol of his Christ-centered spirituality, in the manner of our great seventeenth-century masters. I am reminded of Bérulle, of the Oratory Fathers. Paul VI likes that period, which rethought everything in terms of Christ. Its meditation is related to the moment when Christ will gather to himself all men who were his, and in which he will offer himself, with them, to the Father, *that God may be all and in all.* I contemplate this Christ the Conqueror: He is upright, bursts forth like a spring, like a stream of thought in an inventor, a love that is new, bold, gently sovereign, with the freshness of a new beginning which this time is definitive.

"Filocamo," the Pope told me, "wished to portray glory. 'Look at Christ,' Filocamo says. The colors are pure, he has tried to make them solar; they attract as azure attracts or as white vestments do."

The stained glass shows the nature of the Resurrection, which I tried formerly to speak of in my books, which is not a return to the mortal adventure, but an explosion of being in a new form of existence, the crossing of the forbidden threshold: liberty itself! And this dogma is founded on the witness of men, on experience, on something which was, for the witnesses, incontrovertible evidence of glory and intimacy.

But there are many other scenes, and in particular, on the chief piece of furniture, scenes of human labor, carved in bas-relief by Mario Rudelli. The harvest, the peasant's labor, which for centuries was the very type of human work, for in it is seen the link between the soil, the sun, fruit, and effort; and this bending of the body to the earth, which is the gesture of sacrifice. Factory work tends from henceforth to be the typical work, because man curves the iron, the rail, the rocket which will conquer space. Then, associated with this labor of the masses, the work of the scholar who, faced with the symbolic signs and with the universe, thinks, harvests, and forges on an invisible, spiritual plane; then the work of the man who speaks— the lawyer, the businessman, the man of exchange and conversation.

These works, the color of greenish bronze, are as though written upon a pedestal issuing from the very earth, as if on the trunk of an oak. They decorate and illustrate the hard *cathedra*, in which the Pope renews himself in adoration, before and after his Mass.

I have spoken of the light, but not of the color, which Goethe said is like a suffering of light. Here it is a peaceful suffering. What struck me was the quality of the blues. Blue is the deepest and most transparent color, also the richest in shade and variety. It is to be seen in visiting Chartres Cathedral toward the end of a summer day; then every particle of stained glass, pierced by the dying light, dies in its turn, but with a different agony each time; now calmer, as though by losing consciousness, then resisting, uttering cries of light. In the chapel I admire certain intense blues, almost violet; then the cool blues, those of the distances; and some of those evanescent blues, milky, almost imitating the compact snowy white of the mountains, or the color of Lake Garda around Sirmium. These hues, long observed in his Lombard childhood by Giovanni Battista Montini, have gathered together, without his eye being aware of it, in the background of his vision. In the chapel he can contemplate them, these blues, crystallized, transfigured; deprived of their surrounding air, but with the consistency of precious stones, like the stones in the breastplate described by the Apocalypse. In this oratory, where Christ reigns alone, one might say that the *blue*, set in thoughtful reds and violent violets, gives the Marian *atmosphere*, which I have called, in that book the Pope likes, the virginal sphere, the "Parthenosphere."

A filtered light, a bluish light, white and rosy light of the dawn, light of high noon, softened light of Roman evenings, pale light, nocturnal light, moonlight perhaps, all forms of light are here present in turn as the hours revolve. I think of that, to me mysterious, phrase of the Gospel of St. Luke, where it is said that after the death of Christ "the Sabbath was full of shafts of light": *et sabbatum illucescebat.*[1] It meant, doubtless, the lamps lighted in every Jewish home for the watch and the night. Of the chapel I am describing one could also say that it is illuminated like the last Sabbath of the Resurrection. It is a temple dedicated above all to light, or, more precisely, to the intimacy of light: *lux intima*, in its intelligibility, uniqueness, and diversity, like the Wisdom which Solomon tells us is one, and, being one, can accomplish all and is able to renew all. The pagans of ancient Rome raised stelae to the *sol invictus*, to the unconquered sun; but it is Christ who is that unique sun of minds and consciences.

[1] In English: . . . the Sabbath grew light.

Thy Word is the dwelling of our intelligence
As here below space is the place of our body.

Such is the work of the painter Silvio Consadori, of whom Madurini said so truly that his color, calm and vibrant, dense and at the same time light, gives "the sensation of a vital expansion of our being." In his chapel I imagine that Paul VI has wished to parallel the higher chamber of the Last Supper and of Pentecost, the Cenacle; the chapel has a simple rectangular shape. The Pope reaches it without steps. He can come here at any time of the day or night.

What is secret is the ultimate sense of this chapel. It is rendered secret like a poem or a nest, by a single idea, which is the idea of oblation.

We are in a high place, and this high place is the place of the holocaust, in its two senses, two directions: *mors et vita*—destruction and resurrection, resurrection softening and restoring what has been destroyed. Christ is surrounded by these angels which make me think of those which Adorna-Fieschi—St. Catherine of Genoa— described as "so clear, so happy, so complete that seeing them she could not contain her laughter." The light has crossed the faces of Christ and the angels, we are beneath that wave. But from the floor of the chapel rises the call to the evening sacrifice. Peter crucified head downward, Paul on the other side offering his head to the sword.

In the middle of the nave the stained-glass windows by Consadori recall the creation on the Gospel side and the story of the Virgin, its mysteries, on the other side. The window of the creation allows all elements of nature to be associated with worship; a work that sums up all, should also sum up the summation of all, the work of the seven days, which in raising it higher corresponds to that second and supreme creation which is the Incarnation. This is the idea of theologians and mystics, and of John the Evangelist, that the work of the Word is a second beginning, a creation hidden in Joseph and Mary first of all, as in the early sunless days, and then unfolded in the sunlight of history; a creation which was to become painful and bloody; a creation capable of redeeming the sins of the world, a creation without risk of defeat like that other, which always fails in history. These two works of God, *evolution*, we might say, and *Christogenesis*, are symbolically face to face. The heartrending red and the somber violet are two enmeshed cries of pain and of triumph.

Here the altar does not receive any special light. All is altar, all is light, all is sacrifice. Around the altar is a bas-relief representing Pentecost where are portrayed, it seems to me, Patriarch Athenagoras and Cardinal Tisserant, a memorial already cast in bronze of a prophetic encounter.

I noticed particularly fine work by Scorzelli, the "Stations of the Cross," which presents in one single panel fifteen stations.

"That is because," said the Holy Father, "Cardinal Bevillacqua did not admit that the Stations of the Cross should only reach the Crucifixion. He did not prolong them to the Resurrection or even to the empty tomb. But he wished the fourteen halts on the way to be preceded—so to speak to be enveloped—by the sacrifice of the Eucharist. That is why, beneath the fourteen Stations, you see the Last Supper represented."

I like Enrico Manfrini's work very much: his Madonnas, his Evangelists, his crucifixes. Manfrini knew how to express this recollection of the powers of the soul, so hard to render, in sculpture or in bas-relief: for stone, marble, and bronze require an air of indifference in the faces, and an absence of the soul from the body, which seems to be self-sufficient like the bodies of the Gods. I do not know how Manfrini set about keeping that unfinished quality in his work;

stiffness, clumsiness—which reminds me of Verlaine's poetry—which make the grace, the attentive virginity of the faces stand out. There is in Manfrini a reminder of the primitives; but he is a primitive very aware of his means, who reaches something of childhood through immense, surpassed knowledge. When Manfrini traced the face of Paul VI in a bas-relief, he was really in his element. He emphasized the eyebrows very close together, the big ears and that grave attention which is so hard to catch in portraits and much more so in snapshots, so that this Pope, so secretive, so different from his pictures, can only be rendered well by a sculptor. I find Manfrini's "Annunciation" has something admirable, as has the crucifix on the altar. I would say the same for his "Virgin at Pentecost."

"Will you tell me, O philosopher," the Holy Father suddenly asked me, "how you define beauty?"

J. G.

"I do not define beauty, because beauty has exactly the characteristic that it is indefinable. But if I were obliged to reply, if I were forced to . . ."

HIS HOLINESS

"It is your obligation."

I

". . . I would say that beauty is a radiance, a phosphorescence rather than a light. Or, as one of the ancients said, it is a splendor. It is the projection outward—not very far, like a vapor, a halo, or rather like an aureole—of what is most intimate in anything. And that is why beauty is both more interior than the interior, and at the same time beyond all contour. It is beyond the work of art which evokes it. Yes, even in the beautiful things the earth presents, the beauty is beyond."

HE

"For our part we would say that beauty certainly has a relationship with man which you have forgotten to mention. Beauty is the intimacy of man, it is the 'I' which presents itself in its fullest synthesis—the most painful also, if you will—but also the most joyful."

I

"The poet Mallarmé has a sentence which I think helpful. I know it by heart: 'Poetry is the expression in human language reduced to its essential rhythm of the mysterious in aspects of existence. It thus authenticates our sojourn and constitutes its only spiritual duty.' It seems to me that the poet, while defining poetry, defines the Gospel too."

HE

"The transcendent God has become in one way immanent. He has become the inner friend, the spiritual master. Communion with him seemed impossible. But he came among us."

I

"The Word was made flesh. . . ."

HE

"That reminds me that a very long time ago, in a review where I collaborated with Maurice Zundel, we turned the phrase of St. John around: 'And the flesh,' we said with the audacity of youth, 'was made word.' *ET CARO VERBUM FACTA EST*. We were not understood by all the theologians and I recognize their criticisms as valid, but it should have been understood that we only wished to give a definition of art, and of Christian art in particular. Matter became word, a word of God."

I

"Art is an initiation to beauty, by that harmony which is an image of grace, which it sometimes prepares and invokes."

HE

"I have always kept company with artists, I have always secretly loved them, and every time I can, although they have a ferocious modesty, I try to talk with them."

I

"A priest is an artist who has renounced himself."

HE

"I think on the contrary that there exists an affinity—no, rather a capacity—for a marvelous understanding between priest and artist.

"Our common ministry consists in rendering the world of the spirit, of the invisible, of the ineffable, of God, accessible, comprehensible, even touching. In this art then of translating this world of the spirit, this world of the invisible, into intelligible formulas, artists are masters. And that not in the manner of professors of logic or of mathematics, who make the treasures of the world comprehensible to the intelligence. Artists make the spiritual world accessible to it, while preserving its ineffable character, its halo of mystery, and I insist here again, they have to arrive at this ineffable world both by force and by effort. Inspiration comes, sometimes unexpectedly, like a flash of lightning. But often—as artists know—inspiration requires a slow, gradual, sometimes hard and exacting apprenticeship."

The Holy Father added mysteriously:

"If the help of artists were lacking to us, the sacerdotal ministry would lack assurance. I say it would have to make an effort to become itself. An ascetic and even prophetic effort. Yes," he concluded, "in order to express the mystery of intuitive beauty as it should be expressed, the priesthood must be made to coincide with art."

I

"It could be said that the Mass is the most perfect of works of art. It is music, poetry, architecture. It is a real drama, the most real of all dramas, since it reproduces really what it signifies. And it has, like all works of art, its moment of flight, of ecstasy, its sublime instant linking eternity with time."

HE

"Yes, Mass is a drama which has a sacred moment, which fills the mind and makes the heart beat faster. I think all artists, even if they are not Christian, feel this when they are present at an intimate or a solemn Mass."

I

"But today this coincidence of the priesthood with art is more difficult than ever. Art flings itself into ways that are so inhuman, it touches upon almost infernal realms. Rather, it is not the real, or even the surreal, that it discovers, but the possible, and I mean the possible of the dream, often of the nightmare."

HE

"And I myself also am troubled, my heart bleeds, when I see contemporary art detach itself from humanity, from life. Sometimes certain of our artists seem to forget that art must express things. Sometimes, it is impossible to know what it says. It is the Tower of Babel. It is chaos, confusion. Then, I ask myself, where is art? Art should be intuition, facility, felicity. This facility, this felicity modern art does not always provide. I sometimes am surprised, abashed, staggered. When I said this one day to some artist friends, they replied, 'Whose fault is that? You imposed on us the rule of imitation. We are not imitators, we are creators.' I replied, 'Since that is so, forgive us. Yes, we have not talked enough with you, we have not followed you enough, nor admired you and collected you. We have not explained to you clearly enough what we have in common. If the mysteries of God make the human heart bound with joy, even with exaltation, we have not sufficiently introduced you into that secret cell. We have not had you as pupils, as interlocutors, as friends, and therefore, you have not known us well enough. And may the Pope become again what he always was, the sincere and cordial friend of artists. Transcendence terrifies modern man. And yet whoever does not feel this distance is not aware of true religion. Whoever does not feel God's superiority, His ineffability, His mystery, cannot truly possess His art. For all art reveals transcendence. And I like this thought which, I think, is from Simone Weil: 'Beauty is the proof given by experience that the Incarnation is possible.' "

I

"May art be the inspirer of the spirit! The primal breath carried over the waters of the abyss!"

HE

"Yes, indeed, may art not close itself against the wind of the Spirit! This world in which we live needs beauty lest it collapse in despair. Beauty, like truth, is what puts joy into men's hearts, it is the precious fruit which resists time's ravages, which unites generations and makes them intercommunicate in admiration. This is what I said to the artists at the end of the Council, on St. Peter's Square, on December 8. I hope I was understood by all the artists present in the world, by all the witnesses to the Invisible:

"O blessed voice of art, magic echo, thou that from silent beauty drawest the music of signs and sensible forms, when wilt thou sing again, when wilt thou speak to us again with thy superhuman fascination, of the joyous way, the way open to all, of a sudden intuition of the hidden and profound world of Being, whence all things take their sense and root?"

13

DIALOGUE ON THE MYSTERY
OF THE COUNCIL

The Council has joined the other councils of the past. It has rolled away forever. It is a strange sensation to see disappear into motionless history that which, five years ago, was still *to come*, uncertain, laden with excessive hope. It seems that the unforeseeable and improbable events of the Council were not sufficiently lived by those who lived them, not felt enough, as though the actors were inattentive and hurried. I do not think I ever had so sharp a feeling of the swiftness of time's passing, of the difficulty of stopping that which one is enjoying in order to enjoy it more, of the speed with which an event is engulfed in history, losing its colors, its thrills, its moments of uncertainty to become only a chronicle lacking the thrill of life. It is the eternal passover, which had to be eaten in haste, girt for the journey.

I ventured to ask the Holy Father if he shared this impression of rush. His attention was fixed on what was going on at the heart of history, which was not evident to the superficial mind. For a Council exists on several levels. There is the Council variegated with visible ceremonies, the minor meetings and the votes, the moments of anxiety, of boredom or of triumph. That is the visible. Invisible is the gentle and forceful stirring of the Spirit which, from the movements of men, their zigzags, their schemes, their meetings, their encounters, makes its word, composes its divine movement, advancing slowly through history—all the past and all the future being present, never hastening. The Council is still an enigma, as it is too recent. And one does not yet know what in it will pass away, what will be adjusted, completed, and what will mark the Church's future with new signs, with renewals, with beginnings. It is necessary to wait; time must be given time to arrive.

The mystery of the Council will never be completely grasped by those still navigating in the flux of history. I remember that I had scruples during the first session: Could I, as an "observer," send a report to a newspaper, after I had sworn to be discreet? I consulted a wise prelate, and he replied with this maxim, which is now precious to me because a distinction between two definitions is always illuminating. *About the secret nothing, about the mystery everything.* But where is the boundary between secret and mystery?

HIS HOLINESS

"The secret is a human invention, a protective measure. The mystery is quite something else. It is *the substance of things unseen,* as St. Paul said. The Council should have taken place in secret. But that was impossible because of the great number of Fathers, the modern methods of information, and the world's curiosity. The Council held its sessions in the open. This seeming misfortune had a good result—inconveniences have their advantages as thorns have their roses. The advantage was that the whole world was informed about our deliberations. As for the mystery of the Council . . ."

I

"This mystery, its eternal secret, which will never be fully known . . ."

HE

"We can only have an obscure knowledge, a presentiment, of the place of the Council in the Church's life, in the plan of divine Love for mankind, by which *he creates the centuries in order that the Invisible* become in some measure *visible*. We see it as an enigma."

I

"One must close one's eyes to see."

HE

"Above all, one must be able to forget the accidental. For those who lived the Council from day to day, even hour by hour, in ignorance of the future and without knowing if it had a future (for a check, a delay, an impasse is always possible), for those who lived it in these modern times which are so harrying, it was not always easy to understand what was going on."

I

"Newman said that one does not see Christ directly but that Christ manifests Himself when one looks back and remembers."

HE

"In that way the Council can be seen as having been a time of divine visitation, a time of grace. It was more than a solemn date, a great hour, a mighty moment in the time of the Church. Like a striking clock, the Council was preceded and is followed by silence. We have entered into the following silence, when the echo of the hour that has struck is heard. May I ask you how this hour has echoed in you?"

I

"How can I express what I think of the solemnity of this date, the magnitude of this beginning? History is not an always ascending dialectic, as the disciples of Hegel and the Marxists think. History is made up of rhythms which alternate, like waves, on the ocean of the ages.

"But there are rhythms of various amplitudes.

"Moreover, the extraordinary thing about the present epoch is that three historical rhythms have coincided: We have a slow cosmic, planetary rhythm which is the end of the age when the energies, tapped by the thinking animal, were superficial. Now the power contained in the least grain of matter is being discovered. Here is the end of the first rhythm. The second rhythm which is ending is that era, sometimes called Constantinian, when the Church had to supplement the State, take on temporal duties, associate herself with the so temporary temporal. The third is the end of the age of the great fissions and dislocations which marked the liquidation of the Middle Ages. It is the end of the Protestant Reformation conceived of as a condemnation of the Roman Church. It is the end of that conflict between science and faith, which troubled so many minds, giving rise to lamentable and fallacious conflicts."

The Pope did not reply. The more the Council is described as a turning point in history, the more he feels weighing on him the "terrible and gentle" weight of those responsible.

The Council is one thing when it is recorded, analyzed, seen through the consciousness of lay witnesses or in the consciousness of the two thousand bishops. That same Council is quite another thing in the solitary consciousness of him who bears the ultimate responsibility. I was certainly aware of this difference of viewpoint between *those* who were responsible and *the one* responsible. It is to escape from a burden that councils and commissions are often created. In an assembly, each person leans, rests, on another; feels himself borne, and sometimes excused; he enters into the flow, the drops come together and reassure themselves in the current. The case of him who is alone and who cannot take refuge in obedience or in fusion is totally different.

The Pope could not say all that he had done for, and in, the Council, while respecting the liberty of the Fathers. His interventions, especially that at the end of the third session, were made in fear of a premature move by the Council. His speeches to the Council were an exegesis, a synthesis of conciliar action in which the Pope recalled the aim, often obscured by the debates, where the pilot brought the periphery back to the center, rose above the contemporary, recalled the past, announced the future, and finally, like St. John, gave the ultimate simple advice: "Let us love one another."

THE POPE

"Many possible crises were avoided. One of the most visible results was that the Council took place without too many upheavals. It was never suspended, interrupted. It arrived, in some ways beyond all hopes. It is possible to say that the bishops as a whole set themselves to learn and to listen, and many were surprised how in four years their point of view changed and broadened, how they sometimes accepted what before the Council they would have judged unacceptable or too rash. This action of the Council upon itself was a sign of the divine presence."

I

"One bishop has been quoted as saying, 'Before the Council I believed in the Holy Spirit. I no longer believe. I have seen.'"

HE

"The Spirit acted on the Council to conciliate it. Recalling former councils and even the first Vatican Council, one would have thought there would be a strong minority in opposition. This was not so. The last votes were almost unanimous."

The Pope did not say what he could not say, what all know: that his personal action, his fairness, his respect, his anxiety to place himself above differences, his tact, his talent, too, were the principal human agent of that conciliation. From a conciliatory Council by means of a debating Council to a reconciled Council—that was the dialectic of this council.

I was emboldened to go on. "All my life I have had different ways of saying 'I believe' to the opinions and views of my friends and the newspapers. Their veracity is confused. I would not shed a drop of blood to uphold affirmations of this kind, though in conversation I state them in a peremptory manner, the more so the less I am convinced of them.

"This is not what I believe, that to which I cling with all my inner experience, with all my mind and by a sort of intimate illumination; that which is more true than my truth, more certain than my certitude, that for which I would have to accept suffering at men's hands, that for which the martyrs died, that upon which their testimony was based.

"One has to distinguish opinion from certainty. This demands a great deal of sincerity with oneself and meditation, often anxious and painful meditation. It is necessary to dialogue with the other, not to oppose him, but rather to come together. For if 'my' personal truth is contrary to the personal truth of a judicious man and, how much more, of a wise consensus, that is indeed a bad sign."

HE

"What you are saying about yourself is true for the whole Council. I, too, was struck by the fact that a bishop, giving his opinion in the Council, often disagreed with another bishop, but on voting days they voted together. When a bishop was speaking he was under the obligation to give his opinion; but when a bishop voted, he had to hearken to the thought of the Spirit within him. Here one sees the difference between the human and the divine. In a parliament, the different parties only agree through compromise. And there always remains—I was about to say 'necessarily'—a minority, often a large one. The vote seems a victory for the majority.

"Sometimes in the Council there was a question of victors and vanquished. But if one is vanquished by a truth, or by some aspect of truth of what one had not until then been aware, I say one is a victor. One should not try to *conquer* one's adversary, but to *convince* him. From a healthy and holy discussion, the result is not a 'master' and a 'slave,' to use Marxist terminology, but two servants of the truth."

I

"Your Holiness defines the intellectual beauty of the Council. Yet do you not think everyone keeps his own opinion, that, even when the bishops in the minority come around, it is because they see that nothing is to be gained by opposition and that they prefer to follow the prevailing wind, join the victor's camp?"

HE

"The Council's greatness does not lie in this infirmity, however excusable. It is in the spiritual movement, the fruit of reason and of grace, which drove each Father to seek the profound, universal truth in line with the living tradition which reconciles in itself the private truths, the personal perspectives because it is the place where they dwell, where they communicate, where they range themselves around the mystery of faith.

"The same thing is true of true conversions. The convert never loses what he already possessed of truth and life. He rediscovers it at a higher level, deepened and purified.

"Also in true reconciliation—so different from compromise—each of the partial views should be rediscovered in a form more real than when it was sustained by a single begetter, issuing from a single head, in a perspective that is necessarily private."

I

"I sometimes wondered how in that assembly, with so much movement and so many rumors, it would be possible to follow the traces and the leaps of this *invisible* presence of the Spirit. I sometimes wondered whether one would not see in this Council, toward the end of a session, an event analogous to Pentecost. I did not expect a whirlwind, or 'tongues of fire,' but some kind of event or rather of advent. A sudden enthusiasm might have seized that assembly of thinkers. There are many surprises in human gatherings (I am thinking of the night of the fourth of August) ; all the more such things are possible during a historic meeting of the sons of the Spirit.

"In fact, nothing of the sort ever happened in the Council. And even the summits it reached (at the end, at the time of the kiss of peace between Your Holiness and the representative of the Patriarch) were not blazing. Rather one felt a restrained, respectful emotion, more intellectual than effective. Were there too many bishops? Were they too sophisticated, in this twentieth century which knows everything? Even the sky gave no hint; there were no signs in the clouds. The bronze did not sweat. There was nothing like the storm of 1870 which shook the walls of the basilica of St. Peter when infallibility was defined.

"I have often thought about the Church, not the Church of today, but the Church of yesterday and of always. For she should be seen as a living being, as a rocket that has not completed its course. What are called her marks, such as unity and holiness, cannot well be seen unless one sees that the Church traverses cultures and epochs assimilating what is vital and substantial in each culture and in each epoch without allowing herself to be assimilated. It is that, to my mind, which is highly improbable in the phenomenon of the Catholic Church, if it is regarded over a long period."

HE

"The Church lives, the Church thinks, the Church speaks, the Church grows. We should appreciate this astounding phenomenon. We should realize its *messianic* significance."

I

"The difficulty at the present time, such a pathetic time, is that the Church endures, grows, without seeming to deny her past; this is because without being assimilated by what is not herself, she assimilates."

HE

"The Church can only insert herself in the world according to the norms established by tradition. Look at the past; you will see that the Church *selects* what is valid. From Latinism and Hellenism she rejected idolatry and the inhuman elements in those civilizations, but she preserved the treasure of their classicism and their culture. She removed the violence and barbarity from feudalism, but retained the positive strength of medieval man. She put aside the pagan humanism of the Renaissance, while maintaining its artistic power. Do you not agree?"

I

"It has always seemed to me that, if one looked with a deep, inner, and total vision, one would see that the Church is the *form* of everything. To whatever occurs in the realm of the mind or of history, she is ready to give a *form*, that is to say, to prevent its corruption and to encourage its development. Whether it is a question of Scriptures, or prophecies, of theological doctrines or mystical states, of kingdoms or social advance or antiquities, of renaissance, novelties of culture and civilization, the Church can assume them while letting them be what they are, and even enabling them to be more what they are. When one is loved, one feels more oneself."

HE

"In the same way, I am sure that the Church, while denouncing modern materialism, could never condemn the vast and marvelous civilization of science, industry, and technology characteristic of our time. She will try to *assimilate* it, that is, to breathe into it certain principles still lacking, and to open to it the horizons of spiritual truth, prayer, and redemption. She will try to accomplish today what she has done for centuries: to give men peace and brotherhood and make them children of God in Christ."

I

"I would, Holy Father, go even farther, pursue the mission to its conclusion, in proposing a hypothesis which is improbable but not impossible."

HE

"Which hypothesis?"

I

"That of the plurality of worlds. Since the cosmonauts, this idea disturbs us. Here we are at a time when we must think of the *cosmos* as a whole. Is man alone the thinking reed? Perhaps our descendants will enter into contact with another type of 'reasonable' beings. What will happen then? This is how I see it:

"Either those reasonable beings will not know Jesus, or the Word will also have communicated itself to them in another form. In that case the Church can no more be two than can human reason. The terms of this other Church should have their correspondences in our language. There would be, for the truths of faith, as for those of science and of reason, a transposition to be made, as when we decipher an unknown language. Certain prayers of the Catholic eucology, like the common Preface where the officiant calls upon the celestial choirs, certain sealed books, like the Apocalypse, suggest that the Catholic Church is as vast as the worlds she possesses.

"But the Catholic Church is the church of all the worlds. This beautiful word Catholic must be extended to all the universes. The revelation made in Christ Jesus extends to every humanity."

HE

"The greater the universe grows, the more this extension of creation allows us to grasp the greatness of Him who has created the worlds."

I

"Might it not be said that Catholicism is the name given in human history to the mystical Body of Christ, to that communion of consciences united to Christ by the bond of love, which is the mystery of eternity already present temporally, in miniature?"

"That might in fact be said. I would add that Christianity is characterized by a mutation. It is the great upheaval of history and of life. '. . . when a man becomes a new creature in Christ,' says St. Paul, 'his old life has disappeared, everything has become new about him.'[1] The Christian will never stop at a given stage, or at a virtue acquired. This impulse is dynamic. It sets souls in motion; it raises up saints, the friends of God; it communicates a continual and reforming impulse to human society, a bold and confident enthusiasm.

"We see at this time this spirit of renewal. After this Council, exhaled by it and in its wake, a state of expectation, of suspense, of openness and of active fervor appeared in men's consciousness, on which later will depend, in great part, the fruits of the Council. Both he who has the responsible voice in the Council and he who has to listen to this voice and make it his own can offer up nothing more noble or more just than this spiritual attitude for the happy issue of the Council, for the facilitating and fecundating of the mysterious action of the Holy Spirit in the direction, the vivification, the sanctification of the Mystical Body of Christ which is the Church and which is us, ourselves, when we are united, as we should be, to Christ. If we wish the Council to attain its objectives and to become a decisive moment of renewal in the life of the Church, it is necessary to maintain a state of spiritual vigilance. And by vigilance I mean attention, knowledge, confidence, tension, humility, and a

[1] II Cor. 5:17.

capacity to accept and to enjoy the new things the Council has brought.

"It is not merely a question of application. Creation in that same direction is always necessary. The Council is no new thing. It is Tradition itself, but with more interior truth, authenticity, and charity. We are recognizable throughout the whole history of the Church. *She is the same.* Accidents are accidental, and the accidents appear to us as such, because we judge them with our culture and with the progress of our culture due also to the Gospel. Is it not the Church which is to a great extent at the origin of this civilization, of which the world today acknowledges the truth and which it appropriates? Humanity is hers, by a mysterious hope which certain major features of contemporary history seem to validate; for example, the search for truth and liberty, the necessary progress toward unity, the need for fraternity and peace, so many values which only acquire their fullness in the light of the Gospel."

I

"What I saw in the Council was, if I dare say so, my own mystery. I saw projected there the mystery of every human conscience, magnified, multiplied, dramatized. We are all a kind of conciliar assembly. We try to unite ourselves to ourselves, which is difficult. We try to unite ourselves to others, which is almost impossible. Across this dual disunity we endeavor to unite ourselves with the Supreme Mystery."

HE

"Since you are in the mood for confidences, tell me what you felt on a certain December morning when you spoke before the Fathers of the Council. I had read your text; and I do not believe I asked you for the slightest modification. I had asked you to speak of your experience. The layman, young or old, should never be prevented from speaking of what he has experienced or thought. This is the freedom of the Spirit. Where the Spirit of the Lord is, there is freedom."

I

"My impressions? I did not look at the bishops. I could not see them from where I was. The day before I had been given advice. Some had said to me, 'Above all, express yourself with conviction, with warmth.' Others had told me, 'Above all, no ardor; a calm, grave, and impersonal tone.' I decided to be what I was. I was told to articulate and, like Demosthenes, the evening before . . .

"At the very moment I spoke I saw only Your Holiness, who seemed to be saying to me to *run in my way*. I have noticed that in difficult moments another moves in and lives in your place. One only notices quite small details. And I think death will be easier than one fears. The Lord will carry us away while we only pay attention to our breathing."

HE

"Your agony was soon over. But since the Council is ended, may I ask you what in it now seems to you to have been most important?"

I

"It is very difficult to know the real importance of what is happening. History shows us spectacular events without outcome. And, on the other hand, seeds which fall unnoticed modify everything. Tacitus, that profound observer, saw in nascent Christianity only a quarrel among Jews. I believe that many aspects of the Council which filled the press will soon be forgotten, while the unnoticed seed will grow."

HE

"And may I ask what is this 'unnoticed seed'?"

I

"The Synod."

HE

"I have not yet called it."[2]

I

"It is instituted; and that is the essential.

"I have often been asked: But how is it that there have been so few ecumenical councils in the history of the apostolic Church? Why did Peter not gather together the Twelve to form with them a single body, as it evidently was at the beginning?"

HE

"And what did you answer?"

I

"That there are two reasons for this. One technical, which was the difficulty of communication, the partitioning of the world. The other is the role of the Papacy which, at the fall of the Roman Empire, took over the care of western culture and history. The bishops

[2] It met in Rome in September 1967. *Ed.*

virtually formed a Council, but it did not materialize except in critical conditions."

HE

"You seem to have forgotten the Sacred College."

I

"The Sovereign Pontiff chooses the cardinals in complete freedom, according to a system which recalls the election of emperors. The Pope chooses those who will choose his successor. This flexible process has assured a great continuity to the spiritual power. But on the fifteenth of September 1965, we were to learn from Paul VI that he was instituting the Synod of Bishops. His every word must be weighed. 'In attentively observing the signs of the times, we endeavor to adapt the methods of the apostolate to the growing needs of our epoch and to the evolution of society. Also our apostolic solicitude requires us to affirm by ever closer ties our unity with the bishops, which the Holy Spirit has constituted while awaiting perhaps the Church of God.'

"Thus, for the first time in history, several of those who will assist the Pope in his councils will be elected by conferences of bishops. Paul VI has interpreted the votes of the Council on collegiality; he has incarnated them, if I dare say it, in a permanent institution. It looks new, but it reconstitutes the situation of the early church: Peter and the Twelve.

"And now, may I say what comes into my mind about the future?"

HE

"It is never forbidden to speak of the future. And if one is wrong, nobody will object."

I

"I asked myself if the Council at which I was assisting was the last."

HE

"I have heard the opposite thesis, that proof has been given that henceforward an ecumenical Council could easily meet again."

I

"I asked myself: Is what I see visible for the last time to human eyes on this planet?"

HE

"And why this final twilight?"

I

"Because an assembly of three thousand thinking, governing heads outdistances human scale, rendering a mutual dialogue very difficult. Now the number of bishops will increase with the world's population. Can one conceive a deliberating assembly of five thousand Fathers? And, on the other hand, the means of communication are so rapid that every bishop on earth will be able, easily and without fatigue, to come for a weekend to Rome, while television will carry the face and words of the Sovereign Pontiff to all the world.

"But, if it is true that an ecumenical Council for discussion such as that we have just seen will never again meet at length, it is equally true that the Council will continue meeting, for the Synod will be this permanent micro-Council. It is in and through the Synod that the Council will have its continuation.

"Only time will show how the relations between the Synod and the Curia will be established. Should one conceive of the Synod as analogous to an administrative council and the Curia to an executive board? The Synod making the plans, the Curia watching over their execution?

"But may I ask you an insidious question?"

HE

"I was born to listen to what one dare not say. And [with a smile] I am made for hearing what I should not know. The things unsaid around a Pope are those important for him to know.

"What are the criticisms you have gathered of the Council? The Jews eat bitter herbs during Passover. One should not be afraid of bitter herbs.

"I am not speaking of inevitable criticisms. When a step forward is taken, some find the step is timid, that it has changed nothing; others, that it is too bold, that it changes everything too much.

"But outside the Church, in non-Christian circles where there are loyal and true hearts, or among non-Catholic observers, and even among philosophers, have you gathered some such wise and profound observations—as Socrates might have made in hell?"

I

"I recall an Indian Socrates—that is to say, a Buddhist philosopher—who said to me, 'How peculiar your Catholic position at the Council is. We orientals have preferred life to truth. We have exalted the values of life, of joy, of peace of soul; we have plunged into the waters of the Ganges, that is, into the river of time, or reincarnation, of what you call *history*. But you westerners, you Christians, above all, you Roman Catholics, that is where you were once. Vigilant, stable, assured, proclaiming, defining axioms which never changed;

truths, aspects of the immutable Truth. Our Indian sages sometimes envied you your assurance, your certainty. You spoke with the authority that revelation, possession, gives.

"But, after the Council, we asked ourselves if you had not, *in fact*, lost your immutable certitude. The Church seems to us to doubt that she possesses the Absolute.

"She is more proccupied with life than with truth. She wishes to adapt to the world, to speak the language of the world. She is afraid of the solitude which the feeling of truth, rejected by many people of this century, gave her. She goes along with changing history."

HE

"I would answer that one must not separate what should be distinguished. Charity and truth will never be opposed, because charity, at its highest point, in its sublime aspect, is the charity of truth. What the Indian philosopher said to you arises from the fact that the Council's perspective was pastoral: There was no question of defining new aspects of truth but of rendering this truth more accessible, more assimilable to the minds of today, consequently, still more true, because better loved and more efficacious."

I

"Our contemporaries have the sense of *becoming* rather than that of *being*, so truth seems to them subject to history. The Council may give them the impression that the Church, henceforward, submits her truth to becoming. And not a few wonder how they can reconcile Vatican Council II with Vatican Council I."

HE

"In our age time goes very fast, and history seems speeded up. It is true that in four years of the Council the Church has traversed an immense interval, has made a great leap forward and moved very quickly, at least in appearance. It will not surprise a disciple of Cardinal Newman that this was done not in order to say really new things, *nova*, but in order to illumine, to bring out, to make explicit, to formulate what the Church has always thought, what was implicit in the Gospel itself. The texts on religious liberty, which seemed to some people so new, are founded on texts taken from Holy Scripture. They make explicit the idea, which is at the base of all Christianity, that faith is an act, that this act implies freedom of faith. Where would be its merit and its glory without real liberty? And the same thing might be noted with regard to what the Council has said on ecumenism, on revelation. Here there is nothing new in an absolute sense, but if certain ways of doing, of thinking, or of feeling, if certain expressions are new, it is in order that what was always admitted should be further studied in depth. And especially so that this may be in agreement with the needs of our contemporaries, who desire more liberty, more authenticity, and a more personal knowledge of the mysteries of faith.

"The postconciliar period will be, as has been said, a continuous creation. The Council has opened up avenues, sown seeds, given bearings. But history reminds us that the times that follow councils are inert and troubled. Apostles and prophets must arise to incarnate the spirit of the Council."

I

"May doctors, may prophets and mystics arise; may new forms of sanctity appear!"

HE

"Many are tempted to believe that only what is new, what is modern, what is indistinguishable from the contemporary world is alive. And, instead of starting from the substance of the faith as it has been lived during twenty centuries, they take as their point of departure temporal reality: the state of mind of their contemporaries. Many, even in Christian circles, think that Christianity strives above all in order to make the world better. But the end of Christianity is not to make a better world, by which I mean the material changing world. The world of the supernatural order escapes the wear and tear of time. Sometimes one imagines that the order of grace is in some way a marginal structure. This would seem a messianic naturalism. But you will see that the more materialistic aspirations approach their realization, the less they satisfy the essential needs of life.

"Further I would say that Catholics should not give way to the temptation to raise questions about everything connected with the Council, for this corresponds to the great contemporary temptation which is noticeable everywhere now: *to start from the beginning.*

"In the spiritual life, as one ascends higher, the soul as it climbs upward goes through a period of disarray. It sees the old synthesis which it has criticized, which it had to undo, to take apart; it does not yet see the superior synthesis to which it must attain.

"In every growth, in every mutation upward, every time, as St. Paul said, when one is *stripped* of one's habitual garment in order to be *clothed anew*, there is a moment of nakedness, of disarray—which an ill wind makes use of, in which the devil insinuates himself. This undoing is in itself a good. It is the undoing of something growing. If the rosebud were to see itself in the spring, would it not feel that it was undone when it was about to flower?"

I

"I remember Bernanos' remark: 'To what depth must one dig to rediscover the blue vault?'

"But in the spiritual life, when one mounts higher, consciousness passes."

HE

"We have not taken the side of life, forsaking the side of truth. We wished to give the truth a more abundant life. What our Indian friends make us understand is the unbelievable privilege we possess. 'We have a treasure, then, in our keeping, but its shell is of perishable earthenware.' "[3]

I

"The difficulty is to reconcile truth and life in a single way."

HE

"The order toward which Christianity tends is not static. It is a developing order, an advance toward a better norm, an equilibrium in movement. Founded on the absolute, it exploits the contingencies offered by history in order to prove its vitality. It arouses a need for spiritual renewal in men's hearts; it procures peaceful means for their social renewal.

"Christianity is not a puritan, abstentionist religion, inclined to self-preservation by isolation from the realities where humanity struggles. It is made for humanity. It is the religion of humanity. Its mission is to penetrate collective and individual consciences, to renew and revivify them. It is the light of the world, the spirit's ferment, aggressive if need be. It does not underestimate the strength of the masses; it aims to convince and serve them. It has a genius for reform and novelty no less than for tradition and fidelity. Christianity reaches out toward its own reformation and toward the

[3] II Cor. 4:7.

reformation of the world. It is essentially unsatisfied. But it is optimistic."

I

"The mystery of the Council is the very mystery of the life of the Church in time. 'What Jesus Christ was yesterday, and is today, he remains for ever.'[4] To my mind the Council was an almost instantaneous incision in this historical continuum—what indeed are four years in the age of the Church?—but this incision allowed everyone to see the intimate life of the Church, Christ at work in His creation, hearts expanding, spirits blossoming, the hidden powers in us receiving a kind of increase. Who did not feel his being expand during the Council? And now that the Council is over, it seems that I experience this tension, this expansion of my intimate being even more. I catch myself thinking, like the disciples at Emmaus, after Christ had vanished: Did not our hearts burn within us when He spoke to us on the way and opened to us the sense of the Scriptures? I think that all the bishops on earth, all the observers, will retain all their lives this same impression of having lived a fleeting moment of the eternal mystery, and that they did not entirely grasp it at the very moment in which this mystery was present in their midst. But they will always live off this privileged moment, drawing from its radiance things ever new. For it is not in a single generation that the riches contained in the decrees of the Council will be understood. Several will be necessary, perhaps all till the end of time."

HE

"The Council was an uplifting, unpredictable, sudden, swift, providential, illuminating act, recalling the past, announcing the

4 Heb. 13:8.

future, a work of greater faith, stronger hope, fuller love. An encounter, a fourfold encounter: with all other faithful Catholics, with our still separated brethren, with all who believe they do not believe, with the present world as it appears, that is, tormented, complex, redoubtable—magnificent."

I

"Oh, yes, what intimate, sweet, fruitful, and marvelous meetings!"

HE

"How these will deepen our hearts and our minds, how they will transform the horizon of coming generations, whose ardent steps, whose confident voices I hear! Listen . . . What an immense hope is this youth of the Church and of the world!"

I

"Those who are entering upon life, impatient youth, are not aware of their good fortune. They find in the doctrine of the Council a catechism which corresponds to their present needs. They can no longer complain of the gap between the language of the Church and the progress of minds. The conflicts which have devastated us may reappear. . . ."

HE

"They will be clear-cut confrontations, free from misunderstanding. They will be painful conflicts, but they will be in the light."

I

"In a word, were I to tell you all my thought, all my experience (however obscure) of this mystery of the Council . . ."

HE

"You should."

I

"I would say that the mystery of the Council is a double mystery, a mystery of progress, a mystery of assumption, a historical mystery, an eternal mystery."

HE

"What do you mean?"

I

"That there exists a movement in some way horizontal which pushes the Church forward, and a vertical movement which draws it upward. The first is that of continuing time. The second is that of eternity already present in her."

HE

"But the two movements are not opposed. They complete one another. They call to one another. They join together. They are one."

I

"At this Christmastide one might say: not only the arms outstretched toward the shepherds and the kings, but the eyes lifted to the sky and the motionless star."

HE

"Gladly, I would say, thinking of the Easter mystery: no, not only the pierced hands stretched out toward the universe, as though to bless it, but also the head upright, crowned with thorns, and the look toward the Father."

I

"The giving and the leaving."

HE

"Better still: the two forms of a selfsame gift. Love in its two movements, the gift of self to others, the gift of self to the Father. It is the daily and plenary crossing. It is the sign of the Cross."

I

"This crossing ends at the last hour, when there is no more *before*, when the crossing comes down upon the *above*, then there is but one vertical, that is, *death*."

HE

"That is life."

PART FOUR

The Pope Before the Mystery

14

THE PRIEST

Pauvre âme, c'est cela![1]
PAUL VERLAINE.

J.G.

"In our day the despairing are many. I ask myself—and dare not admit it—if it is not despair of attaining the ideal, of being loved by God, of being worthy of God . . . which begets atheism."

HIS HOLINESS

"What do you mean?"

I

"I mean, Holy Father, that in the impenetrable depth of conscience, this is what is found: How mediocre I am, the All-Perfect cannot truly love me. And that kind of despair makes desirable the admission that the All-Perfect does not exist, and that what exists is nothingness. So that, I repeat, despair begets atheism much more than atheism begets despair, as is commonly said without sufficient reflection."

HE

"Perhaps! In any case, that is a very roundabout way of saying something very simple. In short, what is difficult for man's heart is to

[1] Poor soul, that's it.

believe in the love that God hath for us. St. John said: 'As for us, we have believed the Love.' That fear and certainty can be joined in a Christian conscience, that is what is difficult to believe and make understood. And it seems, as I was saying, that your poet Verlaine translated that in those candid and subtle verses, in which the broken alexandrines betray the emotion."

I

"C'est vrai que je vous cherche et ne vous trouve pas.
Mais vous aimer! Voyez comme je suis en bas,
Vous dont l'amour toujours monte comme une flamme."[2]

HE

"Et pourtant je vous cherche en longs tâtonnements."[3]

I

"Je te ferai goûter sur terre mes prémices,
La paix du coeur, l'amour d'être pauvre, et mes soirs mystiques."[4]

HE

"En attendant l'assomption dans la lumière,
L'éveil sans fin dans ma charité coutumière . . ."[5]

[2] True—that I seek you and I do not find.
To love you! See lowly I am here,
You, whose love rises always, like a flame.
[3] And yet I seek you, groping and at length.
[4] On earth I'll bring you tastes of a beginning,
Heart's peace, poverty's love, and mystic gloaming.
[5] While waiting the assumption into light
The endless waking, in love's daily sight.

"Oh! How fine that is, how precise and well expressed!"

I

"I have sometimes heard a Lutheran friend say to me that the Catholic seeks too hard for palpable security. He insists on knowing, he said, that the mystery is accomplished, that man is pardoned, that he can die in peace. Roman assurance, he said, diminishes faith, abandons man unaware in the night."

HE

"Everything comes together and fuses in a Catholic heart: the uncertain and the certain; the idea that one is the elect and the idea that one is unworthy. A burden can be both soft and overwhelming. You remember the line which resumes Paul Verlaine's last book of verse, *Sagesse: J'ai l'extase et la terreur d'être choisi.*"[6]

I

"The terror and the ecstasy. How well they agree! Perhaps a man become Pope is the only human being who can understand such a line, understand it in its depth, in its fullness. Poets never know what they do, and Verlaine more than any other is a mad, dark prophet. Perhaps he wrote this line so that a son of the Church, knowing it, should say it?"

HE

"It is not only the Pope who can say that. Every Christian is priest and victim. Each Christian is elected from among all, with a particular love. Don't forget your Pascal's phrase: 'I shed that drop of blood for you.' "

[6] I have the ecstasy and terror of being chosen.

I do not remember how the conversation continued. A little later, we found ourselves speaking about a subject difficult at any time: "What is a priest?" And how today, in the present time, does the problem of the *priest* appear? It is an ecumenical subject of the first magnitude, because, since the Reformation, the idea of the priest had been put in question. The whole Reformation centers around that. Will the Council not lead to some new conception of the priest, which will bring the priest closer to the layman? There is indeed a burning question, complex, fundamental, setting future courses. For it is very likely that tomorrow's priest will determine the pattern for the priest for a long time to come. In this moment of mutation we do not see this priest, so old and so new, clearly.

HE

"It seems to me that European literature understands the priest better today than ever before. What progress the idea has made since Lamartine's *Jocelyn*, Balzac's Abbé Bonne, Monsignor Myriel of *Les Miserables*[7] and, for example, that priest whose *Journal* George Bernanos has left us."[8]

I

"The movement has been from the exterior to the interior. But the interior of a priest cannot be explored even by himself. He is invested with a character which isolates him from the world of men; I would even say, which isolates him in the interior of his own being: How indeed can he understand his strange powers? How many secrets bury themselves in him and require that memory itself must

[7] Victor Hugo.
[8] *Journal d'un Curé de Campagne.* (Diary of a Country Priest.)

die! Memory, whose action is so sweet to most men, in a priest can only be painful and suppressed. All of which makes it difficult to analyze a priest's conscience, even his confidences. Everything that the arts, literature, and even the cinema translate of him has always seemed to me superficial, false."

HE

"On the contrary, it seems to me that modern literature has to a certain extent penetrated to the interior mystery of the priest. He is no longer represented as that conventional, slightly comic, moderately agreeable person, who avoids dialogue with the world, with the world's problems, who seems above all afraid to do what should above all be his job: to have a sense of the present, to be aware of the minds' dramas. No, it is not this retiring, timid man whom novelists or cinematographers show us. Quite the contrary, it is a priest full of mystery but also of love. A being—how to describe him?—strange and mysterious, having a personal experience of this world and of mankind, woven of suffering and mysticism, fated to have no practical success because of the deafness of the world around him."

I

"Literature has not always seen the priest thus. Paul Valéry tells us that the priest is an incomprehensible creature, to some extent absurd and exasperating."

HE

"Inheritor of the bygone Middle Ages, allied to conservative egoism, mandarin of an outmoded liturgy, a stranger to life, that's what the priest is for many. I know that."

I

"The priest to modern existentialist or Marxist eyes is the symbol of what faith is: the ambiguous one."

HE

"I know. But do not think that we, the priests of Jesus Christ, are unaware of the confusion the presence of the priest in the world causes in modern minds."

I

"The modern priest, unlike the priest of yesterday, sees himself through the eyes of others. He asks himself, he asks them, as Jesus did: 'Who do you say that I am?' "[9]

HE

"And is today's answer to that question?"

I

"The priest can become for each man the symbol of the best or the worst: of the sublime or of bad faith."

HE

"The clergy has been conscious of a wave of interest in literature for their souls' secrets. They also know that people would like to eliminate the priest from current affairs. But you know what has happened? The priest has recollected himself. It is necessary, he has said to himself, to become conscious again of oneself, one's powers and duties, and adjust one's own mission to conditions in the world, which has changed so profoundly.

[9] Matt. 16:15.

"This instinctive movement was at first defensive, of recoil. And it is what I saw, formerly, before the Council.

"Some people thought that it was primarily a question of defending, not the mysterious grace of the priesthood, unknown to the world and which, being unknown, was not questioned, but of defending the sheath of that grace, that is, the external, social, and canonical forms which protected it, which defined the priest's life; his habit, language, style. Yes, certain people conceived that the whole question was there. Or at least that there were the most threatened points."

I

"Each time the spirit is expressed in the letter, it is imagined that to safeguard the spirit it is sufficient to maintain the letter."

HE

"Exactly. Other priests I knew well consecrated their efforts to revitalizing from within the expression of the cult in which the priest is engaged, more than anything else. The liturgical movement gave significance, and poetry anew to the worn-out prayers; the rite reappeared in its garment of austerity and beauty. The celebration of the mysteries rekindled the sense of the ineffable union of the divine with the human in the sacramental action. A quiver of mysterious joy, of divine presence, of human charity ran through the communities of prayer regrouped around the altar. The priest was filled with joy; spring flowers again in the Church.

"But these gatherings were often only groups of the elite, the masses were missing. The populace seemed, in the vast majority, to be inexorably absent. Would they come back? It was up to the priest to make a move, not to the people."

I

"Perhaps there is the point of difference."

HE

"That is, indeed, the sign of the times."

I

"The sign of the times is the return to the conditions of the
Gospel, of the primal mission: not to wait for them to come to
Jerusalem, but for Jerusalem to move—that is Pentecost."

HE

"Useless, in fact, for the priest to ring his bell; nobody is listening.
He must hear the sirens sounding from the factories, those temples of
technology in which the modern world lives and throbs. The priest
must become a missionary anew if he wishes Christianity to remain
and again become a ferment. The apostle is shepherd and fisherman;
that is, he adapts to all the exigencies of the goal in view, which is to
seize souls and lead them to Christ."

I

"I remember what Stendhal's hero, Julien Sorel, says at the end of
his novel, *The Red and the Black*, which has been a bible for so
many, many people: '*Oh if I could find a priest, a real priest!*' "

HE

"Yes, indeed; it is in the many-sided and eager search for the true
concept of the priesthood that the spirituality of our day has made
the most effort. Toward that have been turned the hopes of so many

visionary minds in the lay world, especially after the tragic experience of the war; a real good, human, and holy priesthood would save the world.

"The mission of the spirit is indubitable. Even atheism creates its militants, devoted to the ideal of their cause. The devotion of brethren to their brethren's good is the only means for raising up the world. The idea of sacrifice and redemption is, still today, in the midst of a triumphant materialism, the guiding light of every authentic moral and social effort. I hope that one day humanity will be astonished to find, in the Catholic priesthood, a unique world, the world of the sublime and the heroic: a world always growing, as is all perfection in this world and, as such, inadequate and requiring renewal; a superhuman and yet a most human world; a world both extremely ideal and extremely concrete."

I

"The totality of being; its two infinities!"

HE

"The art of the priest, if one can speak of art here, is, as St. Gregory said, the supreme art. It needs every faculty, especially the most human. And in him must be found everything that is in man, excepting sin. What is looked for in him is an echo, a welcome, a comfort, not necessarily forgiveness, counsel; no—simply to be listened to, to be understood."

I

"But how can the priest speak as man to man if he has not the experience of a man? I remember these words of Simone Weil:

Purity is the power of looking at filth; it does not demand experience of it but, on the contrary, the lack of it."

HE

"It is not for the priest to make experiments in the scientific sense. The poet does not make experiments, but poetic talent permits feeling with men, having the essential of the experience without being committed to it. Take Dante, for example. The priest is the ultimate poet; he has not only the vocation of feeling with, but of suffering with. His chastity signifies that he does not wish to specialize in any vocation, any special situation, so as to assume in himself whatever is human, radiant, and painful, in all situations and states of man. You will tell me it is a hopeless ideal. All true ideals exalt and exasperate."

I

"Holy Father, if I have understood you right, the ideal you set the priest is to aim at the sublime in man."

HE

"Beyond the good, there is the holy. Beyond the beautiful, there is the sublime."

The Holy Father continued to meditate on today's priest, to penetrate the essential, to trace an ideal portrait. He spoke, and I noted his very words in my memory.

HE

"The priest should seek to express the ineffable truths which call and compel us; to approach the mystery which surrounds the universe, without profaning it. I would go further: to extend the liturgy to the whole cosmos, which silently sings of God, and also to its humblest forms, to give things significance and to spiritualize language. And further, further still: He must penetrate the hidden secrets of human existence, which people today value so highly."

I

"For his existence concerns us above all."

HE

"Yes, the priest must interpret, express, sublimate every moment of existence lived."

I

"And how do you conceive, Holy Father, of his doing it?"

HE

"In giving a resonance to the pain, grief, and love of man."

I

"That is prayer."

HE

"Yes, that is prayer, as the Church sings daily in the Psalms. Prayer is the true, the continual light. Light which is poetry, life, and, dare I say it?—still more . . ."

I

"Is what?"

HE

"Priesthood."

I

"In what sense?"

HE

"The light is for each object it touches, sustains, haloes, sur-rounds a sort of silent oblation and consecration. It seems to me that this love of light, this complete sense of light, is still alive in the heart of the twentieth century."

Listening to the Holy Father speaking in such tones, so emphati-cally on the subject of the priesthood, I said to myself that there was certainly its secret, its very substance.

All its other burdens, so obvious, seemed to me secondary. Or rather, they seemed to emanate from this primary vocation.

And I divined that one of the sorrows of his life was to have been limited by circumstance, by docility, to those administrative func-tions so far from the priesthood. He was more adapted to individual counsel, to the direction of conscience, to the secret and individual generation of souls—as Peter had been for a craft, for managing a little fishing boat, and not for that universal, absolute fishing. I thought to myself that there must exist within him a painful, un-satisfied side. The pastoral charge, especially at its highest level, does not give many opportunities for the exercises of that inner priest-hood, that begetting of a single soul, equal to a world. His words became increasingly animated as he spoke of the priesthood. They became poetry, uplift, a hymn, as Cardinal de Bérulle would have said, to the nameless splendor of the priesthood. But a priesthood enlarged by its immersion in the modern world, sharpened and tested, made firm and at the same time subtle by its assimilation to man's uneasy sensibility in this twentieth century now drawing to a close.

I could not help thinking that, in the guise of these general ideas, he was revealing, as we all do, something of his own story.

G. B. Montini had received at birth the human but very rare gift of feeling *with* the men of his time. And, through his possession of humanist culture, he is able to translate what he feels. This is actually rather a usual capacity among Italians, whose intelligence and sensibility are so well harmonized in their way of life, in their conversation, and in their daily chatter. It seemed to me that his first vocation—I did not venture to question him on this subject—was a lay one; that it had been a vocation in the world, in the midst of the world, with worldly connotations. That is surely the first criterion of a lay vocation. Then I asked myself, Why did he not choose this layman's road, this road which has been my own?

Perhaps one day in his youth he had heard the supreme law: We possess only that which we have renounced. That is the whole of what Jesus teaches: to lose oneself, yes, to renounce oneself, but with the hope—how shall I put it?—with the certainty that God will raise us up again to a higher level, where he will become the mainspring of our nature, of our sensitivity.

Without doubt young Montini had known that law very early; his Oratorian masters, nourished on the idea of abnegation (even smiling like that of St. Philip), were saturated with this law. They must have emphasized it in a thousand different forms; therein lies the secret of their education of generous hearts, especially of those in whom they find that spark which nothing in the world can replace, the essential originality discernible from childhood, the promise of a certain genius. But even that, above all that, must be immolated, destroyed, or at least hidden away, to be rediscovered in a higher way and in another light.

The lay, human, cosmic, political, social vocation of the young Montini proceeded. It was not repressed; it was sublimated, which is quite different.

And it is that which gives, I was thinking, so much depth and vibrance to what he was saying about the priesthood. I seemed to hear the sounds of a long-drawn violin, something Verlaine has described, a mixture of ecstasy and a sob.

It is the gift of sacrifice, which consumes but also consoles, which is, as Pascal said, a fire. The Pope has often used this simple word: *fire*. He likes to quote the verse of Luke: "It is fire that I have come to spread over the earth, and what better wish can I have than that it should be kindled."[10] He loves to advise, with Paul, the *fervor* of the Spirit. There is in him always, as I see it, something fervent, lively, burning. And that human sensitiveness, present and consummated in the oblation of the priesthood, perhaps explains him in his entirety. We have half-opened the door of a tabernacle, into which one must not penetrate further. Let us keep silence henceforth.

But the reader will understand how and why both at Milan and in Rome, before, during, and after the Council, I came to speak with him about the lay vocation; the world of laymen which, basically, is the entire world.

He said to me:

"Reflect upon what is the essential of the layman—I mean, what distinguishes him from the priest. From that one must go up higher . . .

"Here, the summit is the beginning."

10 Luke 12:49.

I

"Christ, Christ alone, as on the mountain of the transfiguration or on the road to Emmaus."

HE

"Christ and those He sent: the Twelve.

"The layman is, like the bishop, a successor of the Apostles. The bishop alone inherits the pastoral charge, visible, controlling, sacerdotal in the full sense of the word. The layman is also a descendant of the disciples and Apostles, but he has received only a part of the inheritance, which he shares with the bishop. And to be witness is the element which, without being exclusively his, is his privilege, his part.

"The layman is in essence a witness. His state is one of witness."

I was to reflect at length on this idea, of envisaging the layman as above all a *witness*.

It accorded with views I had long held on the philosophy of witness. It had always seemed to me Christian thought had neglected the act of witness. Thus, in New Testament exegesis, biblical criticism considers the authors of the New Testament as writers, as inspired mystics, as repositories and rehearsers of the faith of communities, and very rarely as those who have *seen*, who have *touched*, who have been present at a real event or who have questioned those who saw it. We have lost this sense of the historic reality, which is what witnessing is: the occurrence which transforms us inwardly till that moment when, to sustain the truth of the occurrence, we become witnesses par excellence—*martyrs*.

"It always seemed to me," I then said to the Holy Father—and this summed up my thinking—"that the Gospel and the Epistles of John contain a profound metaphysic of witness."

HE

"These will also then form the charter of the lay apostolate?"

I

"In the Gospel of St. John, *who rested on the breast of the Lord,* to witness is marvelously described. The Word witnesses to the Father, because it *rests eternally on the Father's breast.* The Apostles are witness of the Word of life. They beget witnesses, who are disciples. The disciples have not seen, have not heard, have not touched. But they are witnesses of the second degree, witnesses of the first witnesses.

"To this fundamental witness, which is that of the Church, is added the witness of their own experience, of their personal conviction, going on to the witness, if God wills it, of martyrdom which is witness in its essential act, the witness which does not deceive and the only one men essentially believe. The layman should be a potential martyr.

"The acts of the Apostles show them to us in decisive action: And some of them were men (*quidam* in Latin, *tines* in Greek)—note this word: The laymen have no name, they are not designated! There were, then, some *which spake unto the Grecians, preaching the Lord Jesus. And the hand of God was within them.*[11] These unknown people founded the Church of Antioch before Paul's missions. Still less known were the laymen who founded the Roman Church before the coming of Peter to Rome.

[11] Acts 11:20–21 (retranslated by the author directly from the Greek).

"These laymen were the couple Aquila and Priscilla, who brought to their missionary work the grace of marriage at the time of the founding."

HE

"It is true that, as you say, the mystery of the layman, that is, *of the layman entrusted with a mission,* has always existed in the Church since its beginning; and at each time when it has been necessary, as the prayer for the feast of St. Francis of Assisi has it, again warm the world growing cold. The Third Order of St. Francis was an organization of the lay apostolate . . ."

I

"And St. Francis never wished to be a priest . . ."

HE

"But at the present time this mystery is the more striking because of the increasing rarity of priests, the hostility of certain powers, the trend of culture toward laity. But (O joy, O marvel) this witness of modern laymen brings us back to the origins of the Church, to its very sources, to closer proximity to Christ! And in this extraordinary mutation of the world there is born in us the new hope of a new beginning.

"They are, I would say, witnesses of the faith. I was struck by how Cardinal Newman insisted on this point in his pamphlet (which caused him so much trouble in Rome), entitled, 'On Consulting the Laity in Matters of Faith.' Newman showed that it was the laymen and the Holy See who saved the faith in the period following the Council of Nicea.

"You see," said the Pope with a smile, "that the laity are not forgotten by the Holy Spirit. It may be that a similar situation to the one Newman described is again to be found in the Church. I think that in time to come we will have lay theologians. Who knows? The theology of the future may be primarily the work of laymen.

"I have said that laymen have no power to preach the doctrine, still less to define it, to verify it; those are offices of the magisterium. But they have gifts for proposing the truth to men in every generation, so that in every century the heart of Christ speaks to the heart of man in a more intimate, effective way. That is what Pascal did for your nation, in ceaselessly searching for more adequate ways of uniting man to God."

I

"One could say further that the layman has the vocation of educator. And, from this point of view, it must not be forgotten that every mother is a layman. Who can tell what is the mothers' influence in fashioning the man of tomorrow, the priest in the man, sometimes in the priest."

HE

"The Church is proud, as you know, of having magnified and liberated woman, of having made her equality with man brilliantly clear in the course of centuries, among diverse natures.

"The time is coming, and has already come, when the vocation of woman is accomplished in its plenitude, the time when woman is acquiring an influence in the city, a radiance, a power never before attained. And incidentally, in this moment when humanity is undergoing such a profound mutation, women imbued with the spirit of the Gospel can do so much to help humanity not to be inhuman, the more so as women are essentially religious. Love with woman is love incarnate. I saw it at the time of the Council. There, where learned theologians often were embarrassed, Christian women went straight to the essential, like the two Teresas. We were thinking, praying. They fasted, too. They suffered; it is their way of acting and conquering.

"A woman cannot be a priest. She does not sacrifice. But a woman can be a victim."

I

"A victim, yes; an oblation, immolation, constant, profound; inspiration, succor, counsel; reparation, renewal. She can forget, she can awaken. But we laymen do not lack ideas; the problem is to realize them."

HE

"Women also have a vast kingdom of silence. And in our time silence is spreading through the world."

Later I ventured to confide in him my fear of laicism as a temptation for certain priests. I believe in making categoric distinctions, and that to see truly it is necessary to have distinguished truly. And just as I fear the lay sacristan who is like a frustrated priest, so I fear the purely militant priest who is like a layman barely colored by consecration. The Holy Father asked me to clarify what I was trying to say.

"I am afraid," I said, "that these priests of tomorrow, with the very noble aim of mixing among their lay brethren, may be tempted to follow us onto our own ground. I have a fear they will regret not being like us, people with a calling, specialists, professional people, technicians, politicians, trade unionists, workers, or leaders of sections of the social organization, agents of temporal history, family men. I fear their wearing themselves out in trying to speak our language, in wishing to adopt our methods and attitudes, our nerve-racking life, our temporal worries, our suffering engaged in political affairs—in a word, our modern lay style of life. Or again, I fear their desiring to become what are, with us, lay 'directors' of conscience —psychiatrists, therapeutists, sociologists, psychoanalysts, psychologists, masters in the humanities. There again we are, as laymen working full time, stronger than they are.

"That is when, from a long experience of life, I would like to tell them:

"You will be the losers if you wish to equal or to guide us in our laymen's territory. You will always win if you establish yourselves with strength, with joy, with simplicity, on what is your own incommunicable domain, the priesthood. We ask of you before and above all to give us God, especially in the powers which you alone have, of absolution and consecration. We ask you to be 'men of God,' *Ish-Elohim*, like the prophets, bearers of the timeless Word, givers of the Bread of life, representatives of the Eternal among us, ambassadors of the Absolute in you. In reality we live in the relative, but we move, breathe, and are in the Absolute!

"And without the enfolding Absolute we could not even enjoy the relative."

The Pope listened to these "lay ideas." With his extreme discretion he simply said:

"Laymen have more authority than we have to say what you have said. It is good that such things be expressed in the name of experience."

I grew bold, and ventured on a still more forbidden ground.

"Will you allow me to put forward a thought on the chastity of the priest? It is not in question, I know. But in our days so much stress has been placed on the greatness of the lay apostolate, on the mystical mystery contained in marriage, that I discern still among certain friends who are priests a kind of regret, as if they were thinking: Had I but known! If I had arrived twenty years later! If I were postconciliar, then . . . then . . . would I have chosen this way?"

The Pope asked me to tell him what I replied to my friends who bared their souls to me, who told me their regret at coming too late into a world too new.

I

"I answer them somewhat as follows. I draw my inspiration from talks with the philosopher Bergson, at the time when he was not yet a Catholic, and tended toward the *Latium*. Present-day society, by its images, impulses, he said, is aphrodisiac. Now chastity, in this aphrodisiac universe, constitutes, for anyone, a difficult road. If the laity can practice without a heroic effort a prenuptial chastity, and conjugal chastity, fidelity, it is because in fact they see living outside the cloister, young, strong, virile, radiant, and radiating beings who are joyfully, easily chaste. The self-denial of a few elevates and purifies the atmosphere for all. Without these very human beings, who nevertheless have inscribed in their very bodies a part of the Absolute (that is to say, precisely, whose conduct would be absurd if the Absolute were not), the spiritual level would soon fall. The flesh would prevail, little by little, over the spirit. For one would be soon convinced that the spirit cannot overcome the flesh, or at least only in the exceptional conditions of the monastery or the religious state. There would be a landslide of liberty among souls. Henri Bergson, the friend of 'heroes and saints,' thought about that im-

mense difficulty which the overpopulation of the planet will present.
He said in his reserved, mythological language: 'Venus works for
Mars.' He foresaw that if the tide, the human flood, were not held
back, wars would be almost inevitable. He also thought that no
scientific, mechanical, technical means would be sufficient; that a
mystical humanity must arise; that, if humanity did not agree to an
extra effort and poverty, then it would perish. And he only saw one
possible solution: the return to a simpler life, caring for mastery of
the flesh, for what the ancients termed lordship over oneself, 'temperance.' And it was still more necessary, in his view, for new spiritual
men to appear, new exegetes, new mystics, to show the humanity of
tomorrow that the impossible is possible, and that in a joy, in joy
which rises above suffering."

THE POPE

"Bergson was on the right road. I had the pleasure of reading his
book *Les Deux sources*. What a magnificent mind! Yes, the solution
of the apparently impossible is to rise, to rise above, to go beyond
oneself. It is that very thing which Christ came to teach us and give
us power to do."

Then we turned to speaking of the mysticism which, that year,
was the subject of my courses at the Sorbonne. The Pope asked me
in what sense I had oriented my research. I answered that I had
considered that there were three levels in the consciousness; that
relating us to the body, the cosmos: that which is the selective level
which might be called the *soul;* that of the *Spirit* finally, symmetrical
with the level of the body, by which we have access to a higher
mysterious universe. The mystics, the spiritual men, seemed to be

the explorers of this third world, the cosmonauts of spiritual space. And I interrogate them like scientific witnesses.

HE

"That is a positive method, with which all those (and they are many in our time) who take as their rule to depend on experience will agree."

He was silent for a moment, as if remembering.

"Once," he added, "I translated into Italian a little book by an eminent Jesuit, the director of the review *Etudes*, who was in contact with the most able minds before the First World War, Father Léonce de Grandmaison. The little book was called *La religion personnelle*. And he spoke of the mystics, of mystical experience, in a way that I liked very much.

"I recall a passage in which this Father showed the difference between the two ways of reaching God. The first, by the intellectual faculty alone, 'the God of philosophers and scholars,' negatively perceived as distinct from all that is not himself, infinite, incomprehensible, and positively, as being, beauty, supreme goodness—and the same God when one dimly feels His immense attraction, when one tastes His adorable mercy, when one listens in one's own depths to that voice, in truth so different from others.

"I was very interested in Abbé Bremond's works. His *Histoire du sentiment religieux* had opened new paths to me, had restored the mysticism, renewed the vision, of the seventeenth century. What admirable pages, what discoveries and windfalls from your French mystics! I had been since 1930 the friend of the person who was, so to speak, our Bremond: Don Giuseppe de Luca. He was writing a *History of Italian Piety* with a whole philological preparation, which had not been done by Bremond, on the Italian High Middle Ages. He met Bremond in 1933, and the two priests were perfectly matched. It was Don Giuseppe (to whom Fausto Minelli had introduced me at the Morcelliana publishing house in Brescia) who took on the direction of a collection of spiritual works. And among the first books published figured just that translation of *La religion personnelle* with a volume of *Aphorisms* of St. John of the Cross. One has to go back to the highest sources. We can only breathe freely in the sublime."

The Council raised problems; it gave precision to, and defined, pastoral counsel. But the heart of the Council was much deeper in a mystery of silence, prayer, and supplication: the mystery of this life, a shining cloud, in which we, priests and laymen alike, must be ready to advance in the sight of God.

It seemed to me that after the Council and through its mystery, priest and layman would be more at one. In the soul of the Pope, the mystery of this union would be more significant than elsewhere— perhaps because it is at the center rather than in the rays, despite their convergence, that the peripheral points concentrate, console, and support one another. It is by the Pope *alone* that pioneers, messengers, the bold spirits of the advance guard, the lay leaders, can feel themselves truly counseled, truly understood. For the circle needs the center to reassure and strengthen itself; that is its source, that is its principle.

The center is the point from which the motionless compass arm takes strength to trace ever vaster circumferences.

15

THE VIRGIN AT ST. MARY MAJOR

November 24, 1964

I have just returned from a very familiar ceremony: Paul VI's visit to St. Mary Major, where relics of the Crib and a very old ikon of the Virgin are venerated. After this morning's assembly of the Council in the Basilica of St. Peter, what contrasts! The absence of the diplomatic corps, a states' eye view, gave a greater intimacy to this gathering. The absence of the Protestant observers on this Marian occasion removed a kind of embarrassment, that of the host who would not willingly shock his guests. For the Catholics, this evening ceremony was a family occasion, which made me think of Vespers on the fifteenth of August in a little provincial town: the good folk, the canons, the choirboys, the hymns, the incense—there was all that, and what used to be called "solemn Benediction," that liturgy of Vespers where the dogma of the Real Presence is affirmed. At the Council, the Pope, with very clear insistence, had proclaimed the Virgin Mother of the Faithful, Mother of the Church. In this Council, which has renewed the concept of the Church by describing her as the people of God, Pope Paul VI had said it was suitable that all should be completed and summed up in a more appropriate view of the Mother of Jesus. Of this people on the march, Mary is the first, the perfect type, the pledge fulfilled.

I think that the title, "Mother of the Church," if one accepts its strong and precise meaning, necessitates a simultaneous rethinking of the human mystery of every motherhood. The divine mystery of the Word of God entered history through a woman. The result is a kind of maternity for all the sons of men. Finally, the title of Mother of the Church, bestowed at the end of the Council on the Church, was the most discreet and the richest of all possible terms. When in the Middle Ages the people built a cathedral and called it Notre Dame, they felt this idea obscurely. Perhaps it is one of the most secret meanings of the Apocalypse.

That evening at St. Mary Major there were not as many people as one would have wished. As a result of having noised it abroad that no one would be able to get into the basilica for lack of space, many of the faithful had been discouraged. Those who filled the nave were the good people of the parish, those bishops still remaining in Rome, the canons of St. Mary Major in their white ermine. And, in their midst, a Pope without retinue, indistinguishable from his people, all in a familiar and delightful improvisation, as so often in Italy. I was expecting Paul VI to speak. He was silent. Silence, prayer, and hope are often more convincing than words.

HIS HOLINESS

"Mary is a model. Mary is a mirror, reflecting the invisible perfections of God. We can see in her the highest, the most complete and most splendid example offered by one of God's creatures. We should purify ourselves at this source. It is as though today man has lost the idea of man. More than ever before perhaps, humanity appears as a fallen species, degraded by sin, invading with all its ramifications the tree of our terrestrial life. And when we make studies of man— researches and analyses on this subject enjoy a great vogue today —we find innumerable imperfections, miseries, and, as they are called, *complexes*. There are certainly some noble elements, but these are accompanied by such deep deficiencies.

"It seems to me that this view of contemporary man, of his anguish, of his problems and troubles, of his faults, helps, by contrast, to understand Mary, in whom is realized the divine intention of making man the reflection, the image—how shall I put it?—the photograph and similitude of God.

"That is why, at the very moment when the world throws itself headlong toward the absurd, toward despair, perhaps toward annihilation, the Church presents anew, forever luminous in her celestial splendor, the Virgin Mary. To the darkening of shadows. Mary replies by the dazzling of light. To the most desolate discouragement, she replies by the most intoxicating consolation. What a spiritual drama!

"It happens that when I think of the Virgin's character, as the Gospel shows her to us, I see her so discreet, so gentle. Never overwhelmed by fear or uncertainty. The ideal, difficult for us, is easy for her."

I recall this text of a Russian Orthodox mystic, Merezhkovsky: "The whole of paganism is the insatiate anguish of the Son. All Christianity is the insatiate anguish of the Mother. The night of the Father came and the sun of the Son arose. The night of the Son is coming and the sun of the Mother will arise."

The Russian thinker was expecting from the Virgin Mother the kind of help which the Johannine Christ attributed to the Spirit, to the advocate and consoler, the Paraclete. It could be, I thought once more, that the Virgin's time is approaching. It is strange that this idea is to be found in several spiritual writers. The Virgin anticipates the final flowering of creation. She consummated with Christ an alliance which the Church will only realize at the end of time. She achieved instantly a fullness which cannot be accomplished for humanity until after the last day. She possessed, nay, rather she drew forth from her body, from her nature, from the history of her race, this body of Christ, which completes itself throughout history, which will be fulfilled only with the last sigh of the last man. Thus the Virgin, recapitulating the whole course of time, is the image of the alpha and omega: of the first enfolding, when everything was in God in a state of thought, and of the last unfolding, when the Son will return all things to the Father and *God will be all in all.*

HIS HOLINESS

"You remember the sublime verses with which the *Divine Comedy* ends?"

Naturally Paul VI knows them by heart, doubtless since childhood. He repeated them in Italian, in a clear, slightly lilting voice:

> "O Virgin Mother, daughter of thy son,
> Created beings all in lowliness
> Surpassing, as in height above them all;
>
> So mighty art thou, Lady, and so great
> That he who grace desireth and comes not
> To thee for aidance, fain would have desires
> Fly without wings . . .
>
>   Whatsoe'er may be
> Of excellence in creatures, pity mild,
> Relenting mercy, large munificence
> Are all combined in thee."[1]

After the service the Pope knelt in the left-hand chapel, in front of the celebrated ikon, which is one of the oldest images of the Virgin

[1] Dante, *Divine Comedy. Paradiso,* Canto XXXIII. Translated by Henry Cary.

and is constantly visited in Rome. It is sometimes attributed to St.
Luke. But St. Luke was a doctor. I do not think he ever ground,
chose, or put on colors, although his Gospel is the most picturesque:
I mean the one richest in scenes which have inspired painters, from
the Annunciation to the Pilgrims of Emmaus.

16

LIGHT ON SOME BURNING QUESTIONS: LOVE, VIOLENCE, AND PEACE

"Let us always think about it, but never speak." There is something improper about speaking of the things which come too readily to mind, and especially about those which are beyond one's control: One does not discuss life or death. . . . This tacit rule, so long accepted even among pagans, even more in the East than in the West, weighs lightly upon us, more especially on the minds of the young. Even the catechized raise questions at catechism, the Church herself is under interrogation.

Proverbially deep resounds to deep: *Abyssus abyssum invocat*[1] in the words of the psalm. Have you not observed that the ultimate questions, the burning questions, intercommunicate by subterranean channels and that their obscurity seems to increase and thicken? Inversely the smallest ray of light communicates itself; one has the impression that could a little light be thrown on any point of such a closed circuit, then that light, like all light, would illuminate it. And confidence would be spread from person to person. That is what gives such hope even in the darkest moments. For one still hopes (and this I feel very strongly just now) that the *worst* and the *best* are under the same star: that the outcome may be either catastrophe or the restoration of all things; war or an enduring peace.

[1] Psalm 42:7.

What then are the questions which obsess us, believers and un-believers alike, questions which we hide even from ourselves? Every epoch has its cursed lands, its forbidden zones.

It seems to me that *love* and *death* have always been such lands of fire and of silence, or, if you prefer it: sex and violence, the more so since present-day techniques on each of these two points, by the methods known as contraception or by nuclear armament, can change the face of the world. In both cases they are inventions hostile to life and directly contrary to the primordial precept of Genesis: "Increase and multiply!"

I sometimes wonder whether there is not a kinship between these two problems, the one touching on life, the other rather on death. Is the premonition of the author of Genesis being realized before our eyes? Will Adam and Eve not lay hands, at last, on the tree of life?

But how to bring up these questions, buried as they are beneath shame, anguish, or silence?

And yet dare this, O my soul! In these dialogues, which I have wished to be authentic, direct, and never evasive, it seems as though an element of truth would be lacking did I not, perhaps by going outside the set bounds, dare to ask my interlocutor some unavoid-able questions, and had I not gathered from his words some guide-lines for thought, some gleam of courage, some reasons for increased hope and greater strength.

THE POPE

"You do well to raise secret and serious questions. You are right to ask the Church for a rule of human conduct. But you must not expect from her an instant, automatic answer to the problems raised in our times, which are often so difficult, so little analyzed, so new, and so continually changing. The face of today's science changes so fast. And, within the space of ten years, yesterday's scientist must go to school and learn anew.

"Burning questions are also complex ones. Simple honesty demands that they be considered without haste. We should have respect for the complexity of things, listen, weigh them. If the past teaches us anything, it is that it is better to wait, to risk disappointing the impatient, than to make hasty improvisations. And the higher the authority, the more it must wait. It is easy to study, difficult to decide."

As his habit is, sensitive and considerate, anxious to inform himself about everyone, whoever he may be, about his thought, his experience, his competence, his undertaking, the Pope questioned me about the studies I have made regarding the problem of *Human Love*.[2]

I should like to indicate briefly here how I have tried to approach the problem of sex.

For five years I was a prisoner of war in a camp of between five and six thousand officers. Meditative perforce, deprived of the families which they had founded or were yet to found, they could not fail to reflect on the human condition. I remember one melancholy evening when we did not know what to do. One of us conceived a strange game: Each had to tell how the man who had become his father had come to know the woman who was to become his mother. It may be imagined how alike these stories were in spite of their diversity. What had provoked the man's love for the woman, the woman's for the man, was often a tiny detail: a missed train, a furtive glance, a lock of hair, a single word, or a prolonged silence.

[2] Guitton, J., *Human Love*, Chicago, Franciscan Herald Press.

. . . After these confidences, in the prisoners' barracks, a metaphysical silence fell, each felt how that to which he was most attached, his self, his existence, whatever made him what he was, and not another, had at its origin almost nothing—a meeting, a chance expression on a face, or a color of eyes. Each one felt the disproportion between the origin of his being, a chance, a shiver, and this very being, this immortal being.

Such is indeed the mystery: a disproportion between something fleeting, contingent, and the spiritual universe emanating from such an accident. Love is a bauble, a nothing. But this nothing is everything because it is related to everything in the individual and in society. How many problems come to be reflected in this problem which is a kind of mirror of the whole! It would seem that if man had been able to achieve harmony between his spirit and his flesh, then indeed, all his difficulties would be solved as well!

HIS HOLINESS

"May I remind you of the teaching of the Church from the beginning, which is essential, invariable, regarding this problem which we should always keep in mind?"

I

"I admire that thought of Emerson: 'To understand anything well, it is necessary to come down to it from above.'"

HE

"Good! Go to the summit from which you will descend like Moses.

"In everything one should begin from the supreme mystery, which is the mystery of the eternal love.

"God is Trinity. In the divine and mysterious Persons the essence and the relations are profoundly identical. Each person is an eternal gift and thus man and woman, created in resemblance to, in the image of, the Trinity, are called upon by that resemblance to give themselves mutually to one another.

"That is why marriage and the family are not simply a human and sociological structure, linked to the changing conditions of life, of culture, of technique. Marriage and the family come from God. They correspond to a design which is invariable although circumstances change. No! Marriage and the family are not carried away by the *horizontal* movement of history. Marriage and the family have a relation which is constant, transcendent, and I dare to say *vertical*, with God. Families are founded on earth. They live on earth. But they are destined, in a form which is unimaginable, penetrated entirely by the divine love, to be reconstituted in heaven.

"By marriage and the family as intermediaries, God has wisely joined two of the greatest human realities: the mission to transmit life and the love of man and woman. Through love, man and woman are called to complete themselves in a reciprocal giving, not only physical but above all spiritual. Or, better, God wishes the pair to participate in His love, in the love He has for each of them personally, in the love through which He calls them to help one another attain the fullness of their personal lives; and, at the same time, for the two things are inseparable, in the love which God has for humanity and through which He desires to multiply the children of men, in order that they may participate in His life and happiness.

"Now that that has been said, it must be noted that in the light of history, like everything that is sublime, human love is vulnerable. You said so a moment ago. The people of ancient times were little aware of it because they did not admit that the person of woman was an equal to man in dignity; it is the light and strength issuing from Revelation which has enabled fallen humanity to conceive fully, and then to realize completely, conjugal love: only one man, only one woman, for ever.

"It was St. Francis of Sales who said: 'Love—we abuse the word, vilify it! it must be upheld, for it is of incomparable beauty.' "

I

"It is so true that the love of a man for one woman alone, for ever, love understood in the sense of a profound attachment, tender and lasting, of one only for one only, is a tardy achievement, still vulnerable and still threatened. At first woman was divided into two: the matron, mother of warriors, and the woman of the streets. The woman at the fireside was not the mistress. It is Christ who has united in a single being the woman as a mother of children, and the beloved: It is He who practically instituted the *spouse*.

"The Hebrew word which designates sexual love is not translated in the Greek Bible by *erōs* but by *agape*: It is also the word for divine love. And the Shulamite woman who describes conjugal love in the Song of Songs says that flames are divine flames, 'Yahweh-flames.' "

HE

"This sublime subject is so obscured that it is important to put first things first. It is my turn to question you. What do the philosophers of love think? And in particular, how do you look at the widely spread theories of Dr. Freud?"

I

"I think that all man's possible thoughts on the mystery of human love can be summarized in the alternatives expressed by Vergil in *The Aeneid*:

"Dive hunc ardorem mentibus addunt?
An sua cuique deus fit dira cupido?[2]

"Do you come down from the highest heaven or do you rise up from the abyss?

"The first solution is that of the spiritualists, of Plato in the *Banquet*, of Solomon in the Song of Songs; one might say, of all mystics. Conjugal love is a 'flame of Yaweh'; its origin is divine. The flesh is an expression, disfigured by sin, of this eternal love.

"The second solution on the contrary explains love by need, desire, biological instinct. And if love appears spiritual, if it becomes cult, passion, religion, it is because the vital and animal instinct has been transfigured. I do not know if Vergil foresaw Freud: He expressed, in my view, the essential idea of Freudism.

"Between these two a choice has to be made. For they cannot be affirmed at the same time."

HE

"If one must accept Vergil's couplets, I will say that the Church has always chosen. She wishes to preserve in human love what is the essential, the real. And it is there that the world does not understand. The world conceives the laws of the Church as interdictions, taboos, obstacles to true love, as condemnations of sexual intercourse. I do not say that that state of mind has not existed among certain representatives of the Church. Let us always place ourselves at the summit of things.

"The Christian law is not a law made to condemn or to restrain life. It is a law designed to make life more abundant, to make man happier; more truly, more continually happy. It is a law of love, a

[2] Is it the gods who have put this ardor into our spirits?
Or on the contrary does each man make a god of his desire?

law which preserves and increases true love, in protecting it from illusions and deviations. And it must be said and repeated that all which appears to diminish the liberty of love is done to help love to reach its purity, its plenitude, to prevent its becoming perverted, so that it may attain its goal, which is to unite us to another being, to other beings, and by that finally to unite us eternally to God, who is Love.

"That is what must be repeated constantly, time and again. Love is not made for the law. But the law is made for love. *The fullness of the law is love.* Married people will accept what appears to lessen their free choice the day they understand that this restriction gives life and increases freedom and deepens mutual love, inner peace, the power to bring up children, relations with other families—not to mention the life of intimacy with God, the joy of fulfilling his will, and suffering for it.

"The fundamental problem of love is to make what is of the flesh rise above the flesh, to lift what only belongs to the realm of the senses to the realm of spiritual life, to the realm of the heart and of sacrifice.

"In love there is infinitely more than love. We would say that in human love there is divine love. And that is why the link between love and fecundity is deep, hidden, and substantial! All authentic love between a man and a woman, when it is not egoistic love, tends toward creation of another being issuing from that love. To love can mean 'to love oneself,' and often love is no more than the juxtaposition of two solitudes. But when one has passed beyond that stage of egoism, when one has truly understood that love is shared joy, a mutual gift, then one comes to what is *truly* love.

"If it is true that love is what I tell you it is, one can understand that it cannot be separated from the fruit of love. Even Plato taught us that love's spring is in the generation of souls in beauty, for the education of spirits. Love reaches out toward fecundity. It imitates the creative act. It renews. It gives life, it is a sacrifice on behalf of life.

"What is to be feared in modern technique is that separation which it introduces between love and fecundity. People will tell me that this separation is sometimes sadly necessary for budgetary or health reasons. But one must realize that that separation is not normal, that it is dangerous. When one uses a technique for dissociating the act of love from its end, one must be aware that something has been subtracted from happiness.

"The problem which it raised touches the very sources of life. It touches the most vital feelings and interests of man and woman. It is an extremely complex, an extremely sensitive problem. The Church recognizes its many aspects, it questions the many spheres at issue, and among those spheres it is clear that the experience of the married couple takes first place, with their liberty, their conscience, their love, their sense of duty. The Church must also affirm her own sphere, which is not hers, but is that of the law of God which she preserves, which she teaches, which she interprets, which she applies. But the Church ought to proclaim this immutable law in the light of scientific, social, and psychological truths, which have recently been the subject of very intensive research, and of a very vast documentation. The Church must always follow attentively the developments, both theoretical and practical, of this question. It is exactly what the Church does. The question, at this very moment, is being studied, as widely, openly, and profoundly as possible, as seriously and honestly as this human problem demands.

"As to chastity, by which I mean the spirit of chastity, the world must be given to understand that it is not a marginal, accessory energy, necessary for certain states of life, which most men can dispense with. The mastery of the spirit over the flesh is not a speciality of those who have renounced, for a greater love, the ways of the flesh, this mastery is essential to human dignity. It is part of the virtue that the ancients called temperance, and which is nothing other than self-possession; I dare to say that chastity obtains something that people of today value highly, and rightly: freedom, autonomy, liberty. Do not let us be afraid to say out loud what most men think to themselves: There is no true liberty without the spirit of chastity.

"And I would say that chastity, and in particular conjugal chastity, is linked to faith and love. When the sense of chastity diminishes in peoples' conscience, the power of receiving the word of God in oneself is seen also to diminish, the desire for eternal life, the thirst for conversation with God. In sum, the whole spirit of the Beatitudes can be summed up in the Beatitude: *Blessed are the pure in heart, for they shall see God.*

"And I know that the objection will inevitably be raised: 'You impose too heavy a yoke on human nature.' But where is human nature found? Is that called nature which is the ordinary man with all his faults and conditioning, or is it what man should be, what he *can* be, with the grace of Christ?

"Must the moral law be aligned with *what is generally done*, reduced in this case from morality to morals (which, in parenthesis, are in danger of being even lower tomorrow than they are today— and where will it end)? Should the ideal be maintained, on the contrary, at its sublime height, even if this level is rarely accessible, even if the common man feels incapable or guilty? With the sages, heroes, and saints, I would say: All true friends of human nature, of human happiness, believers and unbelievers, even if they protest, even if they resist, deep in their heart will thank the authority which will have enough light, strength, and confidence not to lower the ideal. The prophets of Israel and the Apostles of the Church never accepted a lowering of the ideal; never did they whittle down their sense of what is perfect, of perfection, nor diminish the gap between nature and the ideal; never did they attenuate the sense of sin; quite the contrary."

"But," I said, "did not St. Paul say that the law made sin abound, and that Jesus Christ has freed us from that law of death, to put in its place the law of life, which is faith, which is love?"

"The law of which St. Paul speaks there is legal observance, social law, the *letter* of the Pharisees, dead and static law. But faith in Christ is a living law, a dynamic law, a law which limits and constrains us only to give, as I told you, more abundant life, the fullness of life. The way which leads to that life is a narrow way, and there are few that find it.

"The thought comes to me of a phrase from Manzoni. It occurs, I believe, toward the end of *I promessi Sposi*, translated . . . as *The Betrothed*: 'Trust in God mitigates and renders difficulties useful to a better life, when they arise through our own fault or even through no fault of our own.'

"And to return to the spirit of chastity about which you were asking me, I will repeat that it is not only necessary for the foundation of the home, for the education of children, brothers and sisters —but it is also so for scientific research. What economies, privations, and sacrifices our scientists, engineers, and technicians undergo—especially our Russian or American astronauts, who are often perfect family men! How touching it is to see their children at prayer at home for their father, orbiting in the heavens!

"And finally, speaking chiefly to artists, I will say that the spirit of chastity draws us toward beauty, which may through it be reached by a surer and shorter road. It lends youth, refreshment, and renewal to inspiration. It is a golden key to open the world. I mean that it gives us back something of our lost paradise; that vision which is the goal sought by all the arts. If the world mistrusts this spirit of chastity, it is because it despairs of having it. Or again it is, through the same despair, that it questions and denies what it has lost.

"There are days," the Pope went on, "when the scandals alarm me. Evil has a freedom, an extent, an organization, and a power which one would say was that of irresponsible people. And yet those people are responsible. I should say: Woe to you who write certain pages; who project into our homes amusements of the most abject kind; who corrupt life at its source, at its roots: existence, innocence, hope, and love. One day, alas, you will have to give account for every scandalized soul. You wish to get rid of war? But the deep-down origin of wars is there! The Gospel has said so with fierce emphasis. I know that what I am saying is harsh and severe . . . but what contrasts in the soul of Jesus when faced with evil!

"Jesus poses in liberal, generous terms the current problem of tolerance. He is merciless toward scandal. He caresses the child. Then he pronounces these fearful words: 'Woe to him who scandalizes one of these little ones!'

"As to peace, on which you have also questioned me, it furnishes endless food for thought. It is related to a reality of supreme importance and is always subject to the gravest, least foreseeable changes; it concerns the whirlwind in which the fate of humanity today is tossed.

"It should not surprise us that the human ascent toward the

heights of civilization includes moments of doubt, weariness, and difficulty. We are aware of the complexity of the problems raised by the life of man in society. We know the weakness of man. And that man, at a certain point of his difficult road, feels the temptation to halt and go back; to advance in words and to retreat in acts; this hurts but does not surprise me.

"Man is like that: not only weak but often incoherent; more confident in his own empirical reckonings than sure of the soundness of great ideas—human, true, and forward-looking ideas. And though man in his march toward peace is thus oscillating and intermittent, we should not lose our conviction of the rightness of the cause of peace, nor our consequent courage to continue defending and promoting it. We should always maintain that peace is possible. We should always make every effort to render it possible.

"Yes, humanity must rest faithful to the great ideal conceived after the horrible tragedy of the war: We should all always seek peace; peace for all.

"And though this formidable resolution arose from the searing experience of the war and the fear and terror of seeing it repeated on a greater and apocalyptic scale, today it should rather be love which supports us, love for all men; and I repeat: love of peace rather than fear of war."

I

"It seems to me that humanity has come to a crossroads, and that here again there are only two possible roads: either war or peace. I mean these two words in the absolute and unlimited sense. I would say: either absolute, total, irredeemable war; or perpetual peace, a peace which if finally humanly possible through a single government —what empires dreamed of."

HIS HOLINESS

"The *positive* concept of peace is in fact being developed. Peace is not blind pacifism, or indulgent egoism, or indifference or disinterest in another's needs. Peace is the fruit of a concrete, continuous, and unanimous effort for the construction of a local and universal community founded on human solidarity, in the search for a common, universal good. And if we look at the great needs of humanity, as also at the great dangers which menace its tranquillity, peace, I say, is called in our day *development*: development of peoples who are still in need of too many of the necessities of life and who still constitute a great part of the human race. I am pondering an encyclical on this central and vital theme, which I would like soon to place before all men."

I

"But that is no easy matter, and it will entail (always, perhaps?) a continuing risk, like life, more vulnerable as it grows more precious. And we must live on a tightrope over the abyss."

HE

"Peace is indeed difficult! Peace is great, peace is necessary, peace is the object of much search and much devotion; but it is very difficult, extremely difficult. All the same, as I said just now: It is not impossible."

I

"Will man's forces, prudence, treaties, and progress be adequate to maintain peace?"

HE

"I prefer at this time not to give a complete answer to this agonizing question, which involves the most difficult theses of thought and history. I will simply conclude by applying the words of Christ to the solution of the terrible problem: 'Whatever may or may not be possible with man, all is possible with God.' One can always pray for peace. This act of prayer is founded on faith, that is, on the faith that man is not left to his own strength alone to reach his destiny, but that a powerful, gentle, and paternal force can intervene in the development of decisive events concerning him— even by a miracle, were we fallen so low that only a miracle (by that I mean a visible intervention of God) could at the last moment save this humanity so dear to the heart of God.

"In the context of the period we have just lived through, the word 'peace' has, alas, like so many others, been degraded until it is used to oppose men instead of to unite them. For some people, peace means peace at any price. Peace without justice, without dignity, peace through capitulation to evil is the mark of fear. Peace in justice, a just peace, enduring peace, was defined by John XXIII in his testament, the encyclical *Pacem in terris*. This is the peace of Christ, *Pax Christi*. For the peace of Christ has no frontiers, it is a common good offered to all, which takes root and grows stronger as it spreads."

I

"And what do you think is the European ideal?"

HE

"Everyone knows the tragic history of our century; if there is a way of preventing it from repeating itself, it is through the construction of a pacified, organic, and united Europe. A peace based on the balance of power, on a truce to antagonism, or on purely economic interests is bound to be fragile. It will always lack the necessary energies for resolving the fundamental problems of Europe, those which concern the peoples of which Europe is composed, and the fraternal and community spirit with which Europe should be animated.

"The Catholic Church wishes the process of European integration to proceed without undue delay. This process corresponds to a view of contemporary history which I consider as modern as it is wise; it corresponds to the goals of unity and peace which I have set myself; it puts into practice the virtues of courage, impartiality, trust, love which should form the basis of civic education in a world advancing in the light of the Christian calling, the highest and noblest human calling.

"The dynamism of peace can only manifest its whole strength if it is nourished from within by a deep and true conversion of hearts, which the Church is striving to obtain: This was one of the principal objectives of the Council.

"The road is sown with generous, disinterested initiatives which have nothing in view except human happiness and the means to assure one prime element, the rolling back of the terrible scourge of malnutrition. Still today, in spite of staggering technical progress, this keeps a large part of the human race in a state of painful physical and, in consequence, intellectual and moral inferiority.

"Yes, this for humanity is a matter of life and death. It must unite to survive. First it must learn to share its daily bread. For the Christian, who recognizes the suffering face of his Saviour in every starveling, the text of the Gospel of St. Matthew remains his charter of action; '. . . For I was hungry, and you never gave me food.'[3]

[3] Matthew 25:42.

Hunger! Armaments! Armaments preferred to food for the starving! What a scandal!

"I cannot regard without horror this militarism of which the conception is not the legitimate defense of each country, in order to ensure thereby the maintenance of peace, but which aims at procuring ever more murderous armaments, mobilizing energies and means on a colossal scale, feeding a power psychology, leading to the foundation of peace on an inhuman basis of reciprocal fear. In this context I dare to hope that those who guide the peoples will one day learn to pursue disarmament in a prudent and magnanimous spirit, and that they will envisage with a generous heart the future attribution, even if only partial and gradual, of certain military expenditures for humanitarian ends, not only for the benefit of their own states, but no less to help the developing countries. Hunger and misery, sickness and ignorance cry out for help.

"And who will dare maintain that the world of labor, that vast world, is at ease in the order willed by God! Indeed, who would dare maintain that the sociological phenomenon arising from modern organization of labor is a model of perfection, balance, and tranquillity? Is it not exactly the opposite? Does not our history evidence proof of this? The mechanical and bureaucratic structures function perfectly. The human structures not yet.

"In a celebrated Russian novel, one of the most representative characters cries out: 'Christ has called me to carry the Cross!' How many workers could say these words! How many could discover in the very slavery, pain, and suffering of their condition that key which would open to them the mystery of Jesus the obedient, patient, innocent, carrying the burdens of others, with courage, with love, and thus becoming the example, the hero, the Saviour, the Lord of the world. I do not lose hope.

"It is possible that modern labor draw a new and true inspiration from the Christian view of life.

"It is possible for the rich man to prefer the riches of love to the love of riches.

"It is possible to render the social doctrine of the Church efficacious historically, economically, and politically.

"It is possible to obtain effective and original results in the realm of economic and social progress without having recourse to modern materialistic theories, those intoxicating stimulants which finally prove debilitating and corrosive with their formidable but crushing power.

"The Church's interest in the laboring classes has never been merely religious, verbal, and doctrinal; even less has it been purely rhetorical and ineffective. No, it has always shown itself practical, positive, real. It has sometimes proved limited, for the Church's means themselves are limited; but the Church has never neglected, side by side with the gift of the word, the gift of bread, that is, the gift of practical and concrete aid for the benefit of those for whose benefit the word was destined."

I curtail (for it is late, *the day is far spent*, and this day is ending) this one evening's conversation on burning questions. I shall be forgiven for having asked them.

I was quite sure that all these vital problems had secret links. I asked myself, but wherein lies this link, this connection, this convergence? And what would be the single focus around which all our thoughts are gathered? I have always liked this motto of Mallory, the conqueror of the Himalayas, whose body, frozen in light, was never found: *Solvitur in Excelsis*: "the solution is at the summit." And, like the centurion, I asked the Pope for one word, but *the word*. It was a word about what I might call the invisible frontier, the river of peace, the *love-and-thought curtain* which invisibly separates the atheist world from the believing world of the children of Abraham in our three families of Israel, Christ Jesus, and Islam—which one day perhaps will bring them together. This word could be: the infinite value of every single human person.

HIS HOLINESS

"There is an immense difference between what one might call the logic of atheism, when this logic is radical, and the logic of faith.

"We Christians, believers in God, if we knew that a single person were in danger of death, we would move heaven and earth to save him, because for anyone who believes, and much more, for a disciple of Christ, every single being has an infinite value. . . . But let us imagine the master of a great empire capable of deciding the fate of hundreds of millions of men, and he is an absolute atheist and has no hope. Let us suppose that this master of destinies finds an occasion to dominate the whole earth forever, but at the price of the sacrifice of a hundred million men. If he is logical, this will be absolutely indifferent to him. This is where one reaches the limit between the consequences of the idea of God and the consequences of the negation of God. May the world understand this before it is too late."

17

THE EIGHTH OF SEPTEMBER, 1966

Quindecim annos
Grande mortalis aevi spatium
Tacitus[1]

The Castel Gandolfo gardens which Pius XI laid out after the Lateran Treaty in the Barberini villa give an impression of a secret collusion between solitude and beauty.

For these gardens exist for themselves, for themselves alone, and almost without witnesses. They await Adam and Eve.

This solitude in beauty is to be found to some extent in all works of art: They are made to be admired, they are also made to consume themselves alone in a high place, or in silence, like a lamp hung in an empty house. Then, Mörike says, it is beauty in itself blessed.

The garden, as any "beautiful thing," resembles consciousness. Even more is this true of the Castel Gandolfo garden because, unlike so many others, it was designed by an architect who was also a philosopher, after he had heroically participated in the public life of his country, had known exile, sorrow. This garden was to some extent deliberate, chosen, determined in its entirety and in every detail (and how many details there are in a work of art, wearing out patience) before being laid out and dug in the earth. Finally it is a mirror, a recapitulation of the most perfect gardens in the world:

[1] Fifteen years; a large span of mortal age.

French gardens with their complex symmetry, their architecture a bit too knowing for my taste; Roman gardens, Italian gardens, with their farm, their kitchen garden and the gray-blue foliage of the ilexes, of the stone pines, punctuated with black cypresses and sometimes with a paler cedar—all mixed up with broken columns, ancient walls, white statues, reminders that all passes in this world, everything, even beauty, so vulnerable when it is not that of nature always beginning anew. And I divine also here an influence of oriental gardens, the secret inspiration of the Song of Songs; here I breathe Arabia and the gardens of Spain, those arid, impenetrable gardens, where the tiniest drop of water is preciously saved. I am glad that this pensive garden is made up of separate spaces, juxtaposed or rather superimposed, which are like dwellings—dare I say?—are like those courtyards in *The Interior Castle* described by Teresa of Avila. And yet the architect of these gardens wished them not to be closed in, but that each paradise should open out onto an expanse.

I said to myself, "These gardens are an image of thought, made up of solitary perspectives, linked by a secret architecture," that at least is what I think. That is how I composed these *Dialogues* which are now drawing to a close: I wanted a pyramid of terraces, of mirrors for the mind, and avenues, long avenues reaching to the moment of arrival at a summit, at an inspiration.

It must be added that the promontory where these gardens are laid out and are gathered is a frontier upon two very differing spectacles: that of the Roman campagna, of its expanse that in the distance merges with the sea, and, on the other side, the Albano Lake, a Cyclopean eye which seems to engulf the whole sky. Between these two worlds Domitian, a bald Nero, had a road built. And it is said that to calm his madness he went from one to the other.

The eye turns always from the plain to the volcano, to this motionless lake. It is the privilege, the curiosity, the charm of this place to have two aspects, and as it were, two faces, which require one to be always somewhere else, always to be remembering the opposite—or to be awaiting it.

Sixteen years have passed, *"grande mortalis aevi spatium,"* Tacitus said; as it happens he said it about Domitian. It is true: In human life that is a long time. And, since 1950, humanity has covered a lot of space. Time has greatly accelerated.

In this fall of 1966, in Europe a late summer, the sky is transparent; September, I was told, is the best month for Castel Gandolfians. I could not help commenting on it to the Holy Father, who replied: "Did you know that formerly in Rome the gentle, peaceful papal administration gave an extra day's vacation every week for the enjoyment of the beauty of Rome in October, the *Ottobata?* In the papal states the holidays were formerly in October. At Castel Gandolfo, as you see, September is a month of plenty. In his day in the fifteenth century, Pius II, a humanist pope, noted in a 'Travel Diary' the sweetness of this landscape. It is said that it is from this promontory that the first Roman came. This Pope did not lack humor. He said, 'Since Piccolo has become pope, he has many nephews.' He was also a precursor in his own way. He had had the first idea of a sort of 'League of Nations.' He had summoned the chiefs of state to Perugia. He waited a long time for them. I think not a single one came. See in the distance the Tiber estuary, Ostia? Eight days ago I went to Fumona to pay my respects to Celestine V. You know his story. He was a very simple man who mistrusted himself. At the moment of the election of Pietro di Murrone, the Apostolic See had been vacant for twenty-seven months: there were only twelve cardinals left and they could not agree among themselves. Those were terrible times. Pietro di Murrone, a holy hermit, was elected and invited to ascend the chair of Peter. After having hesitated, he accepted from a sense of duty, and made his entry into Aquila on a donkey, like our Lord. But he found there two kings waiting for him." "He abdicated," I said, "is that exemplary for a Father? Paternity cannot be renounced."

"But," the Pope said, "Celestine found himself duped by his attendants. He had accepted out of duty. The same sense of duty brought about his resignation, not from cowardice, as Dante said, if Dante's words really refer to Celestine V. After Fumone, I went last week to Perentino, near Agnani, where it is said that on September 7, 1303, Sicarre Colonna slapped Boniface VIII. Everywhere in the countryside the history of the Church can be found, and its continuity, in spite of so many obstacles and difficulties: That is what is so improbable, that is the miracle of the Church in time, according to our Lord's promise."

Then the Pope looked out into the distance. He quoted Vergil: *"Silentium late loca"* (space makes silence). Then he added, "Consider the peace of this September evening upon which the liturgy celebrates the birth of the Virgin Mary. The sun is at the end of its course; see that golden globe through the evening mists? And if you went to the other side, you would see the Albano Lake, and perhaps the reflection of the moon in the lake; but I do not know if you would have the patience to wait for it. On September 8, it is after midnight that the last quarter rises in the east. *Pulchra ut luna. Erecta ut sol* (Lovely as the moon, elevated as the sun); so the Song of Songs says, speaking of the Bride.

"See that dark stain, that long reddish smear to your right? That is Rome. There is mist tonight. In a few moments we shall see the lights.

"In front of us lies Ostia; there are the mouths of the Tiber, *Ostia tiberina*, which have not changed, this melting of shore and of sea in a haze. Stendhal claimed that from here he saw ships and sails.

Ships, perhaps? But to see sails he needed a strong imagination. Doubtless St. Augustine was on a terrace. Fifteen centuries have passed, a brief interval. We can communicate with his very thoughts."

And the Pope continued:

"What thinker ever had such a sense of the passing of time. He is very modern in that respect. Yet I will not surprise you when I say that he had even more the sense of permanence. . . . "

I allowed myself to interrupt the Holy Father and to say to him, "I recall an untranslatable Latin phrase: *Non haberent vias transeundi nisi contineres ea.* . . . Things, beings, histories, people could not pass at such a terrifying speed unless You contained them."

"That's it exactly. What rapidity! Time slips by. I would rather say it slips down like an avalanche. Our life is so short and time is so long. But this time which passes does not in any way affect God's permanence, in whom everything is always and forever present. . . . This is a great mystery."

Then the Holy Father commented to me on St. Augustine's conversation with his mother, St. Monica, at Ostia, shortly before Monica's death. I knew the text well; in my youth I had made it the subject of a thesis. The Pope told me that formerly his mother at Verolavecchia, after having, as we say, "put the children to bed," candles out and prayers said, used to come to the bedside of Ludovico, of Battista, of Francesco, and whisper a private word to each, a special message for that one alone. And the children say they still remember the timbre of that voice in the dark no less than the substance of what was said to them.

"Look in that direction," said the Holy Father: "That is Ostia." Once more the evening breeze was billowing out his cassock.

Night was falling. Rather, there was a change in the lighting: fire, incandescence, phosphorescence suddenly took the place of the daylight.

"See," the Pope went on, "the little towns of Latium; the *castella* are lighting up." And he pointed out, on the nearby heights, the twinkling lights of Marino, of Rocca di Papa. I thought of those lines by Baudelaire:

> *Sois sage, ô ma Douleur, et tiens-toi plus tranquille*
> *Tu réclamais le soir; il descend; le voici.*[2]

In this strange moment of twilight (a sad word which really should have a dawn resonance), I was present once again at this spectacle of which I shall never, never weary; the passing of the light of things into the mystery of beings.

It was a painting by Turner, not in misty London but in the golden haze of the Roman campagna: a decomposition of light into atmosphere; a symphony of orange, purple, crimson, pale carmine, a liberation of the spectrum proceeding from its two extremes of violet and red.

"What I admire here most," said the Holy Father, "is variety in unity. No sunset is ever like another. But, on this eighth of September evening, you have perhaps the most beautiful day and the most beautiful evening of the season. Here, one understands St. Augustine when he describes eternal felicity in terms of sensible joys; when he says, if I remember, that to imagine the beatitude of the saints one must start from *delectation*; more exactly: the delectation that one receives from corporeal light. My old friend Bonomelli (to whom we owe this terrace, these gardens) told me, when in September 1932

---

[2] Be wise, O my pain, and be more still.
You cried out for evening; it falls; it is here.

Pius XI came onto this terrace for the first time, he remained looking
at the horizon, at the sea, for a long time. He was, it seems, amazed
by this vision, which gave him an idea of the infinite variety of the
infinite."

Then the Pope went on:

"You remember the ascendant rhythm of the conversation between the son and his mother. Augustine and Monica went up
together, as we have just done in this garden, terrace by terrace.
Then they arrived at a moment of ecstasy where they thought they
had grasped what eternity would be, were this moment to last and to
absorb everything."

Of course I remembered this famous passage which brings us to
the summit of all experience. The Pope made this comment on it:

"It is eternity, it is its mystery of love, which is the secret of all
our desires."

"Which is, doubtless," I said, speaking in the same vein, "what,
without knowing, without saying, we seek everywhere, even in our
pleasures. Can the ephemeral be loved as such? Can one become
truly attached to what passes?"

I remembered what Father Teilhard de Chardin had told me about
his first sorrow as a child: He had seen a lock of hair burn. This had
given him the idea not only of nothingness but of the absurdity of
the nothing. Being, finally, is what can in no case be annihilated.

"I think," the Holy Father said, "that children understand this
very well. I also recall the kind of desolation I felt as a child to see
the fire burn wood, paper, a toy, a letter."

This was the moment to ask the Holy Father a question which
always had preoccupied me about eternal life, about immortality,
about the persistence of the present life in the future.

"How," I asked, "will the memory of what we have lived, what we
have loved, be preserved or transformed in eternal life—and, to give

an example, the memory of this moment with you, facing Ostia, on this terrace?"

The Pope replied:

"Monsignor Colombo told you that, in life eternal (and I think this was St. Augustine's idea) memory, deep memory, is preserved. How could one magnify the Lord, sing his mercy eternally, if one did not remember? But one must add the mystery which is contained in the communion of saints. The happiness of some will not be separated from that of others, as these hanging gardens are. Everything communicates, everything communes, everything is united. Saints Augustine and Monica have the feeling of a shared beatitude, where man loves man; each with the others, each for the others, no happiness which is not shared happiness.

"How could those who love each other think they would cease to do so because God will be everything in their love?"

Then the Holy Father forcefully developed this idea of the link between the love of men and the love of God. That conversation of Ostia remains in my memory as an instruction of the love of God. I took out my jotting pad and noted this very exactly:

"There are two loves, the love of God and the love of our neighbor, and the two loves are Commandments. Jesus Christ says these two Commandments are similar. Jesus Christ does not say they are equal. And the First Commandment, 'Thou shalt love thy God,' comes before the Second Commandment, 'Thou shalt love thy neighbor as thou lovest thyself.' But I do not know if these days the final reason why man must love man is well understood. Philosopher, allow me to question you."

I was surprised by this interrogation, which is not the way the Holy Father usually proceeds. I recalled an anecdote Chateaubriand tells in *The Martyrs*, which Alain repeated: "A pagan and a Christian meet a beggar. The Christian gives him his cloak. The pagan says to the Christian, 'You thought he was a god.' The Christian replied, 'No; I thought he was a man.' "

The Holy Father said:

"And yet that is not enough. Chateaubriand did not get to the heart of the matter. The final reason, the deepest reason, as the scholastics say, the 'formal cause,' which makes us love man is not man; it is God. If one does not connect man with God, it is impossible for men to love each other. Without an absolute who commands them to love everyone, to love universally, do you know what happens? Men make what Bergson calls closed societies, and these closed societies oppose one another, and make war upon each other. I say: If men do not love God, known or unknown, they will not love each other, as I said in New York at the UN, but will be against others, or else they will love each other in little groups, in nations. How shall I put it? It means that they will hate other groups, other nations. War and violence have as their deep cause this failure or this absence of a love which is addressed to all without exception. There is the crux of the problem. Today man has taken the place of God. Men are anthropocentric. The 'formal cause,' that is to say the real, substantial cause of love (and even of the love of the husband for his wife) is not the qualities, which may pass. The reason for love of others is not the attitudes of others toward us: For these others can be our adversaries. The others can be sick, ungrateful, fallen, or vile. We cannot love them for themselves. The true motive for the love of men is that they are made in the image of God, that, like us, they are God's creatures, brothers of a same Father. Without the love of God, men will never be able to love each other. And that is why," the Holy Father added, "in this moment it is heartbreaking to see men coming together without really loving each other. And they do not really love one another because they ignore the love of God."

I then quoted from memory the somewhat sibylline phrase with which Bergson ended his last book:

"Whether one chooses big or little means, a decision is unavoidable. Humanity groans half-crushed under the progress it has made. It must itself first see whether it wishes to continue to live. Then it must ask itself if it only wants to live

(A long silence, a long pause.)

. . . or to make the further effort necessary in order that on this our refractory planet the essential function of the universe, which is a machine to make gods, may be accomplished.

"Bergson meant to say 'saints,' " I added.

"That's it," said the Holy Father. "An extra effort must be made, a sacrifice, an oblation. . . . That is the tragedy of this historical moment.

"It might be said that the Council was a cry, an appeal, a prophecy begging humanity to accept the making of this effort. To the code of purely human hopes it opposed the hymn of truth and of Christian hope. To the sign of atheism and egoism, it opposed the sign of God and of Love. Here is a question vital for humanity. Either it must rise above itself, or perish. It is perhaps the meaning of what the biologists call a mutation. In very truth, there is only one who can take upon himself this mutation; that is Christ."

We began to discuss the possible end of the world. I then said something like this:

"Some people are afraid of the 'end of things,' others find it natural. After all, since the world is not eternal, in a sense it is *already* finished. In a hundred years, we shall all have disappeared. My wife often says to me, 'When I was a little girl, I heard this joyful cry: Beatrice is saved! And I thought, *Saved?* No, since Beatrice will die.' I answered her, 'What is called the end of the world is the *simultaneous* death of all the living, whose *departure is generally staggered in time by generations.*'

"If the perspective of the end of the world were limited to the idea of 'all dying together at the same time,' it would not be sad. It would remove the great solitude of death. The soldier dies more easily than the civilian; it is because he is not alone. It might even be that an atomic death—above all if the weapon is perfected and becomes *absolute*—would not be hard: conflagration, a fainting into light.

"And each of our personal deaths is atomic, in the sense that the universe fades out completely for each one and that we find ourselves *alone with God.*"

I added that in our days biological hope, the hope necessary to the survival of humanity as a living species, must have a religious source: that we had come to the admirable and tragic point where we *biologically* need faith, hope, and love; that between *believing* and *perishing,* humanity would doubtless be brought to belief. That there was the reason for the favorable reception given by humanity to the Council, which is so surprising when one thinks of the pervading atheism and frivolity.

When I see the cosmonauts enter their steel capsules like creatures become seeds and germs, then launched into the sky, where they live an ascetic life, after the manner of the great contemplatives and sometimes float in space in a sort of levitation, I tell myself that the interest the public takes in such performances is not purely scientific. The astronaut is the symbol of a *new man,* freed from weight, raised to a sort of celestial life of anticipated glory. In every human consciousness, there is room for this expectation. If this planet is destined to grow cold and its pale sun also, humanity will be obliged to emigrate elsewhere in order to survive. But this new habitation will itself be precarious, so that those that have an earthly dream of immortality cannot expect it from the succession of generations. We all have the idea, the hope of a superexistence, of a superhumanity, of a "kingdom of God," of a "kingdom of saints," of a *new creation* that is spiritual, where what here is mortal, material, will be raised up, transfigured (but not destroyed) *swallowed up by life*, as St. Paul so magnificently puts it. What we hope: to exist still, but in a higher, purer manner: to be what we are, but in God, who will be all in all! The word so devalued by the Freudians, *sublimation*, explains this need.

THE POPE

"I will tell you a little story, since you like them. When I was at Milan, there was a mountain village without any means of access, not even a muletrack. One had to go there on foot. I went. It was an extremely poor village. And I noticed mistrust in the faces. These good folk, seeing the archbishop, were afraid he had come to take away their vicar. Just as I was leaving, I saw them again, and asked them: 'What do you need most?' A big silence. One of them stood up and said, 'What would be the most useful thing for us would be an oven, as we do not have an oven in which to bake our bread.' When I got back to Milan, I arranged for enough money to be sent to them to build an oven. I have yet to tell you the most extraordinary part and which shows how unmaterialistic people are when they are Christian. And which, in parenthesis, proves how much a simple, empty, and poor life raises the mind. I had forgotten my villagers and their oven. But at some point I asked if they had built one.

Would you believe it? Since the bell of their little village had been removed in 1944, they had bought a bell."

Then he asked me if I could tell him *what time was*, since I had spent my life asking myself this question. And I was tempted to answer him like St. Augustine: "I only know what time is when I am not asked to tell it." However, I tried to reply: "Time is a delay, a reprieve, a respite. For me the more difficult problem is this: Why did God not give Himself all at once and without waiting? Why must He be seen only through shadows? And after so many detours, so much anguish, such tedium. Why time?"

"*Why?*" he said, "but when one is as I am, in that solitude where there is no longer anyone to obey, except the Lord, then one understands better the confidence made by St. Paul to the Philippians: 'I am hemmed in on both sides. I long to have done with it and be with Christ, a better thing. . . ; and yet, for your sakes, that I should wait in the body is more urgent still.'[3] All of us, being human, are torn between the desire of being at the end and the joy of the journey, between the desire of being with God and the love of the others, the love of the world, the need to bring to the world the only good capable of rendering it happy."

The Pope then asked me which was the text of St. Paul that I would choose from among all if I were shipwrecked on a desert island, and I had to live with only one text of St. Paul. I said, "Perhaps this: '. . . not because we would be stripped of something; rather, we would clothe ourselves afresh; our mortal nature must be swallowed up in life.' "[4]

"And why this passage?" he asked.

"Because it seems to be the most profound definition possible of

[3] Phil. 1:23–24.
[4] II Cor. 5:4.

life and of death. We all of us, believers, unbelievers, we all want to be sublimated, raised yet higher, to be redeemed, washed, crowned, and without losing anything, without any abyss (except that of evil) to keep what we are in an eternity of life."

"And I," he said, "this is what I find the most sublime thing in St. Paul!"

And then he recited, in a half-whisper, in the night now grown very dark, under the stars, these verses from the Epistle to the Romans, that hymn of invincible, inalterable hope. I copy them to conclude these unfinished dialogues:

"For I reckon that the sufferings of this present time are not worthy to be compared with the glory that shall be revealed in us. The whole of creation groaneth and travaileth in pain together until now. But if we hope for that we see not, then do we with patience wait for it.

"All things work together for good to them that love God. If God be for us, who can be against us?

"Who shall separate us from the love of Christ? Shall tribulation, or distress, or persecution, or famine, or nakedness, or peril, or sword? As it is written, for thy sake we are killed all the day long.

"Nay, in all these things we are more than conquerors through him that loved us.

"For I am persuaded that neither death, nor life, nor angels, nor principalities, nor powers, nor things present, nor things to come, nor height, nor depth, nor any other creature shall separate us from the love of God, which is in Christ Jesus our Lord."[5]

[5] Romans 8:38–39.

INDEX